Past Life Visions

William L. de Arteaga

PAST LIFE VISIONS

A CHRISTIAN EXPLORATION

THE SEABURY PRESS | NEW YORK

1983
THE SEABURY PRESS
815 SECOND AVENUE
NEW YORK, N.Y. 10017

LIBRARY OF CONGRESS CATALOGING IN PUBLICATION DATA

DE ARTEAGA, WILLIAM L.
  PAST LIFE VISIONS.

  1. VISIONS.   2. REINCARNATION.   I. TITLE.
BV5091.V6D4   1983   248.2'9   83-4690
ISBN 0-8164-2414-4 (PBK.)

Contents

Introduction: The Problem / 1

Part I: The Methods of Theological Analysis / 9
 1. The Logos and Its Shadow / 11
 2. Ambiguity in the Mature Spiritual Life / 19
 3. Discernment: From the Bible to Saint John of the Cross / 29
 4. Discernment: From the Reformation to the Present / 50
 5. The Roads to Spiritual Death / 67

Part II: PLVs in a Non-Christian Context / 75
 6. Karma, Spiritualism, and the Metaphysical Movement / 77
 7. Induced PLVs: The Amateurs / 93
 8. Induced PLVs: The Professionals / 107

Part III: PLVs as Authentic Christian Experiences / 119
 9. Preexistence and the Elijah–John-the-Baptist Relationship / 121
 10. Inner-Healing / 128
 11. Christian PLVs / 139
 12. The PLV and the Ministry of Inner-Healing / 151

**Part IV: Toward a Christian Understanding of the
         PLV Phenomenon / 165**
 13. Evaluating the PLV Hypotheses / 167
 14. The Afterlife / 177
 15. The EJR Ambiguity: Empathetic Identification / 190
 16. The EJR Ambiguity: Reincarnation / 197
 17. Testing the Fruit / 210

Notes / 217

Past Life Visions

Introduction
The Problem

Case Studies

This book is *not* another study of reincarnation. Rather it is a critical examination, from a Christian perspective, of a special class of visionary experiences which have led many people to assume that reincarnation is a reality. The chief characteristic of these experiences is the reception of information, visions, emotions, and impressions that seem to belong to a deceased person. Most often these visionary experiences deal with incidents that seem to have occurred in the distant past, often thousands of years before.

In one of the many recent books dedicated to this type of vision, *Lifetimes: True Accounts of Reincarnation*,[1] there is recorded an experience that occurred to a GI in Vietnam while he was undergoing the trauma of an enemy mortar attack. He later described his unusual experience at length:

> I saw several lifetimes. The one thing that was constant throughout everything I saw was what I can only call a guide. The guide kept telling me when I had learned and when I hadn't learned. For example, I saw several lifetimes in which I was a warrior. There was one in particular in which I was a Roman officer. I wasn't a general, but a lieutenant or minor officer of some kind. I was a good fighter and I loved to fight. I had killed many, many men. One day I was out riding with my troops. We came upon some Christians, and it was our job either to destroy them or bring them back with us. Most of the men wanted to kill them immediately. But I saw one man I thought I knew from somewhere. I rode over to him and commanded him to look up at me. I looked at his face and saw something. I felt that he was a good man. I told my men that these Christians weren't worth bloodying our swords on and that we should pass on. . . .
>
> Now the guide told me that I had done something good. It said that

because I had allowed these people to live, I would advance or progress to a higher life in my next incarnation. . . . The guide told me that doing one positive thing cancels many of the negative things we have done. It told me that the same was true in the life I am currently leading. It told me to help others instead of hurting them. The guide went on to explain that I could rectify my current mistakes if I would only do positive things that would help others. The guide constantly emphasized that the most important thing I needed to learn in my current life was to love those around me. The guide told me that I should not worry about the harmful things I had already done. If I would resolve from that point on only to do the right things, then I could easily overcome the negative things I had done thus far.[2]

This vision took place spontaneously and unexpectedly. The theological implications of what the "guide" told the GI will be examined fully in later sections. Let us pass to another type of experience that is closely related to the above, except that the vision or visions were induced by a hypnotists.

In this case, the hypnotist, Edith Fiore, is a practicing psychologist who uses this type of vision frequently in her treatment of patients. A young man, William, walked into her office. His problem was a persistent obesity that had plagued him since childhood. He was at the time one hundred pounds overweight. After an initial interview session, Fiore led him into a deep hypnotic state where William experienced a vision of himself as a sailor trapped in a becalmed sailing ship in the late 1700s. He and his shipmates were at the point of starvation, and he sneaked into the officer's storeroom and stole a live chicken which he quickly slaughtered and devoured. However he was caught in the act and flogged for his deed.

In the course of several other such hypnotic sessions William experienced other visions of starvation and deprivation, including one as a lost woodsman in the nineteenth century. After every session Dr. Fiore and his patient talked over the vision and discussed how the events described in the vision could have influenced William's eating habits. This therapy freed the young man from his compulsive need to overeat and he was quickly able to reduce his weight.[3]

Problems in Interpretation
Needless to say the visions described above are controversial and susceptible to a wide range of interpretations. For many Christians they immediately trigger a set of negative associations about reincarnation, the possibility of demonic deception, and the whole area of the occult. On the other hand, for many students of parapsychology and metaphysics these visions carry a positive set of assumptions about reincarnation and the inevitable progress of the human soul. In a completely different way many materialist-minded psychologists automatically dismiss this class of vision

as mere fantasy. All of this indicates a need to step back from the prejudice that these visions evoke. In this regard it is important to establish a neutral vocabulary so that Christian fundamentalists, parapsychologists, occultists, and others can describe the visions without "good" or "bad" associations, or without disguised assumptions about their origins.

Let us simply call these visions "Past Life Visions" or, for the sake of convenience, "PLVs." Let us also include under this name the related vision of past existence in the disincarnate state, either as a conscious state preexistent to earth life, or the supposed interval between one life and another.

It is important to establish this neutral vocabulary. Otherwise one can be trapped into confusing a *hypothesis* about the PLV with the experience itself. For example if the PLV is termed "past life memory" there is an assumption that the sensor "remembers" his or her own life, that is, it assumes, the reincarnation hypothesis. If the PLVs are termed "fantasy," there is an assumption that they are merely the product of internal mental processes. The use of "PLV" precludes such association.

Let us now go on to describe the major hypotheses about the cause of PLVs. One of the best discussions of this problem is found in what is considered a modern classic of parapsychology, *Twenty Cases Suggestive of Reincarnation*, by Dr. Ian Stevenson, where the author points out that it is difficult to prove any particular hypothesis about PLVs.[4] He is considerably irritated by those enthusiasts of the reincarnation hypothesis who believe that because a living person receives a vision of a person who is deceased, it therefore "proves" that one person has been reborn as another. In reality the questions with regard to the forms of vision reception, and of what is meant by one "person" becoming another "person" are extremely complex, and Dr. Stevenson does justice to the ambiguities and difficulties involved in dealing with those issues. We will examine Stevenson's contribution to PLV research later, but now we will present as succinctly as possible the five major hypotheses interpreting the PLV phenomenon.[5]

Five Hypotheses

Subconscious Invention

The first hypothesis we consider is that the PLV is the product of the mind of the sensor. We will call this hypothesis the "subconscious invention" theory. It assumes that the sensor in some way manufactures a PLV out of bits and shreds of historical knowledge he or she has gathered through life. The sources of information, the "data" of the PLV, could be as varied as conversations about ancestors, movies, books, other media—

anything that could be a vehicle for historical information. This data is then imaginatively synthesized in the sensor's deeper mind, much like the process by which nocturnal dreams are produced. Thus there is nothing mysterious, supernatural, or "spiritual" at all about PLVs. It can all be explained purely in terms of internal mental processes. This theory was widely circulated at the time of the famous "Bridey Murphy" controversy of the 1950s (discussed in Part II).

A recent article by a clinical hypnotist, James E. Parejko, "A Boy Named Michael,"[6] tries to define the mental factors that lead to a PLV. Parejko believes that four factors are important in producing hypnotically induced PLVs. They are: the expectations of the hypnotist (facilitator), the diminishment of critical thought in the mind of the sensor which accompanies deep trance states, a triggering idea by the facilitator, and, lastly, the hallucinating ability of the mind. He further defined the PLV state as between a dream and a reverie. It is a state that is unusual in so far as the sensor may respond to questions about the vision while in the state, a characteristic not found in pure dreaming. He also noted that the quality of the PLV was something beyond that of a merely invented story, for the sensor often forms a deep emotional tie with the story line of the PLV.

The "subconscious invention" hypothesis pleases those in the mental health fields who wish to credit the reality of the PLV as phenomenon, yet feel it would be "unscientific" to recognize the possibility of nonmaterial influences on the mind. It allows PLV to be fully explained in terms of the individual and his or her biological-mental processes, without mystery or paranormal influences.

Genetic Memory

A second, also materialistic, hypothesis is the theory that the PLV is the product of "genetic memory." This hypothesis asserts that PLV is part of the multifaceted "genetic code" that each individual carries with him. Since so much genetic information is transmitted by heredity, from skin texture to musical ability, then why not even the memories of an ancestor's life? In this view the memory of some ancestor is released to the conscious mind when there is an emotional crisis, which produces spontaneous PLVs, or under the unusual mental condition of hypnosis. In any case, like the subconscious invention theory, the source of the PLV is within the person and a function of the brain's natural processes.

Reincarnation

The next three hypotheses about the PLV are in a different category. They all assume to one degree or another that man lives in a universe that has an important spiritual dimension, and that PLVs involve forces that transcend the sensor's physical brain.

A widely held hypothesis in this category is the reincarnation hypothesis already mentioned. In this theory PLVs are the *memories* of a sensor's earlier lives. In the Western understanding of reincarnation, this hypothesis is accompanied by certain assumptions about the person—that a person possesses a core or spirit which is central to his or her identity, and that this core incarnates in successive individual lives on earth. In the East, on the other hand, some forms of classical Buddhism have no such assumptions about the person, and so no core person reincarnates, but rather a set of forces or energies. The reincarnation hypothesis, as believed in its Western varieties, assumes that all of a person's memories are recorded not only physically in the brain, but in some way imprinted in a nonphysical core or spirit. When a person dies he or she takes along the memories of the old life into the core of the new person, to be released when appropriate.

This reincarnation hypothesis is almost universally adhered to by students of the occult and metaphysical movements, but it is upheld also by a surprising number of Christians who in the present age feel themselves less bound by traditional dogmas than earlier generations of believers. A recently released study of American religious beliefs, done by the Gallup organization, shows just how widespread belief in reincarnation has become in recent decades: almost one-fourth (twenty-three percent) of adult Americans believe in the doctrine. For those in the eighteen to thirty age group it is twenty-nine percent. What is really surprising is that Christians believe in reincarnation as readily as non-Christians: twenty-five percent of Catholics and twenty-one percent of Protestants believe in it.[7]

Demonic Counterfeit

Another hypothesis within the spiritual category, but one diametrically opposite to the reincarnation hypothesis, is the "demonic counterfeit" theory. This hypothesis has gained widespread acceptance among Christians, particularly among those who belong to fundamentalist denominations. According to this hypothesis the PLV is always the result of demonic activity. That is, the demonic kingdom has access to the memories, emotions, and experiences of those who have died, and can inject these impressions into the sensor's mind. One variety of this theory is that PLVs are produced by a form of mediumship in which the souls of the damned dead termporarily possess the seer of the vision and share their past experiences, memories, and so forth with the seer.[8]

In this theory PLVs are not memories related to a previous incarnation, nor are they the products of the seer's own subconscious mind. The PLVs are fabricated by demonic entities for the sole purpose of deception. For instance, they deceive the sensor into accepting the heresy of reincarnation and its associated Eastern doctrines of self-salvation, and so forth.

This hypothesis is closely related to fundamentalist Christian theory of human psychology which believes that the mind is *especially* subject to demonic invasion when it is in an altered state of consciousness (any state such as dreaming, a trance state, meditation, etc., that is not the normal state). This belief has been elaborated in the theology of Watchman Nee, an influential Chinese Christian writer (we will examine his theory closely in Part II), and was succinctly outlined in a magazine interview of Dave Hunt, a Christian writer of books on the occult:

> In a normal state of consciousness, my spirit is operating my brain. But in an altered state of consciousness, I think that connection is loosened to allow another "ghost," another spiritual entity, to interpose itself, to begin to tick off the neurons in my brain. In this way, it can create hallucinatory experiences which I accept as reality; it can convey either false or accurate information and, in general, create an entire universe of illusion, giving me a false notion as to the nature of reality, teaching a lie in place of the truth.[9]

Empathetic Identification

The last PLV hypothesis we will consider is a variation of theory that the great Swiss psychologist C. G. Jung formulated. He believed that beyond man's subconscious mind, which his teacher Sigmund Freud believed to be the deepest level of mind, lay another layer called the "collective unconscious." At this level the individual's identity somehow merged with all of mankind, present and past, and the mind has the ability to gather information of paranormal nature that is far beyond the capacity of the individual to invent. Jung related this area of the collective unconscious to his theory of archetypes, the commonly recurring motifs that occur in dreams, folk tales, and stories of all cultures.

There are several problems with using this Jungian conceptualization and terminology. For our purposes it would be better to modify the Jungian concept along the lines used by C. T. K. Chari, an Indian parapsychologist and PLV researcher. He suggested that the PLVs can be understood as a form of "empathetic identification" of the living with the dead.[10] Chari's concept is similar to the phenomenon of mental telepathy (or travail as a form of this phenomenon is sometimes called in Charismatic Christian circles), whereby a person separated by great distances can feel or experience the pains, anxieties, sometimes even have visions, of another person.

In this hypothesis the PLV does not signify any form of continuity of core personality between the sensor and the person of the PLV. Rather there is some unknown connecting force that brings these two persons into mental and spiritual harmony to the point where visionary exchange results. Like the two immediately preceding hypotheses, this one also presumes a universe in which there are forces that transcend the purely materialistic. This hypothesis has the advantage of generating relatively little argumentative "heat." Under the name of "Communion of Saints" or "Body of Christ" it is easily assimilated to certain orthodox theologies. It does have some difficulties in distinguishing precisely between empathetic identification and mediumship. This hypothesis is discussed more thoroughly in Part IV.

Purpose of Book

This book has two interrelated purposes. The first is to sift through the hypotheses pertaining to the sources of PLVs and to evaluate which of these hypotheses are useful and which are not. The second is to give the Christian some guidelines as to what is helpful and what is spiritually deadly within the area of visionary experiences. In this regard much effort is spent in exposing the biblically described form of heresy called Gnosticism. Most theories of reincarnation currently in circulation are heavily saturated with Gnostic ideas.

Both these purposes pertain to a form of spiritual wisdom called discernment, the ability to correctly evaluate spiritual phenomena or ideas. Achieving mature discernment is not an easy task. In fact the Bible clearly describes discernment as functioning only in an atmosphere of love (the absence of fear) and knowledge. To this end we will carefully examine the biblical criteria for evaluating visions, and add to that the centuries of Christian experience with visions and related spiritual phenomena. We will then apply the criteria developed from these sources to a variety of PLVs gathered from a wide selection of sources: occult, psychiatric, and modern Charismatic Christian. Only after these steps are taken can we come to a mature discernment of this very complex problem.

The structure of the book follows its purposes. Part I focuses on a description of discernment with all its biblical and postbiblical refinements, but also includes a study of other theological tools needed for a mature evaluation of PLVs. It is in this part that we examine Gnosticism, the prototypical heresy of radical nondiscernment that plagued Paul's New Testament churches. Part II shifts attention to the modern era. Here we spend considerable effort in examining spiritualism, a modern variety of Gnosticism, which has influenced most interpretations of PLVs. In Part II we trace the recent history of induced PLVs, from the Bridey Murphy controversy of the mid-fifties to the present day when PLVs are being used by many professionals in the mental health field. The most important task of Part II is to expose how PLVs induced in an atmosphere of nondiscernment or occult spirituality can lead to disastrous spiritual and mental results. However, Part II ends with a positive note as we discuss the pioneer work of Ian Stevenson, whose careful research has been a major step in separating PLVs from their occult and Eastern associations.

Part III centers on the occurrences of PLVs within specifically Christian settings. The first chapter of this part deals with the important biblical revelation of the returning prophet, what we term the Elijah–John the Baptist relationship. We then note several spontaneously generated PLVs that have occurred within Christian ministry and prayer. In Part III we describe the newly developed prayer technique of inner-healing, for it is in reference to inner-healing that PLVs can be useful to the Christian. In these chapters the pastoral potential of PLVs is elaborated, and we believe that here we have made an original contribution to the methodology of pastoral care and Christian mental health services. The case studies we present in Part III are taken from my own case work and give only a hint of the healing and faith-enhancement potential that a PLV ministry might have in the future.

It is our belief that PLVs are significant in both negative and positive ways. Negatively, they show clearly the power of the demonic kingdom to influence and distort mental processes. This should confirm for us, in an age when many Christians do not believe the demonic as real, the validity of the biblical view of a powerful spiritual kingdom which is hostile toward mankind. Positively, a careful sifting of these visions can help clarify important segments of biblical revelation that have been undeveloped in traditional theology and which have significant implications for pastoral practice.

The last section of the book attempts to make sense of all the findings and cases. We stress that what is offered is speculative and tentative. Though this book is lengthy, it is only a beginning at the discernment of PLVs. The judgment of the whole Church is needed in the form of criticisms, emendations, verifications, and dialogue, especially by those who are involved in the pastoral and mental health fields.[11]

PART I

The Methods of Theological Analysis

Chapter 1

The Logos
and Its Shadow

Introduction

In attempting to sift among the alternate hypotheses about PLVs we need to be aware that two factors have deeply influenced contemporary Christendom. The first is the decline of dogmatism or, more positively put, the acceptance of ambiguity in theology. The second factor is the rise of occult metaphysical and spiritualist groups and the spread of their ideas to the population at large.

In the last century there has been a shift away from theologies based on strong dogmatic statements to more open systems of interpreting biblical revelation. Although many Christians still believe their denominational theology superior to all others, very few would enforce their preference to the point of persecution, or believe that Christians of other denominations are hell-bound. Looking at the overall perspective, Christians have learned to be more humble about what they assert as dogmatically true and what they forbid as false. Medieval Christians believed with great assurance that the earth was the center of the universe and that the stars were points of light fixed on a movable sphere. Moderns know that this way of understanding the structure of the universe is not true, but they realize that current understandings, though much closer to the truth, are still provisional. The truly modern scientific mind does not seek to substitute scientific dogmas for religious ones, but rather seeks a method of exploring the unknown and a set of criteria for testing and discerning truth.

The scientific spirit has had a positive effect on most Christians in regard to the way they understand religious truths. Specifically, Christians are now aware that spiritual growth is more than merely accepting intellectual doctrines or creeds, and that maturity of spirit is a multifaceted process. It is generally understood that growth toward maturity is one of the processes that God has established for mankind, and an attempt to reject it for a "safe" area of theological or dogmatic certitude is to counter God's intention for us. That is not to say that everything modern is either better or more mature than what came before. Rather, the problem for the Christian is essentially that of releasing our rigid dependence on doctrines, while retaining and growing in our faith in God through Jesus and our belief in scripture. Without these last elements no authentic Christian spirituality is possible.

The second major fact that influences our study of PLVs has been the wide proliferation of occult[1] and metaphysical ideas of the past decades. We can now see that these forces reached a high point in the mid-1970s, and are currently in subdued postures. Nevertheless these ideas generated much discussion on the nature of man and the cosmos that have been entertained by orthodox Christians for fifteen centuries. The more conservative Christians feel that the best way to confront the issues raised by the occult is to reassert dogma and ignore or suppress occult ideas. This may or may not be effective but, as we shall show, it is neither a mature response nor one that is biblically warranted. Yet to accept occult or metaphysical ideas or to wholeheartedly embrace every new meditation technique would be to repeat at the opposite extreme the mistakes of the 1960s when academic theologians attempted to accommodate the Gospel message to the world view of "secular man," a perspective that excludes the transcendent.[2]

A way that is different from both the dogmatic negativity of conservative Christians and the gullible acceptance of metaphysical "seekers" is needed. This method of evaluation would demand a form of spiritual wisdom called discernment, without which mature judgments on spiritual phenomena are simply not possible. We will discuss discernment fully in chapters 3 and 4. But now we discuss two theological concepts that will assist us in coming to a mature understanding of PLVs. These are the role that the Logos plays in human understanding and the concept of Shadow Truth, both of which are fundamentally biblical.

Logos Theology[3]

The first concept is that of what is called "Logos theology." Logos is Greek for "Word," but it means much more than merely a single word. In the century before Christ, the term logos became much used in Hellenistic culture, both Jewish and Greek, to mean "reason," and a form of world soul, part of which inhabits all men. This was the meaning it had in Stoic philosophy that so greatly influenced Saint Paul and other New Testament writers.

In the influential writings of Philo of Alexandria, the logos was identified with Dame Wisdom of the Old Testament and was viewed as a personification of God's revelatory communication to mankind. It is in this sense that John the Evangelist based his revealed insight that the world-wisdom became incarnate as Jesus of Nazareth (Jn. 1:1–14). Thus, for Christians, Jesus of Nazareth possesses all of the characteristics of the Spirit of Wisdom that we find in Proverbs and other Old Testament scriptures (1 Cor. 1:24).

In modern times there has been a divergence of opinions about the extent and continued action of the Logos. Among some denominations of fundamentalist Protestants, there is a belief that the Logos is now manifest exclusively in the Bible, and that all spiritual wisdom flows from scripture. In extreme forms this belief leads to a disparaging attitude towards secular learning, especially in those fields such as psychology where the spiritual and material interpenetrate.

The more traditional view is that the Logos continues today as in pre-biblical times. It continues to reveal truth to mankind through reason, logic, and scientific methodologies. In other words, the revelatory activity of God is not restricted only to the Bible but has certain "natural" outlets. It should be pointed out that in this view the Bible is the final revelation in regard to the *spiritual meaning* of all things, and that natural revelation must be bounded in its interpretive gropings by divine revelation. It is quite plain from a historical perspective that the latter theory, that of continued Logos activity outside of the Bible, is a more accurate view of revelation than the modern fundamentalist attitude.

The history of the Copernican controversy is the clearest example we have of how the Logos made known a "new" revelation about the nature of the cosmos that was totally independent of biblical revelation. In fact the discovery of the sun-centered universe was a mathematical hypothesis verified and "tested" by the newly developed telescope. It seemed directly to contradict biblical revelation. In the book of Joshua, the sun is commanded to stand still in the heavens and it does so (Jos. 10:12). Theologians and many of the best astronomers of the day believed that this passage, and many others in scripture, verified the earth-centered theory of the universe. The controversy about the Copernican discoveries was long and bitter, with the Catholic Church definitely coming out the loser.

Protestants should not assume that this was merely a "Catholic" problem, for both Luther and Calvin soundly denounced the Copernican discoveries as "heresy." The Catholic Church, however, had the police apparatus to enforce its judgment. Eventually, of course, Christendom learned to interpret Joshua 10:12 and the other passages in nonliteral terms to accommodate itself to the new discoveries. The irony is that our present mature view of the cosmos allows many a pious fundamentalist of our generation to praise God for the planets and the stars discovered by Copernicus's and Galileo's "unbiblical" heresy. This came about because the Logos was able to work a new revelation through the force of reason, logic, and scientific accountability.

Similarly, in the present century, secular psychologists began methodical explorations of the vastness and complexity of the subconscious mind. Their explorations and discoveries took place without any concern for biblical revelation. By no means have the conflicting schools of psychology established their claims as certain. Yet Christians have, however reluctantly, integrated many of the discoveries of modern psychology into their ministry. As we shall see in Part III, the new, very powerful prayers of inner-healing would not have been possible without the discoveries in secular depth psychology. This is another example of the Logos working sovereignly through people outside either scripture or the church.

The irony of all of this is that the modern battles between science and religion were totally unnecessary. In contrast, the very earliest theologians of the church had a great appreciation of the Logos acting through the natural wisdom of their culture. Some of them such as Justin Martyr (d. A.D.165) had a profound appreciation of the Logos working in Greek philosophers.[4] In his work the *Apologies*, he wrote of Socrates:

> In old times evil demons manifested themselves, seducing women, corrupting boys, and showing terrifying sights to men—so that those who did not judge these occurrences rationally were filled with awe. Taken captive by fear and not understanding that these were evil demons, they called them gods. . . . When Socrates tried by true reason and with due inquiry to make these things clear and to draw men away from the demons, they, working through men who delighted in wickedness, managed to have him put to death. . . . [5]

As we shall point out, scripture itself gives us many examples of the Logos, acting as prophecy or wisdom, revealing itself through non-Israelites or, in the New Testament, through *pagan* individuals. This leads us to appreciate that the Logos of God constantly reveals itself to mankind, acting like a solar wind, unnoticed, but ever-present and ever-pushing toward clearer and more complete revelations of the cosmos and of its plan for humanity. *Scripture has been given to us, not to find every single truth, but to be the testing instrument against which all ideas that have spiritual significance must be measured.* Allow us to use a biblical image for this. In Genesis 37–40 we have the story of Joseph as captive in Egypt. There, while in prison, he hears the dreams of two fellow prisoners, and he interprets the dreams correctly for them. Both dreams contained true precognitive information (they were prophecy dreams), so that we may say the Logos worked through their natural minds to give them the "raw data" of revelation. Yet Joseph, who had the God-given gift of interpretation of dreams, had also the final authoritative word on the significance of the dreams. So it is with the church today. It is not the Christian's business to deny that the Logos can work through whom it wills; it is our responsibility to be attentive to its activity and to use our special grace as Christians to be its interpreters.

Shadow Truth

Another concept that we will use extensively is that of "shadow truth," which is closely associated with the revelations of the Logos. It is a fully biblical concept, later elaborated by the Apologists, the first generation of postbiblical writers who attempted to explain their Christian faith to the Greco-Roman World. Saint Paul and the writer of the Epistle to the Hebrews use the concept to refer to the relationship between the Jewish Old Testament law and the Christian faith, and the Apologists extended this relationship to that of the pagan religions and the Christian faith.

The most important biblical source is found in Colossians 2:17. There Saint Paul is addressing the problem of the Jewish festival traditions and observances: "These are only a shadow of what is to come; but the substance belongs to Christ." In Hebrews 10:1 we find substantially the same thought: "For since the Law has but a shadow of the good things to come instead of the true form of these realities, it can never . . . make perfect those who draw near." In both cases the word shadow (*skia*) has a nuance that it does not possess in English. It means not only a literal shadow, but a foreshadowing that is in *contrast to reality*. This negative meaning of the word is important, for this is the aspect that was developed by the Apologists.

In the Book of Acts we have an incident in which Paul dramatizes for us the relation of shadow truth in pagan religions. In Chapter 17 we find Paul in Athens preaching in the Jewish synagogues, and while he was there "his spirit was provoked within him as he saw that the city was full of idols." In other words, his spirit discerned and was angry about the demonic content and degradation of Hellenistic religion. Yet when he was given an opportunity to preach to the Greek audience he did not shower them with a "fire and brimstone" sermon, but began at the point where Greek religion still had elements of truth, and agreed with them where he could:

> Men of Athens, I perceive that in every way you are very religious. For as I passed along and observed the objects of your worship, I found also an altar with this inscription, "To an unknown God." What therefore you worship as unknown, this I proclaim to you. The God who made the world and

everything in it, being Lord of heaven and earth, does not live in shrines made by man. . . . And he made from one every nation of men to live on all the face of the earth . . . that they should seek God, in the hope that they might feel after him and find him. Yet he is not far from each one of us, for "In him we live and move and have our being"; as even some of your poets have said, "For we are indeed his offspring." Being then God's offspring, we ought not to think the Deity is like gold, or silver. . . . The times of ignorance God overlooked, but now he commands all men everywhere to repent. . . . (Acts 17:22–28)

This is one of the few examples we have of Paul's preaching to the pagan Gentiles. There are several features of his brief speech we must note. First he used, as far as possible, pagan sources as a point of contact to get the gospel message to his pagan audience. Both of the internal quotations in his speech are from Gentile sources. This is a scriptural verification of the "broad" interpretation of Logos theology; in this case pagan writers had enough of the divine truth to be incorporated in both Paul's message and, ultimately, scripture. Paul also revealed some of God's plan for mankind: That God *intended* for man to grope for the truth and attempt to find him. After this period would come the appropriate time for a fuller and more accurate revelation. From the setting in Athens we can see that God allowed this probing to take its natural course, which involved both human error and demonic distortion. However evil the whole Athenian scene was, there was reserved a place where the Logos still had an opening: the altar to the "unknown god." This was the base and contact point for Paul's preaching of the Gospel.

From these biblical accounts we can define shadow truth as anything in the spiritual life or theology of an existent religion which points to, clarifies, or helps in making understandable the fuller truths of Christian revelation.

This concept was elaborated in its negative connotation by the Apologists, and especially by Justin Martyr. Like all educated Greek men of his era, he was aware that the mystery cults of his age had ceremonies of initiation and a sacred meal that long antedated Christian baptism and the Lord's supper. Justin was also aware of the debauched nature of these rites: how they often included sexual orgies as part of the ceremonies. Justin and other Christian writers of that era believed that the similarities between Christian and pagan sacramental forms was due to the precognitive ability of demons who anticipated the Christian sacraments. Their goal was to confuse and cloud God's sacramental gift to man by inventing nonsense and debased parodies of the real thing. This was a "demonic counterfeit" view of Greek proto-sacraments.[6]

Since we modern Christians see little relationship between major pagan rites and the Church's sacraments, the issue confronting the early Fathers is not a lively concern in our age. Shadow truth has become an almost forgotten concept. The exception is found in contemporary missionary writings. Missionaries to "primitive" societies have consistently encountered folktales, myths, and religious practices that prefigure the gospel message.[7]

Odo Casel, a monk-theologian and biblical scholar, took a look at the mystery religions from a perspective of twenty centuries and explained the shadow truth relationship more fully. He felt that the mystery religions, however distorted they may have been, ultimately served God's purpose by preparing the Hellenistic world for the ideas of sacrament and redeemer. Thus, in the short term Saint Paul and the Fathers are right; pagan cults were demon worship and did distract souls from authentic worship. But in the long run they served God by "making straight the way of the Lord." This difference between the short-term and long-term effects of Satanic activity goes to the heart of its meaning. The New Testament shows Satan as murderer, destroyer, temptor, and liar, but the Old Testament, especially in the story of Job, shows that, even so, he ultimately works for the Lord.[8]

In reference to a contemporary issue, Christian students of the occult have long been aware that there is some relationship between occult doctrines and truth. Just what this relationship is has always been very puzzling. Walter R. Martin, a Baptist minister and researcher who wrote a first-rate exposé of American new religions and cults, noted that "the cults have also emphasized the things which the church has forgotten, such as divine healing (Christian Science, Unity, New Thought), prophecy (Jehovah's Witness and Mormonism), and a great many others. . . ."[9]

Dom David Geraets, abbot of Pecos Benedictine, and leader of a Catholic charismatic community made of monks and laymen who work, pray, and teach together, reiterates this point. It is his belief that the revealing power of the Holy Spirit (Logos) cannot be stopped by man's stubbornness or defensive theology. The Holy Spirit will flow into occult groups if it is blocked out by orthodox Christians. Abbot David warns Christians that unless they are open to the Holy Spirit they may be overwhelmed by non-Christian forms of spirituality. Further, any truth not taught by Christianity is taken over and distorted by the occult.[10]

In terms of spiritual issues and theology, it seems that God allows the demonic kingdom considerable leeway to distort, confuse, and literally "raise hell" in the short term. However, in the long term the demonic is serving God's purpose by *establishing preliminary hypotheses*. The Logos can then use the preliminary and demonized hypotheses as a *base* from which to mold valid revelation. In this sense many of the ideas found in the occult can be understood as shadow truths.

Both Martin and Geraets are of course dealing with the concept of shadow truth without explicitly using the term. All of this is of critical importance in our study of PLVs; for with this concept we can examine occult writings and ask what forgotten or obscured truth lies here buried and distorted? To the issue of the Truth behind the shadow truth we will turn in Part IV of this work. This will ultimately allow us to hear some of what the Logos wishes to say to us in our time. Right now, however, it is our task to define and examine the issues of ambiguity in revelation, spiritual discernment, and then to examine the biblical form of occultism called Gnosticism, which contains within its doctrines the core of what is truly destructive in the spiritual life.

Chapter 2

Ambiguity in the Mature Spiritual Life

Introduction

The importance of ambiguity in the spiritual life first came to my attention when I came across a well-respected book, *The Natural Depth in Man,*[1] by a non-Christian secular psychiatrist, Dr. Wilson Van Dusen. Van Dusen worked for eighteen years in several California mental institutions for the severely disturbed. He gradually came to believe that many of his patients, especially those who "heard voices," were in fact possessed by evil spirits.[2] This was quite a bold conclusion for someone educated in secular psychiatry. He also noted a peculiar characteristic of these demonic voices: they continuously bombarded the victim with direct commands, instructions, and specific, even picky, advice. The end result of this verbal bombardment was to break down the person's will and decision-making ability.[3]

Van Dusen contrasted this type of demonic activity with the healthy mental life of spiritually mature persons. He found in his survey of mystics and spiritually sensitive persons that they received guidance through indirect processes such as dreams, sudden intuitions, and so forth. These forms of direction were gentle; they respected the decision-making ability of the person, and were essentially ambiguous. (Van Dusen uses the word ambivalence in his book, but its meaning is identical with my use of ambiguity.) This ambiguity is intimately related to the person's freedom; that is, to accept or reject the direction given in noncoercive terms. Also the person who received positive direction had to interact creatively and willfully with the advice. It was a process which uplifted and strengthened the person in the skills of choosing good and avoiding evil (discernment).[4]

For myself, a person educated in the rigidly dogmatic Roman Catholic theology that prevailed before the Second Vatican Council, the concept of spiritual ambiguity was revolutionary. When I began reading modern Protestant theologians I came to realize it was a concept well developed in the mainstream of their thought.

In fact, an attitude of ambiguity, conscious or otherwise, is central to the mature Christian life. On a theological level, it allows a person to accept that there may be more than one system of theology, biblical exegesis, liturgy, way of worshipping, or course of action that is still authentically Christian and pleasing to God. It is the opposite of dogmatism, which is the belief that there is a "right knowledge" or "right theology" about all of these things, or that a specific theological-credal system is necessary for salvation. Many Christians have been accustomed to the idea that their denominational theology and worship are the only authentic response to the Gospel, and that other denominations are to one degree or another "inferior" or "corrupted." Three hundred years ago this idea was so intense that Christians literally killed one another in order to impose their own "right theology" on other Christians. This situation no longer exists, but the idea that one's own denomination does have a greatly superior "right theology" still is prominent in the minds of many Christians.

However, for some time most Protestant laymen have had a functional appreciation of ambiguity through their acceptance of religious pluralism. Many feel complete freedom to shift their place of worship from one denomination to another for such down-to-earth reasons as the quality of the pastor's sermons or Sunday school preferences for their children. Behind this denominational mobility is the assumption that (within certain limits) Protestant denominations are all equally close to the ultimate spiritual truths of Christianity. In effect, though many ministers preach specific denominational doctrines, the public accepts ambiguity as a spiritual reality.

It should be noted that the Anglican Church has been especially open to permitting a wide variety of beliefs and styles of worship within its ecclesiastical framework. Since the Second Vatican Council, Catholics too are learning more and more to accept this attitude, and Catholic theologians have done much in recent decades to move away from the nonambiguous tradition of Neoscholasticism.

Biblical Perspectives

For the biblical view of ambiguity we again turn to Proverbs and other books of the Hebrew Wisdom literature.[5] In certain respects this literature is the "natural theology" of the Bible. Unlike the historical books that relate the special revelation of God's mighty acts in history, or the prophetic books that depend on the anointed and self-conscious revelation of a prophet, the Wisdom Books are the product of the Logos working through man's natural ability to reflect upon moral and spiritual issues.

The Book of Proverbs also gives us an excellent example of how the Logos wove non-Jewish sources into its inspired scripture. The scribes who did the final editing of Proverbs incorporated much material from the Egyptian wisdom book Amen-en-opet (Pr. 22:17–24:22).[6]

The Book of Proverbs itself has many themes, but we need to examine only two of them for our understanding of ambiguity: the idea that wisdom and knowledge must be *actively* sought after, and the contrast between a wise and foolish man.

Proverbs 1:2–6 declares that wisdom and knowledge are acquired skills:

> *That men may know wisdom and instruction,*
> *understand words of insight,*
> *receive instruction in wise dealing,*
> *righteousness, justice, and equity;*
> *that prudence may be given to the simple,*
> *knowledge and discretion to the youth —*
> *the wise man also may hear and increase in learning,*
> *and the man of understanding acquire skill*
> *to understand a proverb and a figure,*
> *the words of the wise and their riddles.*

Why wise men should speak in riddles (or even Jesus in parables) suggests the growth purpose of ambiguity. Further, these skills are not easy to come by, but demand hard, persevering work:

> *If you cry out for insight*
> *and raise your voice for understanding*
> *if you seek it like silver*
> *and search for it as for hidden treasure*
> *then you will understand the fear of the LORD*
> *and find the knowledge of God. (Pr. 2:2–5)*

Further on, in Proverbs 8:17 the personified Spirit of Wisdom reaffirms that:

> *I love those who love me,*
> *and those who seek me diligently find me.*

But for our purposes the most important sections are those which contrast the wise man with the fool. The fool is one who despises wisdom, knowledge, and instruction (1:7, 20), and is "big-mouthed" about his opinions (13:3). This is the very opposite of a wise man. He is not only reticent about what he knows (13:3), but gladly absorbs knowledge and is appreciative of instruction (9:9). The wise man does not see himself as wise in his own eyes (3:7), but, most importantly, trusts in the Lord and does not reply on his own understanding (3:5). The picture of the wise man of Proverbs is strangely similar to that of the figure of Socrates, and perhaps one reason why Christian thinkers of all ages have been so attracted to this "pagan" sage.

The New Testament

In many ways and in many of its books the New Testament repeats the call to ambiguity we found in Proverbs. The ministry of Jesus points to a way of salvation not at all dependent on "right knowledge" or "right theology," but on trust in God through him. Part of Christianity's continuous problem of confusing "right theology" with faith in Jesus stems from the different use New Testament writers gave to the Greek word *pistis*. In the synoptic gospels the word is used to mean "trust," as in trust in the power of God, trust in Jesus for healing or exorcism, or even, in Peter's case, trust in Jesus for walking on the water. In the gospels faith does not mean "belief system" or "right theology." This is clearly shown in the fact that in Nazareth, where the people had the "right theology" but little trust in him, Jesus could do few miracles (Mt. 13:54–58). Yet he did great healings for both the centurian whose servant was sick and the Syrophoenician woman whose daughter was possessed. Both these persons had pagan or semipagan belief systems (definitely "wrong theology"), yet trusted in Jesus (Mt. 8:5–13, 15:21–28).

Paul gave some powerful hints as to the importance of ambiguity in the authentic Christian life. In this sense Paul updated Proverbs to his contemporary situation. In 1 Corinthians 8:1–3 he contrasted the attitude of the religious "know-it-all" (the fool of Proverbs) with the true lover of God:

> Now concerning food offered to idols: we know that "all of us possess knowledge." "Knowledge puffs up," but love builds up. If any one imagines that he knows something, he does not yet know as he ought to know. But if one loves God, one is known by him.

In 1 Timothy, the thought is reinforced by contrasting the unambiguous teachings of the false teachers who make "confident assertions" with the simple faith of the deacons of the Church who "must hold the mystery of the faith with a clear conscience." (1 Tim. 1:3–7; 3:8–9) Thus the Apostolic Church rested on a simple credal base which accepted as normative that many things were a mystery (i.e., beyond the power of the intellect to define or understand). The false teachers were the ones who resisted the elements of mystery and ambiguity.

Paul's letter to the Romans points to another element of ambiguity in the Christian life: the subjective nature of religious practices. Some Christians in Rome were observing dietary regulations and specific holy days while others were not. Paul cites both as pleasing to God as long as the interior motive was sincere. Here as always, Paul mirrors what had been Our Lord's teaching. Jesus spent much of his ministry denouncing the Pharisaic system with its elaborate nonambiguous code of life, and preached a higher, and more difficult, calling of subjective internal responses to the demands of the Holy Spirit. The very means that Jesus used to proclaim the Kingdom of God, the parables, were essentially ambiguous. They had a central meaning that was more or less clear, yet they had a richness and potential for varied interpretation that has been the delight of preachers for centuries. Anyone who considers a parable is drawn automatically into a growth process where in order to understand one must make an effort to understand. Further, as Wilson Van Dusen pointed out about higher spiritual direction, parables are sufficiently ambiguous to permit the person the freedom not to understand.

Perhaps the clearest antidogmatic section of the Bible is the letter of James. This apostle wrote in the direct tradition of the wisdom literature, and some have even called his epistle the "Proverbs" of the New Testament. It is certainly among the most Jewish of the New Testament writings, and it bears the mark of someone, like Paul, who was trained in the exacting process of Jewish hypothesis-reproof.

Chapter three of James's epistle contrasts divine wisdom with the demonic kind, and we can almost see his vision of two Jewish-Christian brothers amiably discussing some point of scripture:

> Who is wise and understanding among you? By his good life let him show his works in the meekness of wisdom. But if you have bitter jealousy and selfish ambition in your hearts, do not boast and be false to the truth. This wisdom is not such as comes down from above, but is earthly, unspiritual, devilish. For where jealousy and selfish ambition exist, there will be disorder and every evil practice. But the wisdom from above is first pure, then peaceable, gentle, open to reason, full of mercy and good fruits, without uncertainty or insincerity. And the harvest of righteousnes is sown in peace by those who make peace. (Jas. 3:13–18, RSV)

It must be noted that in verse 17 the Greek word *adiacritos* that the Revised Standard Version translates as "uncertainty," has two distinct meanings in Greek. One meaning is "impartial" and the other is "uncertainty."[7]

The King James version, as well as other modern versions, including the Jerusalem Bible, chooses "impartial" as the correct translation for *adiacritos* in this verse. It seems that the RSV was in error here, for if the wisdom from above is "unwavering" it cannot at the same time be "open to reason" which is given as a simultaneous characteristic in the same verse.

The Apostolic Church

In the past few decades biblical scholars have discovered just how ambiguous the early Church was in its beliefs and practices. W.D. Davies has shown in his works the depth and scope of the diversity of the early Church. One of his essays in particular, "A Normative Pattern of Church Life in the New Testament?"[8] points out that within the early Church there was a pluralism of worship very similar to the contemporary situation. The Hellenistic churches founded by Paul were "congregational" and loosely structured in their prayer services. Jewish Christianity, which was influenced by the organizational pattern of the Essene sect, followed by a more hierarchical pattern, even to the point of having a "Pope" in the figure of James.[9]

Pluralism and ambiguity of beliefs, far from being a "modern" phenomenon caused by a failure to find "right theology" or "right practice," was and will continue to be the product of different Christian groups responding in their understanding to the living presence of Christ and his gospel.

The Post-Apostolic Church

The public practice of pluralism and the private virtues of ambiguity and reticence eroded in the first centuries of the Church's existence. By the fourth century the bitter struggles against Gnostics, Arians, and others had moved the Church to uniformity of liturgy and elaboration of unambiguous doctrines in the form of the creeds. Thus the Church attempted to counter heresy with "right doctrine," but this inadvertently reduced the role of mystery in the belief system of Christianity.

The effort to reach a perfect "right doctrine" reached its high point in the Middle Ages. The Reformation challenged the whole doctrinal system of the Middle Ages and opened the way for more open-ended systems of belief and worship. This was not necessarily the intention of the Reformers, for they sought to substitute their own "right theology" for that of the Catholic Church. This is especially clear in the works of Calvin, who was noted for his dogmatism.

The Reformation split Western Christianity into two warring camps that established themselves on opposite sides of dogmatic issues, each side assuming that its "right theology" was essential for salvation. There were the issues of human free will versus divine election; of the universal priesthood of believers versus a limited ministry and priesthood; of celibacy as a higher calling versus marriage as normative; of public worship centering on the Lord's supper versus worship centered on the Word. The obvious factor is that both sides had scriptural warrant for all of these positions, and the arguments were based on giving particular weight to one set of scriptures over another.

Ambiguity and Modern Theology

Not only the biblical scholars but theologians as well have come to realize the importance of ambiguity. The first steps in this direction are found in the writings of the nineteenth-century existentialist, Soren Kierkegaard, who stressed the "paradoxical" nature of Christianity. This concept is not exactly equivalent to ambiguity, but it does counter the dogmatic, unambiguous, and rational theologies of that century's orthodoxy. Kierkegaard stresses the irrational nature of faith as against those apologists who assumed that accepting Christianity was a rational and eminently logical process.[10]

It is, however, in the theology of Reinhold Niebuhr that a true concept of ambiguity is developed. Niebuhr sees man as *essentially ambiguous*, caught between the pull of his body and nature to be an animal, unconscious and lacking a desire for freedom; and the contrary pull of his spirit which seeks freedom and escape from the bounds of nature. In his view man can sin in one of two ways. He can surrender to his animal nature and ignore his spirit and sink into selfishness and sensuality. He can, on the other hand, ignore his animal nature or repress it and attempt to live a life of the spirit exclusively. This attempt leads to sins of pride and arrogance. It is, therefore, man's responsibility to accept his ambiguous situation as a permanent state. He must acknowledge himself as a creature of God that is half animal and half spirit, both seeking freedom and being bounded by nature. There is no "resolution" of this ambiguous, uncomfortable state other than total dependence on God for guidance and comfort.[11]

Paul Tillich more than any other contemporary theologian appreciated the importance of ambiguity. In his major work *Systematic Theology*, he dedicated almost one hundred pages to virtually every facet of ambiguity in man's spiritual and moral life.[12] Tillich grew to adulthood in pre–World War I Germany in a social environment that was authoritarian, and a theological environment that was dogmatically Lutheran. His experience as a war chaplain shattered both his politics and his theology, and his discovery of Kierkegaard in the 1920s pointed the way for him towards an ambiguous theological way of thinking.[13]

A major theme of Tillich's mature theology is his belief that religious systems place impossible burdens on man. If these systems are taken with the seriousness (or "ultimate concern," to use his favorite phrase) that should be reserved only to God, they become "demonized."

> There is a phenomenon we could call "the demonization of religion." When we speak of "the demonic" we mean more than failure and distortion, more than intentional evil. The demonic is a negative absolute. It is the elevation of something relative and ambiguous (something in which the negative and the positive are united) to absoluteness. . . . In the case of religion, the deification of the relative and the ambiguous means that a particular religion claims to be identical with the religious Absolute and rejects judgement against itself. This leads, internally, to demonic suppression of doubt, criticism, and honest search for truth within the particular religion itself; and it leads, externally, to the most demonic and destructive of all wars, religious wars.[14]

Against this form of religion Tillich postulated what he calls the "Protestant principle." This is an attitude derived from the ancient prophets and revitalized in the Reformation, which attacks *any* form of "self-absolutizing," and allows for pluralism and ambiguity.

> Where the divine Spirit is effective, the claim of a church to represent God to the exclusion of all other churches is rejected. The freedom of the Spirit resists it. And when the divine Spirit is effective, a church member's claim to an exclusive possession of the truth is undercut by the witness of the divine Spirit to his fragmentary as well as ambiguous participation in the truth.[15]

Tillich believed that what Christianity really demands of a person is his commitment to the *person* of Jesus.[16] Tillich also echoed Proverbs' definition of the "Wise Man" in his belief that the task of a theologian is to be unassuming in order to allow the dogmatic "weakness" to be a vehicle for the ministering strength of the Holy Spirit.

> Nothing is more disastrous for the theologian himself and more despicable to those whom he wants to convince than a theology of self-certainty. The real theologian is he who has the strength to perceive and to confess his weakness.[17]

It should be pointed out that the most important breakthroughs in propagating an awareness of ambiguity among lay Christians have come not from either biblical scholars or theologians, but from the leaders of the present Charismatic renewal. When Charismatic Christians from different denominations prayed together and ministered to one another it was natural that the traditional role of "right theology" would come into question. In this respect the Full Gospel Businessman Fellowship International and Camps Furthest Out have been instruments well used by God. The Charismatics are in an unusually good position to appreciate ambiguity and the limitations of rational theology since more than most Christians they realize the function of the spirit, which is to worship God in a manner that is *beyond* rational categories and verbalization. Charismatic Christians are generally more aware of the relative unimportance of credal confessions as the mark of the believer, and stress the importance of a faith-trust in Jesus. In fact, the trend towards ecumenism based on a sincere appreciation of denominational differences and ambiguity in theology is quite widespread among major Charismatic leaders.[18]

It is now time to place Van Dusen's insight on the role of ambiguity within a specifically Christian context. As we mentioned, he saw ambiguity intimately related to freedom and the development of decision-making skills. In turn we can see that these are the characteristics necessary for the life of a maturing Christian. The first stage of Christian life is to be "saved," that is, to choose to enter the Kingdom of God by acknowledging the personal Lordship of Jesus. This stage has little to do with ambiguity. After this, when the Christian begins to lead a life of deeper sanctification and perfection, ambiguity becomes a prominent part of his or her spiritual life. The situations with which a maturing Christian is often presented are not of the order of good or evil, but of choosing among a variety of good acts. On the intellectual level, as a Christian matures, he or she comes to appreciate more and criticize less the theologies of other denominations.

Qualifications

This brings us to the point where we must begin to limit and qualify the concept of ambiguity. Without these qualifications Christianity would degenerate into an ethical morass of opinions where one idea is as good as any other.

The most important qualification is that ambiguity does not eliminate the role of the ten commandments and other moral imperatives of Christianity. Ambiguity comes *after* salvation and a basic moral life have been established. There is no time when moral laws are suspended. There will never be an ambiguous position on adultery, or murder, or false witness, and so forth. Paul Tillich defines it well by saying that although man's concrete situation is always ambiguous and relative, the moral law itself is absolute.[19]

In this regard there seem to be certain universal patterns in the relationship between the absolute and the ambiguous that are repeated in the lives of most human beings. The great Swiss psychologist Jean Piaget, in his classic study of children learning to play marbles, detected a standard pattern in their understanding of the rules of the game.[20] Very small children understood rules as divinely decreed from the adult world and absolutely correct and inviolable. After ages six to nine they come to understand that rules are man-made and therfore subject to change. In the early teen years they begin to appreciate the value of cooperation in the formation of their own rules. The last stage of moral development is generally not reached before adolescence, and at this stage the person understands rules as internal, relative, and ambiguous, yet necessary and good.

God who is the Father of us all first gave the Mosaic Law, which was absolute and unambiguous; with the formation of the other books of the Old Testament further direction was of a more ambiguous nature. Finally the last revelation of Jesus Christ gave the world freedom from the law by placing it within man's heart and under the power of the Holy Spirit. The Mosaic Law was not cancelled, rather it became internalized with a higher, more spiritual level of imperatives. It is important to clarify that in either ethics or in the spiritual life one cannot merely eliminate the original stage of absolute rules. Rather, this stage must be incorporated and internalized.

Another important qualification of the role of ambiguity in theology is that it must be based on a firm foundation of knowledge, and it must not be confused with the attitude that any idea is as good as any other. Here again our scriptural model is the discipline and training of Jewish theological inquiry (see Lk. 2:46–49). The Book of Proverbs shows that ambiguity is the proper result of the process of diligently and humbly seeking after wisdom and knowledge. Believing that any opinion is as good as any other is what the fool believes, not the man filled with the wisdom of God.

Also, ambiguity in theology is closely related to scientific methodology. A scientist knows that not all hypotheses can be completely disproved, yet clearly some hypotheses are better than others. The process of eliminating the poorer hypothesis involves study, experimental testing, and hard work. Theology should follow the same procedure.

Last is the most important qualification of all. Though it is correct to say that "right theology" does not save a person, it is also true that certain ideas are spiritually harmful and can lead to spiritual death. To distinguish between merely wrong ideas that are irrelevant to salvation, and ideas that are spiritually deadly will be the task of the next chapters.

Chapter 3

Discernment:
From the Bible to
Saint John of the Cross

Discernment Defined

In the history of man's relation to God, the thin line dividing authentic and counterfeit revelation has been difficult to locate. Discernment is the form of spiritual wisdom that makes the distinction between them possible. Discernment enables the believer to distinguish the origins and ultimate nature of spiritual events. The most commonly known form of discernment is called "discernment of spirits." It is given this name in scripture by Saint Paul (1 Cor. 12) and is classed as one of the gifts of the Holy Spirit. Some Christians mistakenly assume that discernment of spirits is a faculty used only in identifying evil spirits or influences. True discernment also has the positive function of identifying the presence or influence of the Holy Spirit.[1]

A second form of discernment mentioned in scripture has no specific name, yet it should not be confused with discernment of spirits. This is the ability to distinguish whether any given *idea* or *activity* is good or evil, useful or not useful, for the welfare of the Body of Christ. Historically this gift has been in constant, though unconscious, operation, for example, in the acceptance of the Copernican view of the solar system, or the acceptance of "Sunday schools" for the purpose of Christian instruction.

Another form of discernment is what might be called "discernment of means." That is, God has apparently chosen certain ways of communicating with man, such as dreams, visions, and so forth, but not others. Thus, as we shall discuss later, trance mediumship, although a "spiritual" phenomenon, has never been used by the Holy Spirit as a vehicle of communication.

The ultimate purpose of all forms of discernment is to guide the person to those activities and ideas which lead to God and away from those things which deflect a person away from him. Some denominations hold that there is little present need for discernment as a specific spiritual gift. Their theology states that miracles, the gifts of the Holy Spirit, and God's communication with human beings through spiritual means ended with the last of the biblical writers. For these Christians discernment is not a spiritual function but rather an intellectual process of judging an idea or action as "orthodox" or not.

However, most Christian denominations, especially those in the Roman, Anglo-Catholic, and Orthodox traditions, have always believed that God continues to speak directly to His people. This belief was given renewed vigor in the Pentecostal-Charismatic renewal and points to an important distinction between biblical revelation and "personal" revelation. All Christians would agree that a unique deposit of revelation is found in the Bible. In it are found the great truths of the origins of man, the nature of God and of Christ, and the way of salvation. This special revelation was closed with the death of the Apostles and sealed with the formation of the canon of the Bible. Thus postbiblical "personal" revelation is of a secondary order, and is limited to and defined by reference to the original biblical revelation. The French theologian Father Laurent Volken has aptly defined the delicate relation between personal and biblical revelation:

> A [personal] revelation, in fact, should teach us something which we did not know. It cannot establish a new doctrine but it should supply something new, whether in a domain other than faith or in the sense that it causes to be understood in a vital way some Christian teaching which has been somewhat forgotten or is only vaguely known.[2]

It is important to realize that personal revelation has always had an important place in dynamic forms of Christianity. It is God's way of giving specific direction, correction, and exhortation to his Church. At times this type of revelation is directed to individual believers and at other times it is directed to groups within the church. Even within scripture itself there are examples of revelations which dealt with not fundamental theological issues, but stayed at the practical guidance level. One example is found in Acts 11:27–30 where the prophet Agabus foretold of a famine. This gave opportunity for the Hellenistic churches to organize relief efforts for the severely afflicted Jerusalem Church. In modern times there was a parallel example when, at the beginning of this century, certain Armenian Christians were forewarned of the impending genocide by the Turks and had time to flee.[3] Yet, at the same time, there have also been countless false prophecies of disasters and of the end of the world. Many an enthusiastic group of Christians have been led in white robes to mountain tops to await the Second Coming, proclaimed by some local prophet and have been rained upon instead of raptured.

Patterns of Discernment in the Bible

Old Testament

It is now our task to turn to scripture and examine what is said there about discernment. By nature biblical revelation is a collection of communications from God to Man. The primary interest is what God has to say to man, and only secondarily are there any warnings about other, negative, spiritual entities also communicating with humans. The book of Genesis describes the original God-to-man communication in its pristine state. In the innocent state of the Garden of Eden there was apparently direct communication between Adam and God through the normal senses and faculties. It was not yet distorted by sin, and was direct, unhindered by the symbolic veil of dreams or visions.

This changed radically with the fall. After that event we see the patterns of God's communication to man that we consider normal: visions, dreams, and locutions (hearing a voice without seeing the speaker). In the Old Testament only Moses was given the privilege of seeing and speaking with God directly (Num. 12:6–8). Numbers 12:6–8 states explicitly:

> Hear my words: if there is a prophet among you, I the Lord make myself known to him in a vision, I speak with him in a dream. Not so with my servant Moses; he is entrusted with all my house. With him I speak mouth to mouth, clearly, and not in dark speech; and he beholds the form of the Lord. (RSV)

The Old Testament describes all the ways that are familiar to us that God communicates with humanity. In 1 Samuel 3 we have the story of Samuel's call to his prophetic vocation through a *locution* from the Lord. Samuel had considerable difficulty in discerning that the voice was indeed from the Lord. He first thought it was from his teacher Eli. Other dreams, revelations, and visions from the Lord are so common in the Old Testament books that we do not need to cite them. It is important to note, however, that the ancient Hebrews made no distinction between vision and dream and often one word was used interchangeably to cover both phenomena. It was assumed that dreams and visions were normal occurrences whereby man entered the spiritual dimension and received his communication from God.[4]

The Old Testament is certainly not a naive document, and while the stress is on the valid revelation and communication from God to humans (and of their usual disobedient response), there is a secondary motif of the confusing and distorting communications from entities that are not from the Lord. The story of the Fall in Genesis 3 shows how the serpent deceived Eve. In a sense, the first sin was brought about by a failure in discernment. In 1 Samuel 18:10–11 and 19:8–10 we see how an evil spirit entered into King Saul and drove him to attempt the murder of David. The entrance of this entity (to my knowledge the only account of demon possession in the Old Testament) was made possible by Saul's sin of jealousy. It appears that Saul was in a normal state of consciousness when the entity entered him.

Deuteronomy is the earliest book to attempt a codification of discernment. Deuteronomy 13:1–5 gives a key rule for discerning a false from a true prophet and it is a scripture that we need to cite:

> If a prophet arises among you, or a dreamer of dreams, and gives you a sign or a wonder, and the sign or wonder which he tells you comes to pass, and if he says, "Let us go after other gods," which you have not known, "and let us serve them" you shall not listen to the words of that prophet or to that dreamer of dreams; for the Lord your God is testing you, to know whether you love the Lord your God with all your heart and with all your soul. You shall walk after the Lord your God and fear him, and keep his commandments and obey his voice, and you shall serve him and cleave to him. But that prophet or that dreamer of dreams shall be put to death, because he has taught rebellion against the Lord your God. . . . (RSV)

Note that this passage warns us that God permits authentic precognitive information to come from false prophets. The most important criterion for authentic prophecy *is not* its validity on the material level, but its *spiritual* message.

Deuteronomy 18:10–11 contains another important revelation concerning discernment. Here certain classes of contact with the spiritual world are prohibited:

> There shall not be found among you any one who burns his son or his daughter as an offering, any one who practices divination, a soothsayer, or an augur, or a sorcerer, or a charmer, or a medium, or a wizard, or a necromancer. (RSV)

These classes of spiritual activity are eliminated from discernment proper. There can be no discernment between "good" or "bad" mediumship, or divination or between "good" or "bad" sorcery. All are forbidden, and to partake in them automatically places one in a disobedient relationship with God. This in turn naturally leads to revelations which are deceptive and destructive.

It was with the prophets that the question of discernment became a more reflective item of concern. The prophets were in the business of mediating God's Word and so were intimately involved in distinguishing true prophecy from false. Jeremiah and Isaiah added significantly to our ideas concerning discernment as they lived in an environment where false prophecy influenced the Israelites. Isaiah paid particular attention to the "atmosphere" of proper discernment. That is, if the people's worship is superficial and not centered in the heart, then God withdraws from them the power of wisdom and discernment (Is. 29). He also warns that those who demand pleasant and reassuring prophecies will be brought to destruction (Is. 30).

Jeremiah echoes many of these warnings and adds a new thought. Not all false prophecy comes from external sources (alien or false gods) as Isaiah implied (28:15), but that some originate from the person's own inner mind:

> And the Lord said to me, "The prophets are prophesying lies in my name; I did not send them, nor did I command them or speak to them. They are prophesying to you a lying vision, worthless divination, and the deceit of their own minds." (Jer. 14:14 RSV)

This thought is repeated in his chapter 23:16 and 26. Chapter 23 of Jeremiah's prophecy is particularly dedicated to discernment. In 23:13–32 he says that prophets who lead immoral lives are not from God (in modern terms this might be interpreted to warn us against those who have "psychic" gifts without holiness). In 23:22 we have a particularly important passage in which it is revealed that the mark of a true prophet is one who leads his people to repentance:

> But if they (the prophets) had stood in my council, then they would have proclaimed my words to my people, and they would have turned them from their evil way, and from the evil of their doings.

It should be emphasized that this is a seminal scripture. In the subsequent literature of discernment the theme is repeated again and again in one form or another. A true vision from the Lord stimulates repentance, humility, and the quest for holiness. The inverse is true, a false vision or one from demonic sources stimulates self-centeredness, vanity, and spiritual self-sufficiency.

One of Jeremiah's roles as prophet was to warn the people about the dangers of what today would be called "psychic extremism." This is the belief that all spiritual experiences are from God and therefore good. We shall see that in the New Testament the Apostle Paul issues the same warning.

New Testament

The New Testament is concerned with discernment in roughly the same way as the Old Testament. Most of it is dedicated to positive revelation, the proclamation of the "good news," that God so loved the world that he sent his Son who pitched his tent "amongst us" (Jn. 1:14). Indeed, Jesus was the perfect revelation (Heb. 1:2). Like the historical books of the Old Testament, the Gospels are not only an account of what happened, but an anthology of *validated* revelations. The Evangelists are not anxious to confuse the narrative by stressing discernment. In essence the Gospels concern themselves with positive revelation, while the epistles confront the practical and pastoral problems (including discernment) of the active Church. As one scholar has phrased it, "discernment of spirits is lived in the gospels and evaluated in the epistles."[5]

In the first chapters of Matthew we are given a picture of Joseph receiving one revelation after another through dreams: a dream message from an angel that Mary is pregnant by the Holy Spirit, a dream to flee to Egypt, and another to come back. At no point are we given the slightest indication that Joseph anguished over these unique revelations. The silent assumption is that his spirit was sufficiently enlightened to discern that these dreams did indeed come from God.

The Gospel of Luke places more stress on prophetic utterances and visions. The Gospel narrative opens with an account of Zachariah's vision of the Angel Gabriel. A parade of other revelations took place even before Jesus' public ministry began. This is not the proper place to elaborate on the visionary phenomena described in the Gospels.[6] It is important to note, however, that scripture is clear that God's revelation is not restricted to the Chosen People. In Matthew 27:19 it is Pilot's wife, a pagan woman, who receives a divine warning about the innocence of Jesus. In Matthew 2:12 the pagan magi are warned not to return to Herod, and at the crucifixion it is the centurion who confesses that Jesus is truly the Son of God (Mt. 27:19, Mk. 15:39). This continues an Old Testament theme that revelation often *first* comes through the pagans, though significantly, must be ultimately interpreted by the chosen people (Dan. 4).

The gospels also raise the problem of what might be termed "multiple inspiration." That is, any individual is subject to use by *both* the Holy Spirit and unholy spirits. In Matthew 16:13–23 Peter gives his great confession of Jesus as the Son of God. Jesus replies by declaring that Peter said this through the inspiration of the Father. Peter immediately follows by urging Jesus not to accept his coming passion and crucifixion. Jesus then rebukes Satan *in* Peter for this. Inversely, the high priest Caiphas, one of the villains of the New Testament, temporarily assumes the role of true prophet of God when he says that Jesus must die for the sake of the Jewish nation (Jn. 11:49–54).

When we turn to the Book of Acts we have a work that stands midway between the gospels and the epistles in its concern for discernment. In Acts, the Holy Spirit proclaims some of the most revolutionary revelations in either the Old or New Testaments. The Mosaic Law was declared no longer essential for entrance into the Kingdom of God, and the Kingdom itself was freed of any geographic limitations. Perhaps because of the radical nature of these revelations the Holy Spirit took the uncommon step of utilizing trance states to bring them forth. Unfortunately, both the Jews and Greeks had relatively few words to differentiate between internal spiritual states. The Greek word translated as "trance" is *ekstasis*, from which we get out word "ecstasy." It literally means being out of oneself or standing beside oneself. The same word was used by non-Christian writers to describe the altered states of consciousness manifest in fortune-telling mediums. The reason that the same word is used for both states is that trance states from God or "the gods" appear from the outside to be similar.

The first incident to note is the famous housetop revelation that Peter had at Joppa (Acts 10:9–16). It is explicitly stated that Peter goes into a trance. While Peter is entranced, the Lord invites him to eat forbidden food, but Peter stoutly refuses to break the Mosaic Law. This is repeated three times. After the vision Peter hears the voice of the Lord (a locution) tell him to receive three gentile visitors. Peter is perplexed by the meaning of all of this and only later appreciates the significance of the vision.

The second incident is an experience that happened to Paul after his conversion, while he was in Jerusalem (22:17–21). This incident is also explicitly called a "trance." Paul was praying at the Temple and Jesus suddenly appeared to him, commanding him to leave Jerusalem and preach elsewhere. Paul tried to *argue* with the Lord, but Jesus merely repeated his command. Again, we note, a trance state that included full consciousness, full possession of will, and full recall.

These revelations came as a mix of the ambiguous and the direct, non-ambiguous. When the Lord wished to reveal to Peter an important new theological policy, that is, that the Gentiles were to be allowed into the Kingdom and that they were not bound by the Mosaic Law, he gave that revelation in an ambiguous vision. Peter had to wrestle with its meaning to understand it and grew in wisdom in the process. Revelation of more simple nature, to stop, or go to a certain place, or to do something were given as unambiguous locutions and direct commands. They required no theological innovation or growth in wisdom.

These divinely inspired trance states shared certain characteristics. To one degree or another those entranced had their bodies immobilized, but their minds, including all the functions of will, memory, and values, were intact. The peculiar altered state of consciousness of the trance state allowed the recipient to *focus* on the revelation.[7] It would be useful to term this type of trance state "lucid trance." This would allow us to distinguish between that type and the trances often found in mediumship and other occult practices. In the occult trance of both ancient and modern times, the person is most often totally unconscious and has no recall of what happened during the trance state. Clearly the will and freedom of the person is not functioning. Essentially there is a vacated body which is "used" by an entirely different entity. Thus although physiologically both trances are similar, spiritually they are completely different. The Holy Spirit works *with* and through the person, while the demonic works in disregard of the person and all its freedom and values.

Epistles

The atmosphere of the epistles is vastly different from that of the Gospels. The concern is no longer for the basic proclamation of the good news, but rather for spiritual warfare against those seeking to pervert the essential meaning of the Gospel. Thus the epistles give a great deal of information about discernment as a basic weapon of spiritual warfare.

Paul, who had the most to say in the New Testament about practically everything, spoke often about discernment. The two Corinthian epistles have large segments dedicated to this problem within the context of the spiritual gifts, especially prophecy and tongue speaking. 1 Corinthians 12–14 deals with the nature and types of spiritual gifts (we have already noted that discernment is defined as one of the gifts). Paul is not concerned that the spiritual gifts are being practiced, but they are exercised in an undisciplined and nondiscerning way, and so he gives practical rules for their correct exercise.

In 2 Corinthians we find that Paul had to defend himself from the attacks of others by listing his spiritual credentials and experiences, a task that he thoroughly disliked (Chapter 11). Paul described his experiences in Chapter 12, which included many visions and some sort of out-of-body experience to the "third heaven." These revelations were so powerful that in order to prevent Paul from being exalted, God gave him a special cross in the form of a "thorn in the flesh" (12:7). Second Corinthians also contains the famous warning that Satan can disguise himself as an angel of light (11:14).

The Galatian epistle closely follows the ground covered in the Corinthian letters, though in more compact form. It is in Galatians that we have a section which is especially useful for an understanding of discernment. This is in Chapter 5 where the "deeds of the flesh" are contrasted with the "fruits of the Spirit."

> Now the works of the flesh are plain: immorality, impurity, licentiousness, idolatry, sorcery, enmity, strife, jealousy, anger, selfishness, dissension, party spirit, envy, drunkenness, carousing, and the like. I warn you, as I warned you before, that those who do such things shall not inherit the Kingdom of God. But the fruit of the Spirit is love, joy, peace, patience, kindness, goodness, self-control; against such there is no law. (5:19–23)

This listing is important because the consistent Christian experience has been that Satan can often counterfeit the *gifts* of the spirit, as in false prophecy, but rarely is successful in falsifying the *fruits* of the Spirit, especially joy.

The letter of Philippians is one of Paul's most personal letters. In spite of this it contains an important revelation about the nature and purpose of discernment:

> And it is my prayer that your love may abound more and more, with knowledge and all discernment, so that you may approve what is excellent, and may be pure and blameless for the day of Christ, filled with the fruits of righteousness which come through Jesus Christ, to the glory and praise of God. (1:9–11)

Note that here we have discernment, but it is *not* discernment of spirits. Rather, it is associated with *knowledge*. The purpose of this "discernment-knowledge" is to test and accept "what is excellent." This is echoed in another scripture of Paul, "Do not quench the Spirit, do not despise prophesying, but test everything; hold fast to what is good, abstain from every evil" (1 Th. 5:19–22). In these passages Paul challenges Christians to do what is most difficult, to accept or reject ideas through the discerning power of the Holy Spirit within. It is far easier to base one's judgment on tradition, doctrine, or creed. This form of discernment-knowledge has no specific name, and has not been noticed by theologians of discernment.[8] This points to the issues we discussed in reference to ambiguity.

Christian theology has traditionally been based on Neo-platonic ways of thinking that trust largely in the power of logic and the mind to arrive at truth. Testing is reduced to a mental process that evaluates the logical qualities of a system and shows less concern for the fruits of that system in the real world. Paul's concept of testing is completely different. It is built upon the reproof system of Jewish Wisdom teachings, but expands it to the point where there is a usable criteria for hypothesis acceptance or rejection. To distinguish this form of discernment from discernment of spirits it would be well to call it "testing discernment."

To finish our study of Paul we should note a passage in Colossians that was directed against the Gnostic tendencies of that church:

> Let no one disqualify you, insisting on self-abasement and worship of angels, taking his stand on visions, puffed up without reason by his sensuous mind, and not holding fast to the Head, from whom the whole body, nourished and knit together through its joints and ligaments, grows with a growth that is from God. (2:18–19)

Thus humility can have an extreme form which is not from God (self-abasement), and false visions can be created in the deeper mind. This was already revealed in Jeremiah, and Paul merely echoes that view. Note also the whole cluster of spiritual errors all related to failure in discernment: self-abasement, angel worship (a form of spiritualism), visions that exalt the person, and, most importantly, being separated from Christ. In these two verses from Paul we have a major lesson in discernment.

Of the non-Pauline epistles 2 Peter and Jude are particularly concerned with false teachers and prophets of the Gnostic variety that were confusing the Church. Both epistles remind the reader that false teachers can be identified by their immoral life styles (especially 2 Peter 2:1–3).

Two Main Themes

We will now focus on the practice of discernment. There are two criteria for discernment found in the New Testament: the "fruit" criterion and the "attitude towards Jesus," or Christology. The "fruit" criterion simply means that an authentic revelation from God must produce good behavioral and spiritual results. Conversely, if the revelation produces evil behavioral or spiritual results it cannot be from God. We must note that "evil" and "good" are understood in the spiritual sense, and are closely related to the "deeds of the flesh" and the "fruits of the Spirit" cited previously from Galatians 5:19–23. They have little to do with the secular definition of happiness or sadness. For example, a prophetic utterance at a local prayer meeting may lead a person to a sense of conviction and repentance, both of which are unpleasant experiences but spiritually "good fruit."

In fact, the ministry of Jesus was introduced by John the Baptist, who proclaimed those great words of "negative thinking": "Repent, for the kingdom of heaven is at hand" (Mt. 3:1). He further warned the Pharisees who came to hear his preaching that they must produce "good fruit" in their lives (Mt. 3:8–10). Paul, writing to specifically Christian churches repeats the warning that moral righteousness is indispensable for continued life in the Body of Christ (Gal. 5:16–22 and Eph. 5:6–9).

But it is the words of Jesus himself that gave the doctrine of fruit its strongest assertion in reference to discernment:

> Beware of false prophets, who come to you in sheep's clothing but inwardly are ravenous wolves. You will know them by their fruits. Are grapes gathered from thorns, or figs from thistles? So, every sound tree bears good fruit, but the bad tree bears evil fruit. (Mt. 7:15–18)

Similarly, in the second criterion, Christology, it was the words of Our Lord that gave us the central scripture. The scene took place at Caesarea Philippi. There Jesus asked Peter:

> "But who do you say that I am?" Simon Peter replied, "You are the Christ, the Son of the Living God." And Jesus answered him, "Blessed are you, Simon Bar-Jona! For flesh and blood has not revealed this to you, but my Father who is in heaven." (Mt. 16:15–17).

Jesus referred here to a conscious saying by Peter, uttered in a normal state of consciousness. In 1 Corinthians Paul repeats this, but in reference to the altered state of consciousness of prophetic utterance and tongue speaking:

> Therefore I want you to understand that no one speaking by the Spirit of God ever says "Jesus be cursed!" and no one can say "Jesus is Lord" except by the Holy Spirit. (12:3)

In the first letter of John we find a similar statement, specifically directed at a heresy which claimed that Jesus did not physically come to earth, but appeared in a ghostlike form (Docetism). Again, as in Paul, the context is that of a Christian church in which prophecy, tongue speaking and interpretation, and visionary experiences are normal events:

> Beloved, do not believe every spirit, but test the spirits to see whether they are of God; for many false prophets have gone out into the world. By this you know the Spirit of God: every spirit which confesses that Jesus Christ has come in the flesh is of God, and every spirit which does not confess Jesus is not of God. (1 Jn. 4:1–3)

Implicit in both the Pauline and Johannine statements is the assumption that these discernment tests are valid for the prophets, visionaries, and tongue speakers while in their prophetic state. Neither statement was meant as a test of human speakers, where lying is always possible, but were put forth as tests for the spirit behind the speaker. The Holy Spirit glorifies Jesus naturally, while evil spirits cannot tolerate to call Him Lord. Both tests belong to the specific category of "discernment of spirits."

We must add here something that is conspicuous in scripture by its absence. There is no scripture in either Old or New Testaments which equates discernment with doctrinal correctness. This, however, is precisely what many Christians believe and live by. It is a reduction of discernment from a *spiritual gift*, which uses the intellect, to a *totally* intellectual function.

Also note a characteristic of the New and Old Testaments which is salient when compared with the scriptures of Eastern religions. The Bible provides little in the way of descriptions of the internal mental states of either prayer or discernment. It is in this area that the experiences of generation after generation of believers can give us insight and direction.

Discernment: The Continuing Christian Experience

The first three centuries of Christianity were filled with a concern for both physical survival from Roman persecution and spiritual survival against various forms of Gnosticism. In the latter case the gift of discernment was sorely taxed, for "Christian Gnosticism" often seemed to be authentically Christian. Yet it was in essence the antithesis of Christianity. The Gnostic sects were many and varied, having in common only their nondiscerning reliance on visions and prophecy.

Closely related to the Gnostic challenge was the task of discerning which writings were authentic holy writ. Gnostic and other spurious writings were examined, discussed, and finally rejected by the Church. Other writings were similarly tested, but found to be "excellent" and were approved by the Church as authentic scripture. Thus, the formation of our canon of scripture was the fruit of the discernment process of the whole Church.

Montanism

Another severe test of the discernment ability of the Church was the rise of the Montanist sect. This was originally a charismatic movement with strong influence in North Africa. It began about the year A.D. 175 as completely orthodox. The peculiarity of the Montanists was their stress on prophecy (which they based on Scripture [see 1 Cor. 14]). However, what destroyed the Montanists as an authentic denomination of the Christian faith was the undisciplined and nondiscerning nature of their prophecy.[9]

The Montanists soon became exceptionally rigorist and pharisee-like in their views and denounced other Christians as heretics.

The Church's experience with the Montanists brought to the fore a discernment of means that was implicit in scripture but not explicit. Namely, that nonlucid trance prophecy (prophecy in which the prophet has no awareness or memory of the utterance) is diabolical. Many of the Montanist prophecies were delivered in nonlucid states.[10] This does not mean that prophecy which is lucid, and spoken by the prophet in full control of his senses, is *automatically* from the Holy Spirit. It does mean that lucid prophecy has the *possibility* of being from the Holy Spirit and must be subject to further discernment. Trance prophecy of the unconscious type needs no further discernment because it is essentially demonic. Again, the principle is that the Holy Spirit works with and through the person, the demonic in disregard of him.[11]

Unfortunately, the Church's experience with Montanism caused it to become unduly suspicious of *any* manifestation of the gifts of the Spirit. From that time until the twentieth century the charismatic gifts did not appear in *sustained*, orthodox setting. In a work of great importance, Father Ronald Knox traced the outbreaks of the gifts of the Spirit throughout church history and shows how irregular and scattered these outbreaks have been.[12] After Montanism the Holy Spirit manifested his gifts most often through saintly individuals, but rarely in public worship and community settings.

Christians in the Desert

At the same time the Montanists were attempting to escape the moral corruption of the late Roman Empire by moral scrupulosity and obedience to a prophetic spirit, other Christians were developing a different way. These Christians sought to carry out Christ's command: "You, therefore, must be perfect, as your heavenly Father is perfect" (Mt. 5:48). They took as their biblical models the prophets Elijah and John the Baptist (the Nazarite way) to forge a life-style in the deserts of Egypt and Palestine. Theirs was a life dedicated to the Lord every moment, and centered on the virtues of celibacy, poverty, asceticism, and solitude. The best-known pioneer of this form of life was Saint Anthony of Egypt (d. 356). Like Jesus, Saint Anthony also experienced great temptations while in the desert, and, like him, after they were over he was much strengthened spiritually. During years of ministry, Saint Anthony displayed the gifts of healing and exorcism, discernment of spirits, and a strong gift of wisdom for counseling others.[13]

Among the desert monks that followed Anthony the most important figure for the study of discernment was the great monk-theologian-psychologist

Evagrius Ponticus (d. 399).[14] His early theological speculations had a wild abandon to them, but his pastoral-psychological writings became classics which enriched the spirituality of both Eastern and Western Christianity.

The desert was the perfect spiritual laboratory for Evagrius. The mud hovels of his monks were in fact ready-made for experiments in sense deprivation. The monk's life and location focused the mind away from the multiplicity of images in secular life and into the spiritual dimensions of existence. Through prayer, scripture reading, self-observation, and the experience of being the spiritual director for other monks, Evagrius worked out a magnificent system of monitoring and discerning the presence of demonic or heavenly influences in the mind.

Evagrius came to realize that the demonic kingdom infested thought processes in any and all states of consciousness. It could be present in the stream of consciousness of the normal waking state, or it could be present in our dream life. In fact, monitoring dreams was an important method Evagrius used to evaluate the spiritual development of his monks. Not even prayer, that state of mind closest to God, was free from demonic assault:

> The devil so passionately envies the man who prays that he employs every device to frustrate that purpose. Thus he does not cease to stir up thoughts of various affairs by means of memory. He stirs up all the passions by means of the flesh. In this way he hopes to offer some obstacles to that excellent course pursued in prayer on the journey to God.[15]

The realization that the demonic can utilize personal memories is central to the Evagrian psychology. In his view, sin leaves a form of energy in the memory that demons can utilize to remind and tempt the person to further sin. To use his words:

> . . . if an image of someone who has done me harm or who has insulted me comes to my mind, it shows the demon of resentment is near; if I remember money or fame it is impossible not to know by their subject matter who is troubling us. It is the same with other thoughts. I do not mean that all memories of such things come from demons, for it is usual to the mind itself, when a man brings it into motion, to reproduce images of past events. But only those memories come from the demons which unnaturally evoke excitation or desire. Owing to the disturbance of these powers, the mind commits mental adultery or quarrels . . . [16]

Evagrius further observed that the demons have a certain power to create visions and images in the imagination:

The demons wage a veritable war against our concupiscible appetite. They employ for this combat phantasms (and we run to see them) which show conversations with our friends, banquets with our relatives, whole choruses of women and all kinds of things calculated to produce delight.[17]

The writings of Evagrius were transmitted to the Christian West by his disciple John Cassian, and they had a tremendous influence on the development of Catholic theology. His insights concerning the process of demonic interference in human thought were accepted as true until forgotten by the modern age.

Christian Mysticism

From the pioneer monks of the desert came not only the main outlines of monasticism, but the ground upon which flowered Christian mysticism. This was greatly aided and directed by several brilliant theologians of the Partistic Era, especially Gregory of Nyssa (d. 395). Today, many people unfortunately associate the whole tradition of Christian mysticism with extreme asceticism. In reality, the heart of authentic mysticism is *contemplative prayer*, which can take place in conjunction with practically any life-style, ascetic or not.

Contemplative prayer is simply a process of quieting the mind, ignoring the normal "stream of consciousness," and prayerfully placing oneself in the presence of God. It is essentially wordless prayer. Normally contemplative prayer is done by relaxing the body and repeating a word or phrase such as "Jesus" or "love" until a lucid trance state is achieved. In this state the body is immobilized but the mind is conscious and, depending on God's grace, intimately aware of God's presence. The classic description of this prayer technique is found in a late medieval work, *The Cloud of Unknowing*, written by an anonymous English monk or nun.[18]

In the West, contemplative prayer has normally been practiced in a reclining position. In its mechanics and superficial aspects it is similar to contemporary practice of TM. It is profoundly different from TM spiritually because contemplative prayer, in whatever way it is practiced, is essentially a worship activity. Its intention is to come to the intimate presence of God. TM and other meditation disciplines aim at deep relaxation and its benefits—emotional stability and healing. Christian contemplative prayer often achieves these effects as a by-product, but its principal goal is always prayer, worship, and the experience of God's presence.

We must note that in the long tradition of Christian contemplative prayer the lucid trance state has been a common occurrence. Most people who have attempted any sort of meditation such as TM have experienced the sensations of bodily tingling, relaxation, and immobilization. At times the degree of immobilization and slowdown of bodily functions is very great. Saint Teresa of Avila, perhaps the greatest mystic of the Catholic Church, would at times go into such a deep trance that she was thought dead. In advanced mystical states, the intellectual functions of the brain also slow down so that the mystic experiences the love of God in its pure spiritual aspect without the distraction of other processes of consciousness. This type of mystic state is intended not as a personal revelation, but rather as a gift of love from God to the mystic.[19]

In fairness to its Protestant critics we must note that Christian mysticism had some of its roots in non-Christian sources. Much of its vocabulary and theology were derived from neo-Platonic sources of the late Roman Empire. This can clearly be seen in the works of Pseudo-Dionysius which were so influential in the Middle Ages.[20] The ascetic and meditative practices may have been influenced as well by Jewish and neo-Platonic ascetic communities located around the city of Alexandria in the first century of our era.

It is also important to note that there are many passages in scripture, especially in the Psalms, which strongly suggest the practice of contemplative prayer. Psalm 4, verse 4 reads:

> *Be angry, but sin not,*
> *Commune with your own hearts on*
> *your beds, and be silent.*

Psalm 46:10:

> *Be still, and know that I am God.*

Psalm 62:1:

> *For God alone my soul waits in silence:*
> *from him comes my salvation.*

And especially Psalm 131:2:

> *But I have calmed and quieted my soul,*
> *like a child quieted at its mother's breast.*

Equally important in the evaluation of Christian mysticism is the "fruit" criterion. Medieval monastic spirituality, that mix of asceticism (poverty, chastity, obedience) and contemplative prayer, produced many saints, known and unknown, who developed to remarkable degrees of holiness. Given that the medieval mind often confused extreme asceticism with holiness, many of the saints did manifest the authentic and universal mark of holiness: love (1 Cor. 13).

It is also clear that many contemplatives in the Middle Ages did have both the gifts and the fruits of the Holy Spirit.[21] Dr. Vinson Synan, a Pentecostal pastor, assistant general superintendent of the Pentecostal Holiness Church, and an important historian of the Pentecostal movement, did an extensive study of medieval Catholic mystics.[22] Dr. Synan, like many an old-line Pentecostal, was reared to hate the Catholic Church, but his own research forced him to conclude that many of the canonized saints of the Catholic and Orthodox Churches were indeed baptized in the Holy Spirit and showed great spiritual gifts and holiness. He went so far as to state that the usual way for Christians to receive the Pentecostal experience during 1500 years of the Church's history was through the mystical way (i.e., contemplative prayer). Further, Pentecostalism has been a relatively new way of receiving the Spirit beginning only in the 1900s.[23]

Howard Ervin, professor of theology at Oral Roberts University, has come to a similar conclusion. In his view contemplative prayer led to a more mature manifestation of the baptism of the Holy Spirit than is often found in today's Christian. In the Middle Ages, a monk or nun who practiced contemplative prayer was a person who had spent years in the conscious pursuit of the Christian life, and any spiritual gift was much cherished. Today it is not uncommon for a Christian to receive the Baptism and the gifts of the Spirit and shortly abandon them for the cares and stresses of the secular world.[24]

Thus far in our survey we have seen that the testimony of both scripture and the Christian tradition is that *any* state of consciousness: normal waking, dreaming, trance state, can be a vehicle of communication for both holy or unholy spirits. We must note, however, that the trance state is one that is especially sensitive to sustained spiritual influence. This is not explicit in scripture (though it is hinted at in Acts) since scripture says relatively little about the trance state. It is evident from the writings of the mystics that the trance state is related to the phenomenon of mental *focus*. As one approaches deeper levels of mind, one's ability to focus on a single thought, or no thought, greatly increases. Thus whatever might be influencing the mind, holy or unholy, has an uninterrupted field of attention. In contrast, during normal waking consciousness spiritual influences can be turned off by ordinary shifts of attention or a fleeting new image.

Christian mystics had, as a natural consequence, an increase in sustained, focused contact with the spiritual world. They were subject to great numbers of visions, locutions, and other forms of personal revelations.

One of the great tasks of medieval spirituality was to order and discipline these spiritual experiences, somewhat in the way that Saint Paul had to order and discipline his Corinthian church. The fruit of this was that the Catholic Church developed a sophisticated system of discernment of personal revelations which went far in describing the *internal states* of true and false personal revelations. We must now look at the high point of this discernment tradition, which occurred in the midst of the Spanish "Golden Age" of literature and political influence.

The Spanish Mystical Tradition: High Point of Discernment

Saint Teresa of Avila (d. 1582) has been rightly considered the greatest of the Roman Catholic mystics. Her life was extraordinary for its holiness, love, patience, courage, and obedience to legitimate Church authorities. She had an intense prayer life, but at the same time maintained an active life as a great reformer of her own order and founder of many convents. On several occasions her spiritual counselors asked her to write about her spiritual experiences and the resultant writings form some of the best literature on contemplative prayer, visions, and discernment found anywhere in Christian literature. It is important to realize that her writings were intended for exhortation and direction to her colleagues in the religious life (people who were definitely "born again," though they would not have recognized the phrase).

Saint Teresa's course in contemplative prayer was begun almost by accident when her uncle gave her a popular book that described in a muddled way the essentials of contemplative prayer. She also learned, almost by instinct, to utilize her imagination in praying. She would imagine herself being present at Gospel scenes in the life of Jesus. As her prayer life developed she increasingly experienced visions and locutions. She was aware that not all of these were from the Lord, and as her life progressed she gained in grace and in the skill of discernment. Like Evagrius she realized that spiritual warfare confronted the believer at every level of consciousness. From personal experience she knew that the closer one came to the Lord the greater would be the attacks from Satan.[25]

Of Saint Teresa's writings, the most important for discernment is her book *Interior Castle*. In this book she warns her nuns to be on guard against the dangers of excessive asceticism. Lack of sleep and food can themselves cause visions that almost invariably come from the self.[26] She also warns that not all quietness of mind is contemplative prayer. It is only true prayer when the soul is actively involved in the joy of the Lord. A relaxed and totally blank mind has nothing to do with prayer—in fact, she considered that to be a sign that the person needed more sleep time and fewer hours of prayer.[27] This insight is especially relevant for today when many Christians have encountered various relaxation techniques and assume that they are "spiritual."

Mansion three, Chapter six is wholly dedicated to the problem of discernment, especially in regard to locutions. Saint Teresa warns her nuns to monitor the *psychological fruits* of any locution. That is, if a locution gives the receiver a sense of peace, joy, and increased desire to praise and worship the Lord, then the locution is most certainly from the Lord. If, on the other hand, a locution produces restlessness, lack of both peace and joy, then the locution is *not* from the Lord. It is understood of course that this discernment is in addition to the standard discernment of biblical compatibility. Saint Teresa's insight is especially relevant today where it is common to hear Christians say "the Lord told me . . . " How much better would it be for all if they instead said, "I had a locution, and it *seems* from the Lord. . . . "

In Mansion six, Chapter four, Saint Teresa gives some rather unique insights into the nature and purpose of personal revelations. She believed that in the advanced mystical state it pleases God, for reasons known only to him, to reveal to the mystic some of the mysteries of his Kingdom. Some of these visions and revelations are so powerful that they cannot be revealed to others. Most interestingly, certain revelations in the trance state do not carry over to the conscious mind or memory and are only spiritually known in a subliminal way. The purpose of this type of revelation is to strengthen the soul and allow it to gain a wisdom that lodges at the deepest levels, but does not manifest directly as intellectual knowledge. Saint Teresa never speculated on why this is so, but I suspect that the reason these revelations were masked from the conscious mind had to do with the need for ambiguity in the spiritual life on earth. Also this "masking" protected the mystic from being theologically too far ahead of his or her contemporary community.

This "infused knowledge," as it is known in Catholic theology, that Saint Teresa describes, is by necessity a "gift" to the mystic from God. It does have additional *practical* "fruit." According to Saint Teresa it gives the mystic a tremendous appreciation of its own baseness in comparison to God's holiness, and, lastly, it encourages detachment from worldly and material matters except as they relate to the Kingdom of God. All of this sounds mysterious and Gnostic, but it is, in fact, perfectly scriptural and is nothing more than an elaboration of what Saint Paul wrote to his church in Corinth when he was forced to reveal his credentials as a mystic:

> I will go on to visions and revelations of the Lord. I know a man in Christ who fourteen years ago was caught up to the third heaven—whether in the body or out of the body I do not know, God knows. And I know that this

man was caught up into Paradise—whether in the body or out of the body I do not know, God knows—and he heard things that cannot be told, which man may not utter. (2 Cor. 12:1–4)

The same thought is extended by Paul in the first Corinthian letter, in Chapter 13, Verse 12: "For now we see in a mirror dimly, but then face to face. Now I know in part; then I shall understand fully, even as I have been fully understood." If we may paraphrase Paul in view of our discussion of ambiguity, "On earth we understand in partial and ambiguous terms, but when we get to heaven the veil of ambiguity will be lifted and we will understand perfectly. But it is not *lawful* (2 Cor. 12:4) to bring back the gift of *unambiguous* knowledge to our earthly consciousness."

It is important to note that within the Catholic mystical tradition there is a school of thought that downgrades the role of personal visions and revelations. This attitude was defined by Saint John of the Cross (d. 1591), a friend and disciple of Saint Teresa. Saint John was a trained theologian as well as a mystic and ascetic. He turned the full force of his considerable intellect to the problems of the mystical way. He was a great advocate of asceticism and contemplative prayer, but he was deeply suspicious of visions or personal revelations.

His classic work on contemplative prayer, *Ascent of Mount Carmel*,[28] is filled with dire warnings about the dangers of spiritual deception in personal revelations. Saint John was very much a child of the Counter-Reformation, and considered *orthodoxy* in theology as essential to salvation. Thus all visions had to be orthodox to the nth degree to fill his criteria for soundness. According to Saint John, not only must one consider the possibility of demonic origins of personal revelations, but even those which do come from God can be distorted by the human mind. He cites as an example the fact that the prophecies of the Old Testament regarding Jesus and the Kingdom were authentic, but largely misinterpreted by the Jews, who sought a material and literal manifestation of the prophecies.[29]

Reading his works one gets the impression that what Saint John really wanted was an absolute prohibition on personal revelation but could not publicly go that far because of his commitment to long-standing Catholic practice. What he advocated was contemplative prayer that disregarded any locution, vision, or revelation and concerned itself only with the process of union with God. Had he been born in northern Europe he might have made a brilliant Reformation theologian.

From Saint John we must take note of his excellent criteria for discerning the origins of visions and revelations. He developed his criteria because he knew others, like his friend Saint Teresa, would go on minding personal revelation regardless of what he said.

In *Ascent of Mount Carmel*, Saint John (Book II, Chapter 24) gives three ways for distinguishing true from false visions. First, demonic visions produce an "aridity of spirit" in regard to communion with God. This means that the desire and joy of prayer are lessened. A demonic vision will also be self-glorifying and the person will consider the vision valuable in itself, rather than as an instrument for further closeness to God. Second, the inverse, a vision that is from God will result in humility, gentleness, and love of God (Saint John did not specifically mention the fruits of the Spirit, but was obviously aiming at these). Third, if the vision is from God, it will not be valued in itself, but will be considered an instrument for a closer relationship with God or deeper Faith.

This last criterion is typical of one of the strongest themes of Saint John's theology, detachment. For him, one must detach oneself from desiring all things but God. No spiritual gift, no vision, is either to be sought or desired. Every vision that does come to the mystic must be accepted in a strict attitude of detachment, with absolutely no emotional entanglement for the vision, no matter how beautiful or holy it may seem. This emphasis on detachment may have been Saint John's greatest contribution to mystical theology. It gives a "fail-safe" system of evaluating personal revelations. When a person receives a vision or revelation in detachment he or she can then monitor the spiritual effects of the vision in an objective manner. If the fruits of the vision are good, the Lord can be thanked for his blessing. If the fruits show signs of being evil, the recipient can disregard the experience as an incident in the spiritual warfare that is the lot of every believer, and thank the Lord for the gift of discernment. Please note that this attitude of detachment will be a cardinal element in our dealing with PLVs.

Note also that Saint John is, in a certain sense, a precursor of Paul Tillich. For Saint John of the Cross, the person should develop emotional detachment from all things, possessions, visions, and so forth, and attach all his love to God. Tillich carried this to an area where St. John would not have dared, to *theology*.

Chapter 4

Discernment:
From the Reformation
to the Present

The Reformation

In the writings of Saint Teresa and in Saint John of the Cross we have the very best of the Catholic mystical tradition. Few others who attempted the mystical path achieved their degree of holiness or skill in discernment. As a matter of fact, a young Augustinian monk named Martin Luther personally encountered many religious who showed neither discernment nor holiness and who considered themselves great mystics.[1] Luther's experience with unbalanced mystics led him to be suspicious about mysticism and contemplative prayer in general.[2] Later reformers went much further in rejecting the whole of the Christian mystical heritage. Calvin was adamant about centering Protestant worship in the conscious mind and avoiding anything that might smack of personal revelation or vision. For Calvin, the Bible was not only the sole depository of revelation, but it was the sole vehicle by which God continued to speak to his elect.

What developed in the Protestant denominations was the theology of "dispensationalism." That is, it was only under the old and unique dispensation of biblical times that God communicated with man through the medium of dreams, visions, locutions, and so forth. But with the perfect revelation of Jesus Christ and the formation of the Bible, such means were no longer used by God. Further, in the old dispensation God had to stimulate the faith of his Church through miracles, healings, and exorcisms, but in the present age these also were unnecessary. The positive search or use of spiritual phenomena was considered as a sign of weak faith. In contemporary times this position has been redefined and elaborated by the theologian Karl Barth.

50 |

While the antimystical element of Protestantism certainly eliminated the excesses of medieval Catholic spirituality, it also lost the rich legacy of Catholic experience in discernment. For where there is no place for personal revelation, there is no need for discernment. Discernment as a spiritual process and gift of the Holy Spirit became confused and replaced by *theological evaluation*. This lack of a viable tradition of discernment has had some tragic consequences in the history of Protestantism. For one thing, when an occasional mystic did come forth, he or she was not protected or guided by either a community or theology that was experienced in discernment. Such was the sad fate of Jakob Böhme (d. 1624), one of the most famous of Protestant mystics, who began having visions and wound up entangled in a theosophical system that had little to do with worship or holiness. To a lesser degree the same fate has haunted some of the early revivalist movements. Auguste Poulain, the great theologian of Catholic mysticism, writing in the early 1900s and observing the Welsh revival of that era, noted that the revival had a great blessing from the Holy Spirit. He also noted that due in great part to the lack of the most elementary concepts of discernment, it suffered from abuses and excesses that ultimately limited its propagation and effectiveness.[3] The same thing would be noted in a careful study of the Pentecostals of the 1900s.

It was through the Pentecostals and their descendants the Charismatics that Protestantism encountered again the spiritual phenomenon of visions and personal revelations in a sustained way. Naturally there also arose a renewed need for discernment.[4]

Discernment in the Pentecostal-Charismatic Tradition

The Pentecostals and Charismatics are united in their keen appreciation of discernment of spirits. It is an often-used spiritual gift in their exorcism and deliverance ministries, which have become important in recent decades. However, like most Christians, they have no conscious awareness of "testing discernment," and their conservative orientation makes it difficult for most of them to "test" anything that is new. This is not always bad, because this natural conservatism, common to all fundamentalist denominations, has prevented the acceptance of many new and deadly ideas current in the secularized liberal churches.

A negative element in the nondiscerning attitude of many Pentecostals and Charismatics is their continued opposition to Christian mysticism and contemplative prayer. In spite of the fact that many of them have had authentic mystical experiences, they continue to draw no distinction between Christian mysticism and contemplative prayer on one hand, and pagan and occult forms of meditation on the other.[5]

The antimystical prejudice of many Pentecostals and Charismatics has been encouraged by several factors. Most contemporary occult groups use some form of meditation and call their visionary experiences "mystical," no matter how immoral their lives or undiscerned and outlandish their visions. There has also come about a wave of chemically induced, hallucinatory experiences pioneered by such men as Aldous Huxley, Timothy Leary, and Charles T. Tart who also equate their chemical "trips" with mysticism. A devastating critique to the claims of this form of "instant spirituality" has been made by the outstanding Christian scholar R. C. Zaehner in his book *Mysticism, Sacred and Profane: An Inquiry into Some Varieties of Praeternatural Experience.*[6] Further, many "higher consciousness" groups, based mainly on Eastern philosophies, claim that their systems of self-salvation are "mystical." These factors, in combination to traditional Protestantism's suspicion of mysticism, have fundamentalist Christians convinced that *all* forms of mysticism are demonic delusions. Again, the main problem is that of not being able to discern the distinction between truth and shadow truth.

The Protestants Rediscover Trance

While the factors just mentioned have strengthened the Protestant belief that all forms of mysticism and trance states are demonic, the Holy Spirit has been moving with gentle irony in the very opposite direction. Protestant Pentecostals and Charismatics in ever increasing numbers have been participating in a special form of spiritual experience called "slaying in the Spirit." This phenomenon, also called "coming under the power," was given wide publicity in the ministry of Kathryn Kuhlman. In her healing rallies people would come up to her stage in droves and by the mere touch of her finger would fall down in a swoon, completely limp and powerless. This phenomenon is not uncommon in Christian healing groups when people are prayed over, but it seems that certain healers like Kuhlman, Kenneth Hagin, and others have a special anointing for this gift.

In recent years this phenomenon has been examined by two noted Christian scholars, Morton Kelsey and Francis MacNutt. MacNutt dedicated a lengthy chapter to what he renames "resting in the Spirit" and stresses the historical antecedents of the phenomenon and its similarity with Catholic mysticism. Kelsey, in his study, focuses on its psychological dimensions.[7]

Both articles are exploratory and much more research needs to be done in this field. MacNutt carefully documents dozens of cases of people being slain in the Spirit: Catholics, Protestants, fundamentalists, and liberals. Universally the descriptions center around the fact that the body is partially or completely immobilized (some persons can talk in this state but cannot move their limbs) while the mind is lucid and keenly aware of God's intimate presence. The mind is generally wordless, though filled with joy and peace. Occasionally, in this state, the Lord exhorts or encourages the person about some aspect of his or her life. Father MacNutt convincingly shows how these descriptions are identical to those of the classical mystical state; as a matter of fact he cites Saint Teresa as a point of comparison.[8]

MacNutt was originally skeptical of slaying in the spirit as really coming from God. He was particularly disturbed at the circuslike atmosphere of the Kuhlman rallies, where he first encountered this phenomenon. It was only after he began speaking to the people who had undergone this experience that he changed his mind. Not only had the people who were slain by the Spirit come closer to the Lord, but they were often healed in profound and dramatic ways. Interestingly, this phenomenon was particularly effective in dislodging evil spirits. MacNutt was forced to conclude that anything that had such good "fruit" had to be from God, regardless of the relative lack of solemnity in its application. (One can see he was educated in the Catholic theory of discernment by "fruit.")

Kelsey's study, though essentially positive, is much more cautious about the phenomenon. He also makes a greater effort to relate slaying in the Spirit to biblical situations in the Old and New Testaments. For our purposes the most important aspect of Kelsey's investigation is his description of slaying in the Spirit "gone wrong."[9] The case was of a Catholic priest who was anointed to a healing ministry by Kathryn Kuhlman. Some time later, as he officiated at a local healing service, people he prayed for began falling over. His local fame skyrocketed and his healing services began to attract large crowds. However, he noted that some who were slain in the Spirit became hysterical and others did not seem to benefit from the experience except for the "good feeling" it provided. In addition several persons experienced emotional breakdowns after they were slain. His bishop was disturbed by the sensationalistic aspects of his sessions and prohibited activities along these lines. He was disappointed but submitted. Kelsey concludes that slaying in the Spirit is similar to any other spiritual phenomenon; one has to be constantly alert as to whether the phenomenon is truly coming from God or if it is being spoiled by psychic or even demonic forces.

Two Viewpoints on the Soul's Power

At this point we need to stand back and assess two schools of thought in Christian psychology. Their variant viewpoints intrude in all that we discuss regarding spiritual phenomenon. They may roughly be called the Medieval Catholic and the Contemporary Evangelical. The point at issue between these two traditions is the role of the soul, or to use the Greek term, "psyche." Saint Paul clearly defined man as a composite creature made up of body, soul, and spirit. It is quite clear that in Paul's view the soul and spirit had independent functions, if not totally independent existence. However, early in Christian theology the distinction between soul and spirit became blurred until it was assumed that soul and spirit were two words for the same thing, the nonmaterial, immortal part of man. Only with the rise of the Pentecostals and Charismatics has there been a renewed interest by Christian thinkers to draw distinctions between one and the other.[10]

According to the concepts hammered out in centuries of discussion during the Middle Ages by Catholic theologians, the soul/spirit of man had certain "natural powers." These powers belonged to the soul/spirit regardless of its state of sanctification, and they included what today we would call "ESP." An example of these natural powers would be the ability of many a mother to "sense" that there is something amiss with one of her children even though much distance separates them, or the experience of having a prophetic ("precognitive") dream. According to Catholic thought, these "psychic" powers were both natural and "neutral." Like any other faculty of the soul, they could be used for either good or evil. In this view the psychic powers could be increased and spiritualized as the person grew in sanctification.[11]

On the other hand these natural powers could be manipulated and enhanced by cooperation with the demonic kingdom. A person in conscious league with the devil would have, in effect, the diabolical equivalent of the spiritual gifts described in 1 Corinthians 12. These "gifts" would be used for witchcraft or, as in the case of a false prophet, to confuse the Christian community.

In both cases the spiritual principle is the same. A spiritual force enhances and completes what is a natural "psychic" power. As one of the sayings of medieval theology phrases it, "grace completes nature." The demarcation between natural psychic powers and their demonic manifestation was of particular interest to the medieval church in trying to discern whether a person was a witch. Inquisitors were warned to be careful not to condemn persons as witches merely because they had gifts of the psychic order; there had to be evidence of its being used for diabolical purposes.[12]

The second Christian viewpoint as regards the role of the soul we termed "contemporary Evangelical." We turn to the figure of Watchman Nee (d. 1972) to find its most clear and influential articulation. Nee was a Chinese convert educated in the missionary schools of the pre-Communist era. He acquired his confidence in the power and truth of scripture from observing uneducated peasant converts take the Bible at face value and heal the sick and cast out demons. From the library of his missionary spiritual director he gained knowledge of the classics of Protestant spirituality. These he combined with his own extensive biblical studies and experiences as evangelist and pastor to form an original theological system. He was jailed by the Communist regime and died in prison after almost twenty years of confinement.[13]

Watchman Nee wrote only one book, a multivolume work called *The Spiritual Man*, considered by many to be a classic of Christian psychology.[14] His disciples, however, transcribed many of his sermons and teachings, and subsequently these have been translated and published throughout the Christian world. It is not an exaggeration to say he is the single most influential theologian among contemporary Evangelicals and Charismatics. Nee's views on the role of the soul are a logical culmination of the antimystical tradition of Reformed theology, and are found in a book called *The Latent Power of the Soul*.[15]

Nee based his analysis on the clear distinction between the soul and spirit. He believed that the soul is the seat of the personality and of self-consciousness, while the spirit is an organ of communication and awareness of God. Before the fall, Adam was a "super psychic," that is, his God-given soul powers were many times more powerful then they are today. As a result of sin, the soul's powers were reduced to a vestige of their former glory. In addition, according to Nee, "This power had fallen with man, so that according to God's will it should not be used further. But it is Satan's desire to develop this latent ability so as to make man feel he is as rich as God in accordance with what Satan has promised."[16] Further, Nee states that God *never* inspires man through the soul:

> Man's soul power is Satan's working instrument, through which he works out his evil end. God, though, never works with man's soul power, for it is unusable to Him. When we are born again, we are born of the Holy Spirit. God works by the Holy Spirit and our renewed spirit.[17]

For Nee, this means that the Christian is to be particularly careful not to inadvertently stir up the soul's power. This means that Christians are specifically to avoid hypnotism, which releases the latent powers of the soul. Nee believed that there are only two ways a person can receive information from other than the ordinary senses: through the soul or through the spirit. All information that comes through the soul (ESP, for instance) is by necessity under demonic influence and cannot be part of God's communication with man. Additionally, only in the Christian person is the spirit alive and in a receptive mode. Therefore, in Nee's theological system only Christians who are born-again can have valid spiritual visions or other forms of nonordinary experiences. Anything of this nature that a nonbeliever experiences is psychic and under demonic distortion.

The way to allow God to work through a Christian's spirit is for the Christian to completely suppress his or her soul-power. This is done by prayer and conscious renunciation of all psychic experiences of the Christian's past.[18] Nee's argument is curiously similar to the position of Saint John of the Cross with regard to renouncing visions. Both thinkers recognize a reality but require that it be suppressed.

The main problem with Watchman Nee's arguments is that they do not concur with the biblical evidence. In both the Old and New Testaments there are countless pagans who either had messages from God or who had valid precognitive dreams. Just to mention a few: in Genesis 40 Joseph interprets valid precognitive dreams from the Pharaoh's cup bearer and baker. In Matthew 2:12 the Magi, whose "wisdom" consisted in what today would be called metaphysical studies and astrology (and by Nee's definition would be *doubly* in Satan's power) received, and had the wisdom to understand, a godly dream not to return to Herod's court. Pilate's wife had a dream which warned her that Jesus was a "just man." According to Nee, since she was not a born-again believer, her soul received that dream; but since her soul was under Satan's control the revelation that Jesus was a just man was under demonic influence.

The continued evidence from the missionary field affirms the biblical revelation: a pagan is in possession of a soul that has powers capable of receiving messages from the Kingdom of Heaven. For example, one of the classics of Christian missionary literature, John L. Nevius's *Demon Possession and Allied Themes*,[19] cites the case of a Chinese woman who often suffered bouts of severe possession. Though a pagan, she had a dream that told her to seek Christian instruction in order to be released from her possession. She did so, and was in fact delivered and converted.[20] In the very recent work by the experienced missionary Don Richardson, *Eternity in Their Hearts*,[21] there is an account of an Ethopian holy man who received precognitive visions that Christian missionaries would some day come and free his tribe from the necessity of demon worship. This, in fact, happened.[22] A major theme of Richardson's book is that even among the most backward of peoples there is a thirst in the soul for the true gospel, and that this often manifests itself in paranormal experiences.

This evidence strongly counters Watchman Nee's radical casting out of the psychic powers as demonic, and his belief that the spirit is the only vehicle for God's revelations. The older Catholic view seems closer to the truth.[23]

Since the Charismatic renewal is so new in the Catholic Church, dating specifically from 1967, formal Catholic theology has not had time to revise its vocabulary or its understanding with regard to the demarcation between the psychic powers of the soul and the gifts of the Holy Spirit. Let us suggest that while the Catholic viewpoint is adequate, it might further be clarified by an analogy from quantum physics. The atom is composed of levels of electrons in orbit around a core of heavy particles. When the atom is "excited" by absorption of energy, the electrons in its orbit jump from one orbital level to another. It is interesting to note that when electrons jump from one level to another, there is no in between state. When the energy excitation reaches a certain level an electron is freed and becomes usable energy.

By analogy, our psychic powers are "low-orbit" energy levels that exist as part of our natural existence. These low-orbit powers of the soul can be energized by outside spiritual forces, negative or positive. In the case of the gifts of the Holy Spirit the low-orbit psychic powers are energized to a much higher level that can do "work" for the body of Christ. The relationship between the psychic and the spiritual can thus be understood as a *quantum jump*. Just as there is a similarity in the atom between the lower orbits and the higher ones, there is a similarity between the psychic and the spiritual. This analogy takes into account that the gifts of the Spirit are often a radically new experience for the person, yet maintains the medieval insight that "grace (the Holy Spirit) completes nature."

Twentieth-Century Contributions

The twentieth century has seen a renaissance of reflective writing on mysticism and discernment. Though none of this century's writers can match the Spanish mystics for personal experiences, they have more than compensated by their scholarly command of the literature and their willingness to assess and refine the collective experience of Christian believers.

Interestingly enough, two of the Catholic writers examined in this section borrowed heavily from the new discipline of parapsychology, which was developed to study the spiritual phenomena that materialistic psychology refused to acknowledge. This does not mean that they accepted the secular viewpoints of parapsychology, but that they utilized it as an independent witness to the reality of the spiritual world.[24]

Father Auguste Poulain, the first author we will survey, wrote before parapsychology had been defined as a separate discipline. He did have, however, an appreciation of turn-of-the-century psychology and an understanding of its limitations. His study of mysticism extended over forty years and included extensive interviews with living mystics and seers. They bore fruit in the classic work *The Graces of Interior Prayer: A Treatise on Mystical Theology*.[25]

Poulain had many things to say about discernment and the mystical experience, but we cannot even begin to summarize his work here. We should note that he aligned himself squarely with the tradition of Saint Teresa of Avila and considered the *Interior Castle* the greatest work ever written on mystical discernment. He wrote for Catholic readers, especially for confessors and spiritual directors and assumed that personal revelations occur in the later stages of contemplative prayer. He also assumed that personal revelations and visionary experiences are valid only if they are compatible with scripture and Catholic doctrine. He felt that all personal revelations truly from God should lead the receiver to a deeper sense of humility, and that any vision or revelation that does not increase personal holiness is suspect.

What makes Poulain's work especially useful for us today is the fine pastoral advice he gives to both spiritual directors and seers. He warns those involved in contemplative prayer that there are three important precautions that must be taken to prevent deception from spiritual experiences. First, the seer must fear being deceived and ask God for protection. Second, the seer must be totally frank with his or her spiritual director on all aspects of his/her spiritual life. Third, no revelation should be requested or desired.[26]

To spiritual directors he gives especially important guidance. The director is to be patient in judging any revelation, as it often takes a long time for the "fruit" of any vision or revelation to manifest. Second, any display of admiration for the vision is to be avoided, as this would injure the humility of the seer, and at all times what is to be stressed is the prayer life of the seer. The director must be *gentle* with the seer, especially in cases of false revelations, for even when they are of demonic origin they are in no way the "fault" of the seer. Lastly, the director is to keep in mind the purpose of the revelation, as this will often give a clue to its origin.[27]

We now turn to a work by the most eminent contemporary Catholic theologian, Karl Rahner, S.J. In a book entitles *Visions and Prophecies* Rahner brings to the subject of discernment a systematic and exhaustive command of the pertinent sources: mystical literature, saints' lives, studies on modern religious apparitions, psychology, and parapsychology.[28]

Rahner firmly takes his stand in the Catholic tradition of man's natural psychic gifts, and consciously disputes the dispensationalist theories of liberal Protestant theology. Unlike Poulain, whose intent was pastoral, Rahner's intention is to give us an understanding of the purpose and process of personal revelations.

Rahner sees personal revelation as a blend of the natural mind (psyche) and God's activity on the mind. In fact, Rahner divides revelation into two classes. In the first class the mind serves as the base upon which God influences and molds, until what appears as natural thought is in fact what the Lord wishes to make known. An example of this would be Saint Paul's sloppy and "barbaric" Greek writing-style, very human, yet truly a vehicle for God's revelation. The second class of revelation pertains to those visions and locutions which are purely "spiritual." That is, they come from outside the historical process of the person's thought or experience, and from God alone. An example of this class would be Peter's vision at Joppa.

However, in Rahner's view, even the "spiritual" revelations that originate from God reach the consciousness *through* the seer's subconscious mind, and it is in that process of transmission that the revelation is distorted by the seer's education, expectations, religious beliefs, and so forth. This is essentially what Saint John of the Cross claimed, but, unlike Saint John, Rahner does not push to the logical extreme that revelations are therefore useless and dangerous. Rather, revelations are seen as helpful when used with discretion.[29] On another point, Rahner found that genuine prophecies and visions are presented to the Church in a humble and tentative way. Indeed, arrogant, absolute confidence that a given vision is from God is a good indication that it is not.[30]

Rahner's system touches on the perennial problem of the subjective nature of spiritual phenomena. It begins to explain why the symbolism and content of personal revelations are so different among different seers even though the message may be similar. For example, Protestant seers have visions of heaven and hell, but Catholic seers often have visions of heaven, hell, and *purgatory*.[31] The essential *message* in both Protestant and Catholic visions is that the choice we make on earth is important and that we are subject to God's judgment, but the actual content of the vision is different. The *content* and details of the visions among those in the same denominations is also substantially different, due in turn to subtle differences in theological expectations, needs, experiences, and so on.[32]

These priest-scholars pushed forward our understanding of discernment to higher levels. Auguste Poulain codified the Catholic Church's mystical experience into a usable pastoral system, and Karl Rahner made the nagging problems of the subjective nature of revelation more understandable.

Two Protestant Seers: Hagin and Wilkerson

It would be worthwhile now to take a look at two seers whose visions have been influential in the contemporary American church, Kenneth Hagin and David Wilkerson. Both are fundamentalists and prominent in the charismatic renewal. Both have had international recognition, though Wilkerson is more important in this respect.

Kenneth Hagin, can be considered one of the great evangelist-healers responsible for the introduction and popularization of the healing ministry into main-line Protestantism. Hagin was born a premature baby in 1917 and spent a sickly childhood with a severe heart defect.[33] When he was fifteen he became very seriously ill and the doctors gave up all hope for recovery. Like the now famous stories related in Raymond Moody's *Life After Life*,[34] Hagin died and resuscitated. Unlike most of the cases reported in Moody, however, Hagin experienced a descent to the gates of Hell. But as a giant demon was about to take him in, the voice of God intervened and he came back to his body. This experience propelled him to an instant "born-again" commitment, and in turn led him to read the Bible and discover the principles of divine healing. The young Kenneth developed into a healthy man and became a Baptist minister and traveling evangelist.

In 1950, while he was in Texas praying with a small group of Christians, he heard a locution, "Come up hither!"[35] He opened his eyes and saw Jesus calling him. In spirit he ascended to the throne of God and there Jesus anointed the palms of his hands. Jesus told him to go and proclaim healing to all Christians.

After the vision Hagin felt a burning sensation in his hands that lasted for days. But subsequently he found that when he prayed for people they would be immediately healed and very often "slain in the Spirit." Hagin has had periodic visions of the Lord all through his evangelical career and has been given frequent revelations about such things as the nature of the demonic kingdom. He has been careful to check every revelation with the Bible. He writes:

> The Holy Spirit always leads in line with the Word. The Word and the Spirit agree. I am not in favor of just following voices, for a person can go wrong following any voices. But we can never go wrong following any voice that leads us to walk in line with the Word of God.[36]

Hagin's theory of "biblicity" was sorely tested in a subsequent vision when the Lord showed him a vision of a demon infiltrating a born-again, Spirit-filled acquaintance of his, which eventually led to the person's damnation.[37] Hagin believed in the Baptist doctrine that once saved a person cannot lose his salvation, so he responded by telling the Lord directly (in the way reminiscent of Peter's argument with the Lord at the house top in Joppa):

> . . . I still wasn't exactly satisfied with this. I wouldn't accept any vision, any kind of experience, if I saw Jesus twenty times a day, if what He said to me couldn't be proved by the written New Testament . . . I would discount it all.[38]

The Lord was delighted by Hagin's challenge (just as he was when Saint Teresa challenged him in her visions) and completely satisfied Hagin with an exegesis of Hebrews 6:4–6 and 1 John 5:16. This revelation brought about an important change in Hagin's theology, and in fact his teaching ministry includes a strong exhortation for Christians to beware the Evil One even after their "born again" and "Baptism in the Spirit" experiences.

It is my opinion that Hagin's visions were authentic revelations from the Lord. They satisfied the double criteria of biblical soundness and good "fruit." The fruit of his first vision was his personal conversion, the second was the tested fruit of years of a powerful healing ministry, and the third vision brought forth fruit of strong exhortations to a life of continued prayer and vigilance.

Even more influential than the ministry of Kenneth Hagin has been the work of David Wilkerson. He began as a small town preacher in the coal fields of Pennsylvania. Through a series of locutions and promptings from the Holy Spirit he was led to intervene in the lives of some delinquent teenagers in the slums of New York. This eventually led to a marvelous and effective ministry in New York and other major cities for the evangelization and rehabilitation of inner-city teenagers. The story of this aspect of his ministry is told in his book *The Cross and the Switchblade*.[39] This book has had a special anointing in its power to inspire people and has been translated into many languages.

In April of 1973, when Wilkerson was already known worldwide for his teen ministry, he received a series of visions. They were prophetic visions and dealt with the events of the next decade (1973–1983), with special attention to the happenings in the United States. It went into print as *The Vision*[40] and became an immediate best seller among fundamentalist Charismatics. Wilkerson first publicly proclaimed the vision in a conference of Lutheran Charismatics in August of 1973. The tape of that session is an amazing document in the history of Christian prophecy,[41] but, although the book contains all the prophecies, one can better appreciate Wilkerson's state of mind by listening to the tape.

As he spoke at the Lutheran assembly he asserted time after time that his message was directly from God, and that it was the "clearest vision I've ever had." He assured the audience that the Spirit behind the vision was the same that guided him to the teen ministry. Several times during his delivery he was practically overwhelmed by emotion and said, "Never have I felt such an anointing," or "I predict in the Spirit!" and so on.

Wilkerson warned of five major calamities that were surely coming on the world by 1983. In economics, the "next few years" would be prosperous (he missed the recession of 1974–1975), followed by a deep depression brought about by financial collapse. The depression is to start in Germany and the Arab countries will suffer the most. At the same time there will be severe earthquakes in the United States and world wide food shortages. On the moral front, the United States is to be invaded by a flood of pornography never before seen, and the courts will take an even more permissive stand on this issue. There will also be a major wave of disobedience by children towards their parents.

The most important and dramatic part of the vision pertains to the churches. There will arise a new Church, really the Church of the anti-Christ, made of a liberal Protestant and Roman Catholic amalgam, in which the Pope will be recognized as the *political* head. The "true" Church of God, a new union of all authentic spirit-filled Christians will of course oppose this Church and in turn suffer persecution. Wilkerson especially warns Catholic Charismatics to expect persecution from their own hierarchy. They will eventually be forced to choose between their Catholicism and the spirit-filled life. As a practical measure he warns all Christian churches to put their financial houses in order so as to weather the coming hard times. Specifically, no new buildings or borrowing should be initiated in the future.

All through the delivery of this prophecy Wilkerson provided ample biblical quotations to give it a sense of biblical validation. That *The Vision* was a false prophecy is becoming more and more obvious as we approach the end of 1983. Was it merely a subconscious concoction of the fears and prejudices of a small-town preacher? Certain elements in the prophecy suggest that they may have had a deeper, demonic source. The very shrillness and lack of humility in his assertions was itself a sign of that. The prophecy did not call Christians to prayer or repentance, nor did it console, edify, or exhort; it frightened and condemned. There was not a single suggestion that might have been remotely *useful*, such as might have prepared Christians for the energy crisis.

Further, the only practical suggestions were *destructive*. The separation of spirit-filled Christians into "one true Church" would have resulted in a new Montanism with results as destructive to the Universal Church as the old Montanism. Even the minor point of financial conservatism most probably had a demonic source, for the many churches have in fact continued to flourish and expand and to build in response to their growing needs (though of course no one should confuse this spiritual growth with a building program).[42]

That Charismatic Christians did not follow the deadly advice of *The Vision* was due in great part to the intelligent and quick response of other, more mature leaders. David du Plessis quickly denounced the prophecy as not coming from God. He further compared it with many a false prophecy he had heard as a young man which claimed the coming world rule of Stalin and the Papacy.[43] Ralph Martin, one of the best-known and respected Catholic Charismatics quickly spread the warning of "false prophecy" among fellow Catholics.[44]

Wilkerson's prophecy goes to the core of the discernment problem. He did nothing wrong in reporting his prophecy. As a matter of fact, according to Catholic theology, he would have sinned had he not. As Rahner helped us understand, the prophet is in a poor position to discern his own revelation because, if it is of demonic origins, it will play upon the fears, prejudices, and belief structure of his own subconscious mind. It is the task of the Church to judge prophecy, not the prophet (1 Cor. 14:29).

It is important to note some other issues. It is clear that Wilkerson's original ministry was blessed by God and has borne much fruit, yet *The Vision* was demonic. This is a modern example of Peter's "multiple inspiration" cited earlier. It is also important to realize that while Wilkerson was experiencing the original vision, and while he delivered his address to the Lutheran conference, he was probably *functioning as a medium for an evil spirit.* Yet in no sense did he commit the sin of mediumship. Rather it is in the nature of the mature spiritual life to be an instrument of either the Holy Spirit or other spirits. Advanced spiritual life is by nature risky (but not as fatal as a mediocre spiritual life, for our Lord makes it clear that he abhors those who are neither "hot or cold" [Rev. 3:15]. Perhaps the major fruit with *The Vision* affair was that he did not have or seek a mature spiritual director with whom to discuss his experience before he went to the public with it.

Discernment in Protestantism and Catholicism Compared

It would be useful to evaluate and compare the two main discernment traditions in the Christian West, that of Roman Catholicism and of Pentecostal-Charismatic Protestantism. Of the Catholic tradition it must be said that it it the heir of a continuous, reflective process from New Testament times. It maintained the double criteria of discernment by "fruits" as well as biblical conformity. However, there have been several serious problems in the Catholic tradition of discernment. Until the spirit of the Second Vatican Council took hold, Catholic theologians assumed that biblical conformity was equivalent to every iota of Catholic theology. Further, in the first decades of this century there has been a major failure in discernment pertaining to the Marian apparitions of the nineteenth and early twentieth centuries. Many contemporary Catholic scholars are aware of the problem and have tried to separate Catholic theology from the extremes of Marian revelation.[45]

A silent assumption in the bulk of Catholic literature on discernment is that God's continuing revelation to mankind is dispensed through those who are in advanced stages of the spiritual life. This is not so much a formal doctrine as it is the received experience of a community whose discernment wisdom arose from the Church's mystical tradition. The rise of the Charismatic element within the Church has seriously questioned that assumption.

Another point of unbalance in Catholic discernment is the repeated emphasis on *humility* as the cardinal virtue in the spiritual life. Humility is certainly important, but it is love that is central to Christianity (1 Cor. 13). In both scripture and in postbiblical history men and women of God have received *commissioning revelations* which, in isolation, do not meet the criteria of humility. For example, Saint Paul's visions and commission to teach the Gospel to the Gentiles did not in itself breed an attitude of humility. In fact, Saint Paul was so sure of his commision that he publicly denounced Saint Peter for conforming to Jewish-Christian taboos about table fellowship with Gentiles (Gal. 2:11). Had Saint Paul had Saint John of the Cross as his spiritual advisor he would have been told to do penance, stay out of the sun, and beware of Satan. It seems that what the Lord did with Paul was to use his energy and enthusiasm for the sake of the Kingdom and later deal with his humility. His exact words on this matter are found in 2 Corinthians 12:1.

> And to keep me from being too elated by the abundance of revelations, a thorn was given me in the flesh, a messenger of Satan, to harass me, to keep me from being too elated.

Paul's example is rather extreme, but the history of the Church shows that many men and women of God have received commissionings which were not in themselves humbling. The grace of humility seems to be given to them as they carry out their assigned work in the Kingdom, whether it be founding convents, reestablishing the healing ministry of the Church, and so forth. As Auguste Poulain suggested in another context, the proper discernment of a commissioning vision may take some time. If, in the long run, the seer maintains an overall humble attitude, and if he achieves what the commission directed him to do in the Kingdom, then the revelation was authentic. Kenneth Hagin is an example of living through a valid commissioning vision.

Concerning the Protestant tradition of discernment, we are forced to conclude that, although it has some strong points, it has a major weakness. Because of its radical break with Catholicism, Protestantism lost contact with the tradition of discernment wisdom of Catholic mysticism, and based its discernment criteria on "biblicity" alone without serious consideration of the "fruits" element. As seen in the Wilkerson vision, this can lead to very serious errors.[46]

The Protestant tradition does have strong points. There is less tendency to confuse biblical compatibility with dogmatic assumptions. Further, since, for Protestants, there is no tradition of the more "perfect" path of celibacy and monasticism they are more open to accepting revelations from all sectors of the Church. Also, in this regard humility is seen in clearer perspective. If anything, Protestant Charismatics and Pentecostals are too ready to accept commissioning revelations as from the Lord as long as they are biblical sounding (or end in "Thus sayeth the LORD!").

Probably the most difficult task that faces every Christian community or denomination is the establishment of the "Pauline" balance between acceptance and the exercise of the spiritual gifts on the one hand, and discipline and discernment on the other. There is no final solution. That which seems innovative and from the Spirit for one group often drifts into abuse and unbalance within a few decades. The facile solution of avoiding the spiritual gifts and discouraging spiritual phenomena leads to bureaucratic forms of Christianity that revolve around dogmatic formulations and try to channel all worship through the intellect. This form of Christianity, whether Catholic or Protestant, loses much of its power to gain converts or witness effectively outside its own circle of believers.

Discernment and PLV Phenomena

We are now at a point where we can make some preliminary discernments concerning PLVs. Recall that for any vision or personal revelation to be from the Kingdom of God it must pass a triad of requirements. The vision must be compatible with biblical revelation; it must have an acceptable Christology; and it must generate good fruit. Not all valid vision must include all three segments. For example, a vision about an impending accident may have nothing to say about Christ, yet still be from God. On the other hand, any vision or revelation that actively gives a negative revelation about the nature of Christ or contradicts a fact of biblical revelation is not from the Lord no matter how good its fruit. Spiritualist visions are often of this order, they often present sound medical or ethical advice which if taken does indeed lead to better health and happiness. Yet because they are given through a familiar spirit, that type of spiritual experience is not of the Kingdom of God. Invariably, continued contact with the familiar spirit will lead to revelations that are of the anti-Christ.

Many readers will immediately assume that any PLV is incompatible with biblical revelation. Later we will deal with the issues of whether all forms of belief in reincarnation are incompatible with Christian scripture.

For now, we should note that PLVs as *phenomena* are in no way forbidden by the Bible, as they can be interpreted in ways that are totally orthodox—such as the concept of empathetic identification.

In regard to the hypothesis that the PLV is demonically inspired and ultimately a form of mediumship, we must again make some preliminary discernments. Everything in the Christian tradition of demonology, biblical and postbiblical, indicates that demons do have access to the mind and memory of man and have the power to conjure images with which to tempt and torment him. Thus the fundamentalist hypothesis is at the very least in the mainstream of Christian experience with the demonic. With these two powers, access to memory and the ability to creatively conjure images, we can see that it is quite possible that PLVs are generated or distorted by demonic influence. However, one must be careful not to make the error that because something *can* be it *must* be. A case in point has been our study of modern prophecy. We have shown in the Wilkerson case that prophecy *can* be a form of demonic mediumship, but that does not mean that *all* prophecies are from demonic sources. In order to condemn PLVs as mediumship it will be necessary to establish that *all* PLVs are in the mediumship and demonic category. Before we make any judgment in that area we must look at further evidence.

Chapter 5

The Roads to Spiritual Death

There are many roads to spiritual death and the rejection of God's gift of eternal life. The most fundamental of all is absolute resistance to the Gospel, or denial that there is a spiritual world to which one is ultimately accountable (Lk. 16: 19–31). Another way is indicated in Hebrews 6:1–8 and 2 Peter 2:20–21. These scripture passages indicate that spiritual death and judgment fall on those who, once Christian, turn their backs on Christ and fall again into pagan ways. But also important to consider in this context is the problem of heresy.

The problem of heresy points to an important relationship between ambiguity and discernment. As we have noted, an attitude of ambiguity allows the Christian to develop a mature and open-minded spiritual life, one that is elevated above clinging to dogmatic assertions, or the assurance that his or her denomination is the "one, true" church. Such theologies can obviously be very sophisticated in spite of their overly rigid assumptions. They ultimately strangle the ability of Christians to love, worship, and trust across denominational lines. Yet this attitude of ambiguity is an open one, and if not protected can be too open. It is the spiritual gift and skill of discernment which *protects* the open-minded Christian and sets the limits of ambiguity in theology. Without discernment a believer could rapidly descend into heresy. "Heresy" is possibly the most abused word in religious literature; often it means nothing more than another denominination's theology. The Greek word that is translated as "heresy" is *hairesis* and simply means "sects." In that sense *every* Christian denomination is a sect and as such a "heresy." Yet it is obvious from the way hairesis is used that there are certain sects which are indeed destructive and whose beliefs lead to spiritual death (2 Peter 2:1 calls them "destructive sects").

In the biblical sense, then, a true heresy is not just a denomination, but a denomination or sect whose ideas are spiritually destructive. This almost begs the question, for Baptists might say that about Catholics, and vice versa. Thankfully, the New Testament clarifies the evidence and points to two such prototypical factions which indeed were spiritually deadly. The first of these were the Pharisees. The ministry of Jesus was largely dedicated to rebuking this Jewish "faction." The other was the Gnostics who dogged Paul's ministry to the Gentiles. These two sects are the biblical prototypes of "heresy" that lead to spiritual death. It is important to realize that these are the heresies of those who have already passed the first steps of the spiritual life. A Pharisee is one who has honestly and radically dedicated his life to the Lord, but his dedication has been distorted by pride. A Gnostic, too, is one who has accepted the reality and importance of things spiritual, but has also been led to fatal error, in this case through radical nondiscernment.

The Way of the Pharisee

A Pharisee was one who believed that the way to God's good graces was through observing an *unambiguous* system of "right" rituals, worship, and morals. Jesus' critique of their system was that it removed the center of man's consciousness away from God and placed it on the system itself. Later, Saint Paul taught his churches how the Pharisaic system deadened and obstructed the true saving relationship, the faith relationship with Jesus Christ. It is amazing how little specific attention has been given to the problem of modern Pharisaism. Perhaps because "Christian Pharisees" are often the "best" church members. This heresy is among the most "spiritual" in the sense that a Pharisee is completely orthodox on an *intellectual* level, while dead in his or her spirit. It is also an extremely difficult heresy to identify properly, since a Pharisee does not *do* anything wrong; rather it is the Pharisee's attitude that is wrong.

There are no declared Pharisees in today's Church, but at the same time the "spirit of Pharisaism" has continuously distorted and caricatured the true meaning of Christianity. Late medieval Catholicism, with its elaborate system of unambiguous ethics (including its classification of "mortal" and "venial" sin) came very close to duplicating Pharisaism. As a matter of fact sensitive Catholic spiritual directors have long been aware of this problem. Though few would (before Vatican II) repudiate scholastic theology, many were keenly aware of the dangers in too structured an ethical and moral code.[1]

Pharisaism is not, however, specific to Catholicism. It is found at times among fundamentalist denominations in the elaborate and specific "holiness" codes, which define going to movies, or wearing lipstick as sinful activities, and judge a member's holiness by the length of the hemline or abstinence from tobacco.

We need not develop our study of Pharisaism further. As a whole, denominations that have a strong Pharisaic spirit give little attention to visionary experiences. They are too busy "perfecting" their external spiritual life to have much energy left for internal, subjective matters. We must, however, examine the other major form of spiritual heresy, Gnosticism, with much more care, for the Gnostics make subjective experiences the basis of their beliefs.

The Way of the Gnostic

Gnosticism: General Patterns

Contemporary New Testament scholarship is making it increasingly clear that the "false teachers" denounced so ferociously in the Epistles were Gnostics. Paul, Peter, Jude, and John all agree that the Gnostic distortion of the original Christian proclamation is so serious that it ceases to be a legitimate view of the Gospel and becomes a system of belief that leads to spiritual death. In fact 2 John 10–11 forbids Christians from having contact with these false teachers.

Until very recently there has been a problem in defining and identifying these New Testament Gnostics with any precision. This is because practically all of the surviving documents relate to the later forms of Gnostic belief (second century and later). It has been even more difficult to identify the origins or to date the beginnings of this belief system. Another complicating factor has been that Saint Paul and other New Testament writers often use Gnostic *vocabulary* to proclaim the authentic Gospel, and many Gnostics of the second and third centuries claimed that Paul was indeed an advocate of their false doctrines.[2]

The latest scholarly estimation is that Gnosticism originated in Mesopotamia and that it predated the Christian era by about a century.[3] It soon spread to different parts of the ancient world, acting as a parasite on existing religions. It associated itself with Hellenistic culture and became Mystery Gnosticism, and with Judaism to become Jewish Gnosticism. This latter variety attempted to infiltrate Christianity. It was fought vigorously by New Testament writers. In a more Christianized form it continued to plague the Church in the first centuries of our era.

Gnosticism has been such a chameleonlike phenomenon that it is important to define and understand its core assertions and not to confuse these with secondary characteristics which it shares with authentic Christianity. One of the most prominent scholars of Gnosticism, R. M. Grant, has defined the uniqueness of this ancient heresy by identifying three interlocking assumptions which are common to all its forms.[4] The first is that salvation comes through knowledge. This is of primary importance and is where the word "Gnostic" originates; it means "one who knows." The second is an attitude that is self-centered, as contrasted with most religions which are God-centered. Thus, ultimately, Gnosticism is almost totally subjective; it relies on personal revelations and continuous spiritual experiences for its survival, with little or no concern for discernment.

The saving knowledge of the Gnostics was the knowledge of "who they really are." That is, a Gnostic believed that once he came to realize that he was intrinsically *spirit*, an emanation from the Godhead that was temporarily trapped in the "lower sphere" of earth, he was saved. This self-realization of his "Godness" meant that all the cares and ethical concerns of the world were in themselves unimportant and could be superseded by remembrance of the God from whence one came. Thus salvation was the product of awareness-knowledge (called today higher-consciousness). Often this would be reinforced, depending on the system of Gnosticism involved, by secret knowledge of magical incantations used after death to escape the demons of the heavenly spheres and to return to the Godhead. Gnostic knowledge had nothing to do with knowledge of an ethical or ritual law as in Jewish orthodoxy. Its practical result was to decrease or eliminate *worship* and place trust in salvation on the glorified self.

Indeed, this radical self-centeredness cut off all need or inclination to worship. For the inner spirit-self was viewed as *identical* to the Godhead. Thus there was not recognition of the difference between creature and Creator that is the core of authentic Judaism and Christianity. The Gnostic group was not concerned with community worship and prayer for others, but with spreading knowledge and helping others to their own self-enlightenment, called "awakening." There was fellowship within Gnostic communities, but not the fellowship of prayer and unselfish assistance and service, rather a quasi-academic fellowship of teacher and disciple.

The third attitude of Gnosticism, radical subjectivism, was noted by Saint Irenaeus, Bishop of Lyons (c. 177–200), and one of the earliest Fathers of the Church. He spent much of his ecclesiastical career dealing with Gnostics, and his great work *Adversus Haereses* was aimed principally against them. He found the task difficult because Gnostic cults and teachings were so disparate.

> Since they disagree with one another in teaching and in tradition, and the more recent converts pretend to find something new every day and to produce what no one ever thought of, it is difficult to describe the opinions of each.[5]

The Work of Walter Schmithals

Recently, Walter Schmithals, a German biblical scholar and disciple of

Rudolf Bultmann, has given us a more exact picture of the specific Gnostic creed that New Testament writers had to confront. Schmithals has concentrated his studies on the "false teachers" who opposed Saint Paul in the churches he founded, paying special attention to Corinth.[6] Schmithals argues that the opponents to Paul's ministry were Jewish "Christ" Gnostics. That is, they were Jewish Gnostics who derived their central attitudes and beliefs from Jewish esoteric centers in Mesopotamia. They were "Christ" Gnostics in the sense that they believed that by adopting their Gnostic "wisdom" every person could become a "christed" being, fully aware of his or her own divinity. They were *not* followers of Jesus of Nazareth; they were not Christians.

Schmithals took on the task of reconstructing the theology of Paul's Jewish Christ Gnostic opponents. This was not an easy task since there are no independent documents about them from this early period. He was therefore limited to the New Testament epistles which he examined in great detail, noting especially where Paul seemed to be on the defensive. With these leads, and with an exhaustive study of other, later Gnostic sources he was able to reconstruct the theology of the Jewish Christ Gnostics. For purposes of convenience I have organized Schmithals's description into a numbered sequence of theological propositions,[7] organized into the four general categories of Christology, salvation, worship, and morality.

Christology:

1. Jesus Christ is not the redeemer of mankind. Every person is his or her own redeemer and responsible for his or her own transformation into a "christed" being.

2. Jesus the man was no more important than anyone else, and only at the moment of his baptism at the Jordan did he become "christed" and enlightened. Because of this it is possible to say "curse Jesus" while in an ecstatic state.

3. The crucifixion of Jesus was an unimportant historical event and has no special significance for our salvation.

Salvation:

4. Special Gnostic "wisdom" is necessary for salvation. This wisdom is all-inclusive and replaces the faith, hope, and love preached by Paul. The Gnostic "wisdom" is the "new gospel" criticized by him.

5. Repentance is an unnecessary process. The gnosis that leads to salvation-enlightenment is an intellectual process not a moral one, and repentance, just like the cross, is another unnecessary detail.

6. The world is divided into those who have received the gnosis and

those who have not. Those who have received it are the "perfected ones" and those who have not are essentially inferior. Thus, boasting and self-glorification are normal and proper for a perfected one.

7. It is *necessary* for the Godhead to gather back to himself all of his emanations (individual souls) in order that he regain his completeness. This must and will happen as mankind comes to universal enlightenment.

Worship:

8. Worship should be exclusively ecstatic, "spirit-filled," and un-disciplined. The amount of ecstatic manifestation displayed is related to the degree of perfection a person has achieved.

9. The Gnostic should know the names and functions of the angelic powers. Worship is due to some orders of angels. Further, a perfected one should develop dominion over the demons of the spirit world. (Note Jude 8.)

10. The Gnostic is allowed to practice magic which has been learned as part of his enlightenment process.

11. Sacramental worship is not to be taken seriously. The Lord's supper and baptism are much like the crucifixion and repentance, unnecessary and "primitive" stages of religion. Real worship is always mystical and ecstatic. Matter cannot have power over the spirit; therefore neither the water of baptism nor the bread of the Lord's supper can in any way affect the spiritual life.

Morality:

12. The body is a trap for the spirit and worthless in itself. Nothing that the body does can affect the spirit once a person has come into the gnosis. The resurrection of Jesus was a spiritual event, his body was not involved.

13. Sexual permissiveness is allowed to the "perfected ones" since their enlightenment has removed them from the sphere of spiritual danger and darkness.

14. Asceticism must be practiced in sexual and other bodily matters. It is through a severe discipline that the "prison of the spirit," the body, can be subdued sufficiently to free the spirit and allow it to come to enlightenment.

15. Women are absolutely equal to men and are entitled to hold any and all the offices of the Church.

The reader must have noted that numbers fourteen and thirteen are contradictory. In fact, Gnostic sects have vacillated between both extremes of sexual morals. Either view is the natural consequence of believing that the body is no more than the spirit's prison and altogether incapable of co-sanctification along with the soul and spirit.

It is also important not to accuse a given Christian denomination or person of Gnosticism if they believe in or practice a few of the above theological propositions. What makes a sect Gnostic is its *general attitude* plus adherence to *most* of the theological opinions we have outlined. There are few denominations in orthodox Christendom that do not assert several of these propositions in one way or another. An obvious example is found in traditional monastic Christianity with its extreme stand on celibacy and fasting. Belief in the absolute equality of woman is held by many contemporary Christians, yet that does not mean they are gnostic. Similarly, some fundamentalist denominations have little appreciation for sacramental worship. Again, in isolation, this does not make such denominations gnostic.[8]

It is difficult to overestimate the importance of Schmithals's achievement, for it gives us a biblical view of the system of "wrong knowledge" that is truly poisonous to the spirit. The Gnostic system he reconstructed is not merely a theology censured by scholars but a system passionately condemned by New Testament writers under divine inspiration.

It is important to note that this Gnostic system made no reference to reincarnation. If the Jewish Christ Gnostics in Corinth or in any of the other of Paul's churches believed in reincarnation, this belief was not seen by Paul as worthy of correction. That they believed in reincarnation is possible because of the widespread belief in reincarnation in the Hellenistic world, and also to the fact that some Jews did believe in some form of *limited* reincarnation. (See Part IV.)

Reflections

The "wrong knowledge" of the Gnostic system is fatal to the spirit not because in itself it is incorrect (as a matter of fact so is much theology), but because the specific set of "wrong knowledge" obstructs the ability of a person to come into trust-faith relationship with the Lord. By trivializing and universalizing the meaning of "Christ," Gnosticism severs the worship relationship with Jesus Christ. By its interlocking attitudes of self-centeredness, nondiscernment, and extremist sexuality, the person is led to a total moral and ethical breakdown where knowledge of the true Christ who could lift him out of the abyss of sin is virtually impossible.

As a whole, Gnosticism is radically subjective and nondiscerning. Yet within any given Gnostic groups there is a system of totally complete and *unambiguous* "teachings" that are "channelled" from other realms. Unlike the teachings of Pharisaism, Gnostic teachings refer mostly to cosmology and esoteric matters rather than to moral behavior. This aspect of Gnosticism is not immediately as deadly to the spiritual life as other aspects, but it does deaden the intellect and obstruct true intellectual growth which is the product of sustained hard work (as we saw from Proverbs).

It is of interest to note that Western Christianity, especially since Augustine, has been influenced by a curious mix of both Pharisaism and Gnosticism. The Church is Pharisaical because it has distrusted the ability of its members to forge a Spirit-led ethical life, and has often attempted to impose its authority and "order" by developing various systems of unambigious ethics. On the other hand, like the Gnostics, Western Christianity has come to believe that its creeds ("right knowledge") are the key to salvation.[9] This is quite clearly observable at a popular level where the fashion about "knowing if you are saved" seems to be of greater importance than an ongoing and growing relationship with the Lord. As we have noted, Tillich called the various forms of credal Gnosticism the "demonization of religion," and ultimately idolatrous. Any time that a theological position is given an ultimate value it automatically destroys the authentically biblical "wisdom from above."[10]

To all of this certain qualifications must be made. Western Christianity, even in its darkest moments of heretic torture and Inquisition, did maintain enough of the essential faith-trust in Jesus that it could inspire and direct many to great holiness. Neither Satan nor Christ has had complete dominion over the earthly Church and the situation is not likely to change until the second coming. The solution to essential or "pure" Christianity is not to scrap all that has come before as "contaminated." That is a sure way of allowing a new round of Satanic distortion through the sin of pride.

All of this points to a reevaluation of the role of theology in the life of the believer. It would be tempting to overreact and throw out all theology, but that is impossible for several reasons. Saint Paul, perhaps the earliest of the New Testament writers, was essentially a theologian, a person who sought to explain the Christ-event in terms of reason and the philosophical language of his times. To reject theology is to reject the spirit of much of the New Testament. We will never have theology as directly inspired as his again. But to limit the attempt is to leave the human intellect starved of the salvation and sancification that is the right of every part of our being. For good theology is indeed an attempt to sanctify our intellect. Theology must always be viewed as an aid to the faith-trust relationship with Jesus and not as a replacement for it. This may seem obvious, but violation of this principle is what made the "death-of-God" theology of the Sixties so arid and short-lived.

PART II

PLVs in a Non-Christian Context

Beloved, do not believe every spirit, but test the spirits to see whether they are of God; for many false prophets have gone out into the world. *1 John 4:1*

See to it that the evil demons do not lead you astray by means of some vision. Rather be wise: turn to prayer and call upon God to enlighten you if the thought come from him, and if it does not, ask him to drive away from you the deceptive one quickly. *Evagrius Ponticus*

Chapter 6

Karma, Spiritualism, and The Metaphysical Movement

Induced and sustained PLVs are an entirely modern phenomenon in the Western World, dating only from the nineteenth century. PLVs before then were rare events and only spontaneous in nature. Many metaphysical and occult books make the extravagant claim that the mystery cults of antiquity and especially the schools of ancient Egypt made systematic use of hypnotism. There is very little evidence that hypnotism as we know it was practiced in any of those settings, or that PLVs were intentionally induced. What we do know is that ancient religions often encouraged trance and relaxation states in their followers, during which visionary experiences would commonly be experienced.[1] In the Buddhist East, on the other hand, where reincarnation has been a basic doctrine for centuries, PLVs have long been used in certain forms of meditative training.

Our attention in Part II will be directed to the PLVs in the contemporary Western World, specifically PLVs induced in the practice of metaphysical and occult groups and as used as a therapeutic tool by psychologists. These groups have little or no understanding of discernment, and thus visions generated by their practices are prone to distortion and demonic intervention.

Reincarnation and Karma in Classical Eastern Philosophy

Before we examine how these groups use PLVs we must look at several concepts that have become established in the Western occult tradition and which have heavily influenced the perception of PLVs. Among these concepts are the Eastern doctrine of reincarnation, especially in association with the belief in karma, and the general acceptance of the concepts used by spiritualists as a normative for understanding the nonmaterial world.

The various Eastern doctrines of reincarnation are based on classical

Hindu ideas about the soul. In Hinduism, as in Christianity, the soul is considered immortal. However, in Hinduism the soul after death does not permanently abide in the spiritual afterlife of heaven or hell, but is reborn on earth into another human body. Some Hindu sects believe that under certain adverse conditions the soul can even be reborn into the bodies of animals. The earth is considered eternal, uncreated, and without a radical end, as in Christianity. It is the permanent setting for the cycles of the soul's rebirth. This cycle of rebirth is broken only when the individual soul has attained a state of purity sufficient to be reintegrated into the God-head. The Hindu mentality has always enjoyed using large numbers, and most Hindu sects believe that the number of rebirths needed to achieve release from the "wheel of rebirth" is astronomically high, often talking in terms of thousands, even hundreds of thousands, of reincarnations.

The techniques for release from the cycle of rebirth fall into roughly two categories: first, "right living" according to the demands of a person's caste and state in life. This includes such things as ritual cleanliness, as in the Mosaic Law. The other category deals with various meditative practices which help the devotee to reach ever-higher states of consciousness. On the popular level there has always been a great deal of liturgical obser-vance and private worship of the gods. In spite of this it is safe to say that in Hinduism the burden of salvation is left to the individual with relatively little need of grace or divine assistance.

Buddhism was an outgrowth or reform movement from within Hindu-ism that attempted to simplify the convoluted system of Hindu religion in much the same way that Protestantism attempted to reform medieval Catholicism. Buddha was silent about the nature of the soul and reincar-nation. His primary concern was to point people on a systematic way to higher consciousness whereby the person could be released from the grip of attachments to the world. Buddha's disciples, however, generally adopted some form of belief in reincarnation.

Karma is a concept derived from Hindu and Buddhist theories of rein-carnation. It is often called the "law of karma" and it supposedly explains the injustice and present suffering of the world in terms of long-term perfect justice and moral equilibrium. Under the law of karma, every moral (or immoral) event has an equivalent aftereffect. Thus, for example, if I lead a lifetime as a cruel man, and mistreat and beat my wife, I would be fated in some future life to suffer a similar fate. I would be reborn as a woman and marry a brutal husband who would mistreat me in the same measure that I had dealt out earlier. Extended infinitely, all of the current suffering and injustice of the world are seen as perfect justice working itself out. It is only the spiritual ignorance of humanity that prevents it from perceiving the "beauty" of the moral world.[2] Under karma, a person must save himself by attaining higher consciousness and nonviolence. To return to our original example, the wife, who was the cruel husband in a past life, and who is now suffering, must put aside her resentment for her husband and suffer patiently in order to erase her karmic debt.

If she responds with bitterness or malice, she has not learned her lesson and must be reborn until that particular karmic debt is paid. The person's obligation under pain and suffering is solely to accept patiently the suffering given to him. Prayer is not only futile, but an attempt to escape justice of the universe.[3]

The Judeo-Christian Rejection of the Karma Concept

One reason why the concept of karma has found such wide acceptance in the West is that it fills an authentic spiritual and emotional need, the need to be reassured that there is indeed a moral orderliness and accountability in the universe. This is especially acute in recent decades when anti-establishment philosophies in the West exalt the rights of individuals to the point where any sense of transpersonal values have become seriously eroded. Karma asserts that every moral (or immoral) action will be dealt with in kind at some point in eternity. In addition, for many, this idea of cosmic justice seems more attractive and fair than the conventional Christian doctrine of infinite punishment for limited sin.[4]

However, most Christians have rejected the karmic view for several good reasons. The great Christian scholar and philosopher R. C. Zaehner has noted in his studies of Hinduism and Buddhism that, even in its "pure" form (let alone when contaminated through the mediumship of Western occultism), the concept of karma becomes the *ultimate* source of motion and activity in the universe. In effect, karma *becomes a god*. The Hindu and Buddhist devotee must directly deal with the law of karma before he comes into union and intimate relationship with the ultimate source of the universe, "Brahmin."[5]

At best, the concept of karma reduces God to a distant, impersonal force. Some observers have called Buddhism a "religious atheism" because of this. The Christian, on the contrary, comes into relationship with a personal, loving Father, and this relationship makes possible the observance of moral laws. Pure Buddhism has no concept of forgiveness or karmic absolution (though in some Tibetan and Chinese forms there is a concept of "savior"). The opposite is true in the Jewish and Christian traditions, where, since the Psalms of David, God's mercy and forgiveness have been revealed as fundamental to the character of God's being and activity.

Also, in the Jewish and Christian tradition, there are functions of suffering that clearly have nothing to do with personal guilt or "justice." At times suffering is a *test* of man's devotion and obedience to God. The Book of Job, perhaps the very oldest book in the scriptures, stresses this very point. Job suffers ruin and illness at the hand of Satan, as a *test* of his devotion to God. His neighbors come to him and present various theories for his suffering and suggest repeatedly that Job has some secret sin that has caused his calamities (quasi-karma). Job rightfully refuses these explanations and maintains his integrity by not cursing God. In the same tradition Psalm 11:5 states:

> *The Lord tests the righteous and the wicked,*
> *and his soul hates him that loves violence.*

At a deeper level, suffering can become, if transformed by love of others, part of the highest aspects of man's spiritual life. This was expressed in the poetry of Isaiah, as he prophesied about the sufferings of the coming messiah:

> *Surely he has borne our griefs*
> *and carried our sorrows;*
> *yet we esteemed him stricken,*
> *smitten by God, and afflicted.*
> *But he was wounded for our*
> *transgressions,*
> *he was bruised for our iniquities;*
> *upon him was the chastisement that made us whole,*
> *and with his stripes we are healed.* (Is. 53: 4–5)

The New Testament reveals that in the new covenant the old path of suffering is even more important than before. Jesus makes suffering an indispensable obligation for discipleship (Mt. 16: 24). Peter verifies the message of Job, that some suffering is for the sake of strengthening and testing our faith (1 Pet. 1:6–7), and James adds a new revelation, that suffering has the ultimate goal of growth in spiritual wisdom (Jas. 1:2–4).

Most importantly, Peter and Paul both show us that the redemptive suffering described by Isaiah is a spiritual imperative of all true Christians. Paul declared, "Now I rejoice in my suffering for your sake, and in my flesh I complete what is lacking in Christ's afflictions for the sake of his body, that is, the church . . ." (Col. 1:24). Peter echoed the same thought in a wordier fashion in his first letter (4:12–19). The thought that suffering is a necessary element of Christianity has been an essential part of practically every denomination in Christendom. Only recently have there arisen theologies which accentuate material prosperity and happiness as normative to the Christian life.[6]

Perhaps the most important and often noted Christian objection to the concept of karma is that karmic theologies tend to make persons passive towards social or personal evil and injustice. A person who believes in karma assumes that what is is indeed good, no matter what the "illusion" of his emotions tells him. In its classic form karma was the rationale behind the injustices of the Hindu caste system.

In the Judeo-Christian tradition, evil and injustice are perversions of what should be. The prophets of ancient Israel reviled against the social injustice of society, and never regarded the oppression of the poor as an expression of spiritual justice. One of the basic motifs of the Gospels is that Jesus came to establish the Kingdom of God by overthrowing the evils of disease, demon possession, and ultimately death. The basic commission of every Christian disciple is to continue the work of destroying Satan's destructive hold on the world. An authentic follower of Jesus is not one who necessarily has the "higher consciousness" to see beauty in evil, but one who has the very power of the Holy Spirit with which to combat it.

The Act-Consequence Relationship

There seems to be no question that the classical doctrine of karma is incompatible with biblical revelation. It would be better not totally to reject the doctrine of karma, but rather to see it in terms of a shadow truth containing elements that are biblically valid. In the Bible, there is a motif that resembles the Eastern doctrine of karma in that some actions do have consequences in this life, others in the afterlife, or in future generations. In this regard the studies of the contemporary Old Testament scholar Gerhard Von Rad are particularly significant. Von Rad studied this motif of ethical and moral accountability with great care and termed it the "act-consequence relationship."[7]

Von Rad calls attention to the fact that the act-consequence relationship (hereforth, ACR) permeates the whole Bible. It defines the relationship between the nation of Israel and God. Whenever they were obedient to his will, they prospered and triumphed over their enemies. Whenever they were idolatrous they suffered defeat and ruin. Von Rad found the personal, individual descriptions of the ACR concentrated in the Wisdom books of the Bible, especially the Book of Proverbs. There the ACR defines not only the moral life, but almost every aspect of mankind's being.

The moral admonitions of Proverbs are among the best known in the Bible. For example:

> *He who troubles his own house will inherit the wind*
> *And the foolish will be servant to the wise hearted.*   *(11:29)*

> The fear of the Lord prolongs life
> But the year of the wicked will be shortened.   (10:27)

On the economic aspects of life:

> Poor is he who works with a negligent hand
> But the hand of the diligent makes rich.   (10:4)

> Ill-gotten gains do not profit
> But righteousness delivers from death.   (10:2)

A thing to note about the ACR as described in Proverbs is that it is not a "religious" law. It is not a series of promises about some future afterlife, but rather is "this-worldly." They may be interpreted by the pious as promises about the future spiritual world, but biblical scholarship (and any honest reading) has shown that indeed they were literal statements about man's willful actions and their consequences in *this world.*

Von Rad also points out that the wise men and scribes of Israel who compiled the Wisdom literature were aware of the ambiguity of the ACR.[8] They do not take the further step, like the sages in India, to proclaim an unambiguous law of retribution (karma). Rather, they saw the ACR as a general force which could be, and indeed often was, canceled by other factors. The book of Job shows this most clearly. There Job's counselors insist that his ills are the result of an unambiguous ACR, that is, Job is suffering, therefore Job must have sinned. Job knows their accusations are unjust, but he does not know the cause of his misfortune. The reader knows from the prologue, however, that his woes are a test of his devotion to God.

The existence of the ACR is not easy to discern in the modern age. Many liberal-minded Christians are embarrassed about the "work ethic" advocated in Proverbs as being an apologetic for capitalism; others see Proverbs as a collection of trite moralisms. Unfortunately even traditional theology has had difficulties in dealing with many of the this-worldly aspects of the ACR. In the first centuries of Christian theology there was a tendency to allegorize or spiritualize them. They were often seen only in terms of ultimate rewards after the Last Judgment.

Only in recent decades have certain fundamentalist groups rediscovered the literal, this-worldly meaning of the ACR and woven it into practical "laws" of prosperity, health, and general well-being. This has caused distress among less conservative Christians for the good reason that often these "laws" are presented in unambiguous terms which do violence to the subtlety of biblical revelation. For example, many Christian evangelists are currently preaching the "gospel of prosperity" that avoids the passages in Luke about the spiritual blessedness of poverty, or what James, in his letter, has to say about the poor.

It is rarely recognized that the New Testament teaches that the ACR pertains both to final judgment and to this-worldly judgment. For example, Jesus affirmed that there was an ACR between sin and sickness in the cases of some forms of paralysis (Mk.:2: 1–12 and Jn. 5:2–15).[9] Perhaps the most dramatic case of ACR functioning on the this-worldly plane in the New Testament is found in the account of Herod's death (Acts 12:20–23). There Herod was stricken by some form of hideous illness for accepting the idolatrous flattery of a pagan delegation from one of his client cities.

Because of the similarities between the concept of karma and the biblical ACR, many occult writers mistakenly claim that they are identical and that therefore the "Bible teaches karma." For example, Geoffrey Hodson, a Theosophical apologist, in his book *Reincarnation, Fact or Fallacy?* has a chapter called "Karma in the Bible."[10] Hodson cites Galatians 6:7, as proof: "Do not be deceived; God is not mocked, for whatever a man sows, that he will also reap." That does sound like karma, but what Hodson does not cite is the verse that immediately follows: "For he who sows to his own flesh will from the flesh reap corruption; but he who sows to the Spirit will from the Spirit reap eternal life." That verse modifies the preceding one so that what is taught is not karma but the doctrine of ACR. In this case it is not even a this-worldly ACR.

Trying to distinguish the subtle distinctions between karma and the ACR may be bewildering, so let us place them back to back. In Eastern religions karma is the central concern of the spiritual life. In biblical revelation the ACR is a law, but it does not play so central a role. The personal Father-God and his loving kindness are the chief concern of the Judeo-Christian religion. Karma is precise and impersonal: willed actions will return to the originator in exactly the same manner as they were given. The ACR is ambiguous. It is subject to modification or cancellation according to God's grace through Jesus Christ.

The doctrine of karma asserts that it functions primarily by influencing future reincarnations, although most Eastern religions also recognize that karma often rebounds upon the person within the period of one lifetime. Contemporary Christian understanding of the ACR focuses on two ways that it operates: the consequences of actions are experienced by the person within this lifetime and are this-worldly, or they are postponed until a final accounting at either death or the Last Judgment. It is not generally understood that the ACR is described in scripture as operating in a transtemporal, this-worldly manner that is similar to karma. An example of this is found in prohibition against idol worshiping:

. . . you shall not bow down to them or serve them; for I the Lord your God am a jealous God, visiting the iniquity of the fathers upon the children to the third and fourth generations of those who hate me . . .   (Ex. 20:5)[11]

In Deuteronomy 5:9, we find that the sin of illegitimate conception excludes membership in the congregation until the tenth generation. This means that the ACR does indeed pass beyond the first individual to future times and generations.

Spiritualism and the Metaphysical Movement

In the West, two loosely related groups have done the most to influence the contemporary Western attempt to understand the PLV. For this reason, it is important to take a close look at them to discern shadow truths from what is otherwise dangerous in their practices and doctrines.

Spiritualism is a religious system which asserts that mankind needs constant, conscious, and unambiguous communication from the spirit world, that is, spirits other than the Holy Spirit. Like ancient Gnosticism, spiritualism is parasitic and chameleonlike in that it adapts itself to a wide variety of host religions: Christian, non-Christian, and even atheistic groups. No matter what the setting, in either the voodoo churches of Haiti, or one of the "Christian" Spiritualist churches of America, the fruits are the same: a cessation of authentic worship, personal subjection to an array of spirits, and the reception of unambiguous cosmic teachings.

A characteristic of all forms of spiritualism is their reliance on some form of mediumship for spiritual communication with the advising spirits. At times the mediumship is of the "classic" type where the "sitter" is temporarily entranced and unconscious, and the alien entity completely controls the sitter's body, using the sitter's own vocal cords to speak. But there are other forms of mediumship that are more subtle. A common form today is called "automatic writing," where the sitter's arm is controlled by the alien spirit while the rest of the body and mind are in a normal state. Other common forms of mediumship include ouija boards and a weight on a string called a "pendulum." All these forms have the same effect, they allow information to be received from the spirit world.

The Bible, particularly the Old Testament, specifically and vehemently condemns mediumship (Dt. 18:10–11; Lev. 19:31, 20:6; 2 Kg. 23:24; 2 Chr. 33:6 and others), but does not at all explain *why* mediumship is forbidden. There are hints that mediumship is always associated with idolatry and the heathen religions that surrounded the Israelite people.

It has been the consistent Christian discernment that the entities contacted under mediumistic circumstances are not really spirits of the dead so much as demons masquerading as those spirits. For example, in the tradition of Christian discernment, if a grieving widow goes to a medium and makes contact via the medium with a spirit who sounds like her husband, and who even knows of all the private details of their lives, the spirit is not really that of the husband, but is rather a demonic entity. By some means the demonic entity has access to all the memories and emotions of the dead husband. This belief is essentially a testing-discernment derived from long Christian experience. It comes in part from the accounts of mediums who have renounced their work and become Christians.[12] For centuries, the experiences of Christian exorcists have repeatedly shown that demonic entities can indeed mimic the voice patterns and memories of any person for their own ends. The Roman Catholic manual for exorcism, developed in its present form in the seventeenth century, warns the priest-exorcist against believing any statement made by the possessing demon, no matter whom it mimics.[13] It is only in the last century that Protestant denominations have again come to take exorcism seriously, and have also rediscovered the similarities between the "revelations" of the demons of a possessed person and the discourses of mediums.[14]

There is every indication to believe that the demonic entities that motivated and formed ancient Gnosticism are the same ones responsible for modern spiritualism. The work of the great psychologist C. G. Jung points in this direction. In his massive early work *Symbols of Transformation: An Analysis of the Prelude to a Case of Schizophrenia,*[15] Jung traced the progressive "insanity" of one of his patients and he was astonished to discover that the patient's "hallucinations" and dreams drew from myths, symbols, and stories of ancient Gnostic and Near-Eastern demonology. These hallucinations were totally beyond the educational and personal experience of the patient. The patient was, in fact, undergoing a process of demonic possession.[16] Jung developed many of his beliefs on archetypes from this case, suggesting that he had poor discernment of the abilities of the demonic kingdom. Morton Kelsey, whom we have cited often, also believes that Jung frequently confused his archetypes with angelic and demonic forces.[17] For our purposes, *Symbols of Transformation* demonstrates quite clearly that the same demonic forces which were behind ancient Gnosticism can be active and present in the modern world.[18]

The human "father" of modern Western spiritualism was Emanuel Swedenborg, the Swedish scientist, engineer, and medium. He had a visionary experience of Jesus Christ, followed by prolonged conversations and revelations with angels, then with the spirits of the dead. In prolonged trance states, he was reportedly transported to heaven, hell, and other locations in the universe. He reported that he conversed with many famous figures from the past. He wrote volume upon volume about his revelations and eventually a church was founded to propagate his views.

The Swedenborgian churches never amounted to much; their principal function has been to translate and publish their founder's interminable writings. But Swedenborgianism has been a major influence of most varieties of Western Spiritualism. The Swedenborgian system proclaims itself to be Christian: Jesus Christ is the central figure in history and Christianity the best of religions, but behind its facade is an essentially gnostic core. Jesus is not the redeemer, his crucifixion was not an atoning act, and man essentially saves himself through moral behavior.[19] Strangely, though Swedenborg was in constant communication with the dead, he did not recommend it for others and believed he had a specific dispensation from the biblical prohibition against such contact.

Systematic contact with the dead through mediumship, for the general public, had its origins in the West in upper New York state in 1848. That year two teenage sisters, Kate and Maggie Fox, began manifesting a "rapping" noise in their home which soon became a code to communicate with spirits of the dead. The rappings drew nationwide attention, and by the end of the century various forms of spirit communications were in full bloom, both in the United States and in Europe. Many different "Christian" Spiritualist Churches came into existence, all based on local mediums and the revelations channeled through them from various "guides." In 1893 the National Spiritualist Association of Churches of the United States was founded (N.S.A.).

Turn-of-the-century Spiritualism had many local variations based on different sets of spirit-guides, but shared a fairly common cosmology and "theology." It was very close to the Swedenborgian system of the preceding century. The Christology was Arian: Jesus was a heavenly being, but not God; salvation comes through self-knowledge and self-effort.[20]

Two elements of turn-of-the-century and early twentieth-century Spiritualism deserve special attention as they disclose its chameleonlike and parasitic nature: the nationality of its "guides" and its rejection of reincarnation. In the 1900s there was very little awareness or appreciation of Eastern religions in Western culture. There was, however, a great reverence for the culture of classical antiquity. Thus, the "spirit guides" manifested as heroes and personages of antiquity. Andrew Jackson Davis, the first major American spiritualist writer, had a guide who identified himself as Galen, the great physician-writer of the Hellenistic world.[21] Very popular at this time were guides who claimed connections with Pythagoras and Plotinus, and esoteric and mythical traditions of the ancient West. The very idea of a Hindu or Tibetan guide would have been unthinkable to the Victorian Colonial mind.

Spiritualist theology at this time roundly condemned reincarnation. The afterlife described in spiritualist communications included tales of a happiness without judgment or ethical accountability, with no mention of worship and prayer. The concept of reincarnation was entirely alien to American spiritualism, and came to spiritualist circles through two sources, the Theosophical Movement founded by Madame Blavatsky in the 1870s,[22] and the influence of the French spiritualist Allen Kardec, who was the major influence in the formation of Brazilian spiritualism. The pro- and antireincarnation debate within spiritualism mounted in the 1920s and became quite bitter. Different mediums, backed by different sets of "guides" argued back and forth about reincarnation. In 1930 the antireincarnation forces of the N.S.A. temporarily won and passed a resolution condemning reincarnation.[23]

Thereafter reincarnation slowly won the upper hand as the newer mediums and their guides turned in favor of it. During this period one also notes that some guides manifested as Eastern entities, because much of the public had now grown in appreciation of Eastern religions. For example, Alice Baily, who split off from the Theosophical Society and who "channeled" an endless series of books on metaphysical cosmology and practice, acquired the guide Djwhal Khul, a supposed Tibetan adept. By the 1950s, both Eastern religions and reincarnation were entrenched among spiritualist circles.[24]

It would be worthwhile to compare here the nature of revelation from the Kingdom of God with that of spiritualist revelation. As we have seen in Part I, biblical revelation is ambiguous, anecdotal, and historical, and for the most part doctrine must be *drawn out* of scripture with effort, "seek it like silver and search for it as for hidden treasure" (Ps. 2:4).

In both biblical and postbiblical revelation, the believer must respond with obedience to God's commands, but always within a context of personal growth and freedom. In postbiblical times revelation has been limited by reference to established scriptures. On the other hand, spiritualist revelation is primarily subjective, and unambiguous. Many spiritualist systems are little more than textbooks of morality and cosmology. The disciple has little input in drawing out the theological implications of the system; they are plainly and unambiguously presented in pretentious language. In effect the disciple responds with obedience and acceptance *without* any process of intellectual growth, or development of wisdom.

One of the most consistent patterns of spiritualism is its tendency to give the disciples vast, unambiguous, unmanageable, and untestable amounts of "scientific" and cosmological knowledge. The knowledge and facts "revealed" are always of a nature that are beyond the level of a contemporary science either to deny or confirm but sound impressive. For example, in the Swedenborg system, the moon is inhabited by beings that breathe through their stomachs and Martians have faces that are half black and half white.[25] We *now* know those "facts" are impossible, but for the reader of the eighteenth century, this was an amazing and *possible* revelation. The result of spiritualist "revelations" has always been to obstruct real scientific growth by claiming that scientific knowledge can be "received" without the humbling, hard work of research, testing (including failing), instrument development, and interpretive debates (the reproof system of science). A person who believes he can discover the mysteries of the universe by attentiveness to any spiritualistic system, ends up with pseudoknowledge that is untestable and absolutely useless on any accountable scientific or utilitarian level.[26]

This spiritualist attitude extends even to a dislike of normal historical research. And why not? One of their beliefs is that they or their guides have access to a universal superlibrary called the "Akashic Records" in which all historical events are accurately recorded. Therefore the tedious process of document evaluation, interviewing, critical conversations, and so forth are all "unnecessary."[27] In essence, spiritualist wisdom and knowledge are "cheap wisdom" and "cheap knowledge," easily gotten and ultimately worth even less than the effort it costs to acquire them. Spiritualism contradicts the biblical commands that knowledge and wisdom must be sought *with* the help of God, but *through* disciplined perseverance and brotherly reproof.

Another dramatic distinction between the revelations of the Holy Spirit and those of spiritualist sources is in the way the human channel is used. The Holy Spirit profoundly *respects* the human host and works *with* the memories, language, educational level, culture of the person. Thus, in the Bible, we have vastly different levels of writing and eloquence as Matthew, the authors of the Psalms, the writer of Hebrews, and Saint Paul.[28] Spiritualist revelations *violate* and ignore the human medium. The language of these revelations has no relation to the education, culture, language patterns, or personality of the medium.

Similarly, in matters of cosmology and science, revelation in Holy Scriptures is scant, ambiguous, and symbolic. Christians have committed their gravest theological errors when they have insisted that the cosmology of the Bible is scientifically precise, and have interpreted it in unambiguous terms.[29]

There is one class of revelation, however, where communication from the Holy Spirit and from spiritualist sources is practically identical. That is in the area of specific *action commands*. As we pointed out in our study of Acts, Peter received an *ambiguous* vision when the Lord wished to reveal to him an important *theological* message, but when it came to direct Peter on a *specific action,* to go down and receive the messengers from Cornelius, the Lord spoke in an *unambiguous* locution (Acts 10:9–22).

The discernment factor in a locution which directs immediate action is not generally in the form, but in the internal state of the receiver. (Is there a sense of joy and peace, or not, as discussed in our study of discernment?)

The Metaphysical Movement[30]

Parallel with the growth of spiritualism has been the spread of the metaphysical movement. This movement is as difficult to define as ancient Gnosticism. Like Gnosticism, every metaphysical group has had its own peculiar doctrine, often based on visionary or spiritualistic revelations of its leaders.

The metaphysical groups that developed at the end of the nineteenth century were generally heavily influenced by Swedenborg, American spiritualism, and by the American transcendental philosophers, particularly Emerson. The Christian Science Church was the most famous of these early metaphysical groups, but as influential, if not as well known, was a grouping of unorthodox Christian thinkers and pastors known as the adherents of "New Thought."

It would be easy to simply label the metaphysical movement a philosophical spiritualism, but this is not quite accurate. There have always been persons within its ranks who have always distanced themselves from active spiritualism. Yet the metaphysical movement has always had philosophical and practical affinities with ancient Gnosticism that are so numerous that many writers identify the metaphysical movement as a form of Gnosticism. This is asserted by both Christian writers who realize the dangers of Gnosticism,[31] and by its own philosophers and writers who consciously and proudly claim descent from Gnosticism.[32]

New Thought

The most important of the New Thought prophets was Emmet Fox (d. 1951).[33] He was born into a Catholic family and raised in that faith. As a young boy he already possessed the gift of healing, and as his own Church could do little to guide his use of that gift he turned to other sources, especially Christian Science and spiritualist writings. With these sources it is understandable how he developed a neo-Gnostic theology. He adopted that ancient exegetical method of allergorizing scripture so that such fundamental doctrines as sin, the atonement, and the divinity of Jesus were reduced to meaningless symbols.

In spite of all this, Fox maintained a love for the Bible as the revealed word of God and so the Logos used him to understand certain truths that were totally alien to nineteenth-century orthodox Christianity. Some of these truths referred to a discerning of the specific ACR of certain attitudes and actions. Thus although his general theology was neo-Gnostic, his pastoral theology (his beliefs about spiritual matters in everyday life) was decades ahead of his own orthodox contemporaries. For example, he discovered that honoring the Old Testament rule of tithing would free a person from serious financial difficulties.[34] He found, on the matters of health and healing, that the emotions and thought processes were the key to good health. Further he discovered that an effective way to healing was to "appropriate" relevant healing scriptures and repeat them until they are firmly lodged in the subconscious mind.

Fox preached a gospel of prosperity and positive thinking that was anathema to his orthodox contemporaries.[35] Eventually, through the writings of such men as Norman Vincent Peale, and a multitude of other channels, many of the elements of Fox's pastoral theology have passed into orthodox Christian thinking. The fundamentalist TV evangelists of today who advocate a gospel of prosperity and healing are in fact greatly indebted to Emmet Fox, no matter how much they may preach against the occult or denounce metaphysics.

Contemporary metaphysical groups usually believe in some blend of spiritualism, interest in parapsychology, Easter philosophies, and "higher consciousness" philosophies. Also, central to metaphysical philosophy is an idealization of evolution that becomes almost a worship of it. Like karma, evolution becomes an ultimate, independent principle of cosmic motion. This produces an assumption that all progress and all current events are for the good, and blinds the devotee to demonic forces and to the possibility of regressive movement and sin.

However, because of the philosophical, cultural, and scientific differences between the ancient world and the present scene, the metaphysical movement does have several differences with ancient Jewish-Christ Gnosticism. The ancient Jewish-Christ Gnostics did not make mediumship a major factor of their religion, while modern metaphysical groups are for the most part also practicing spiritualists. The difference is perhaps due to the fact that New Testament Jews and Christians held fast to the Old Testament injunctions against mediumship.[36]

A second difference between classic Gnosticism and modern neo-Gnosticism manifests in a totally different attitude towards evil. Every religion in the ancient world had an awareness of demonic forces as personal and malevolent, and most developed ritual forms of obeisance to mollify the evil demonic forces could inflict. The promise of the ancient Gnostics was that, with their secret knowledge of incantations, they could contemptuously taunt and overcome all demonic forces (See Jude 10). Evil directed toward persons from the spirit world did exist, but the perfected one, the Gnostic, had knowledge-power over any demon.

The neo-Gnostic metaphysical groups take a different, but equally dangerous, view. They believe that all sin is ignorance and there are no malevolent spiritual entities. There are, perhaps, "lost" souls in the lower levels of the astral world (sheol-hades), who need *illumination*. All evil is ignorance and fundamentally an illusion. This was the core doctrine of Christian Science. It is actually an extreme form of Platonic theory of evil as privation, which became normative in medieval Christian theology. Neo-Gnostics essentially believe evil to be a problem of consciousness. A person with a developed "higher consciousness" recognizes that there is no personal source for evil, and that "all things are one" (a shadow truth of Eph. 4:6).

The problem of metaphysical groups is *not* their impulse to explore in these areas, rather it is their nondiscerning approach. Like spiritualists, their explorations are influenced by demonic sources which feed them "cheap knowledge" and "cheap wisdom." Metaphysical people tend to say "yes" to every new idea (while Christians tend to say "no" to them). Saint Paul exhorted his followers to *test* all things.

In spite of its origins in spiritualism, the Logos made great use of various metaphysical groups for its revelatory tasks. It is fair to say that the Christian Science Church was the first Christian group since the third century to preach healing as a *normal* process for the believer. New thought was similarly influential in bringing to attention the positive aspects of the ACR, especially in regard to prosperity and health. The question comes to mind: Why didn't the Logos move among the orthodox churches on these matters? The answer to such a question is complex, but certainly a part of the answer lies in the fact that the orthodox churches were perfectly satisfied with their credal definitions and theological understandings. There simply was no room in the inn for the Logos; he had to settle for a smelly stable to bring forth his new light.

Before we end this chapter we should take note of the reincarnation system revealed by the American seer Edgar Cayce (1877–1945). No other person has had a greater influence of forming contemporary attitudes for or against reincarnation.[37] As a young man, Cayce developed the gift of medical diagnosis. He would go into a deep, non-lucid trance and see clairvoyantly the medical problems afflicting a person. In addition he would often prescribe herbal remedies that often proved to be effective. After several years practicing this strange psychic ministry, Cayce stumbled upon reincarnation/karma as concepts helping to illuminate the cause of many of his patients' illnesses. Subsequently he spent much of his time giving "life readings," which were revelations of the seekers' past lives and especially the person's karmic debt as it relates to his or her present situation. The information about the past life would often be accompanied by moralistic exhortations toward an attitude of non-violence and forgiveness of others.

If effect, this procedure set up a guru/disciple relationship in which the data of the seeker's past life and karmic debt would not be critically evaluated or discerned. The tradition of "talented seer" dispensing "life readings" has had a major impact on present metaphysical and occult groups. Today, practically every New Age institution has a seer who will give a Cayce-style life reading.

Chapter 7

Induced PLVs: The Amateurs

The Bridey Murphy Case: The Challenge[1]

It was the famous Bridey Murphy case of the 1950s which sparked a revolution in PLV investigation. The case stemmed from a series of regressions done by an amateur hypnotist, Morey Bernstein, on a subject who had a facility for deep trance, a Mrs. Virginia Tighe. Six times, from November of 1952 to August of 1953, Mrs. Tighe was regressed to a PLV as a certain Bridey Murphy of Cork, Ireland, who was born in 1798 and died in 1864 in Belfast. The sessions produced a vivid, if somewhat mundane story of life as a middle-class woman in nineteenth-century Ireland. The sessions also produced a wealth of details about customs, geographic locations, street names, grocery shops, and coins that were verified in subsequent field research by other investigators. In 1954 a series of articles on the regressions appeared in the *Denver Post*. Finally the book itself, *The Search for Bridey Murphy*,[2] was published in January of 1956.

The book became a best seller but was immediately attacked from several quarters. Articles appeared in *Life* and the *Chicago American* and other Hearst papers which attacked the whole thing as nothing more than an invention from the mind of the subject. The *Chicago American* articles in particular attacked the veracity of the PLV by pointing out supposed parallel experiences in the lives of both the hypnotic subject and Bridey Murphy.

By the end of 1956 a group of medical hypnotists who worked within accepted professional bounds produced a book on the controversy. It was edited by Milton V. Kline, who today is considered an authority in the field of medical hypnosis and hypnotic theory.[3] One after the other the contributors took Mr. Bernstein to task for being an amateur and unqualified for the dangerous business of hypnosis. As a matter of fact, several of the authors had experienced PLVs spontaneously occurring in some of their own patients, but just how they handled these is not fully explained.

However, every article asserts that the *only* possible mechanism for the formation of the PLV is "cryptomnesia," that is the mind's power to recall long-forgotten bits of information. One article attempts to discredit belief in any form of afterlife as unacceptable to the scientific mind. The real issue, that the regressions produced substantial amounts of verifiable information about Ireland in the nineteenth century that could only have been acquired by paranormal means, was not addressed by either the articles or the book.

One article appeared in the immediate post–Bridey Murphy period in the professional psychological journals: "An Experimental Investigation of the Psychodynamic Implications of the Hypnotic 'Previous Existence' Fantasy".[4] The title discloses the basic assumption of the researcher, Edwin S. Zolik, that a PLV cannot be anything more than fantasy. The declared aim of his experiment was to show how PLVs are pieced together by crytomnesia.

Zolik hypnotized an undergraduate volunteer to a deep trance level and proceeded to age-regress the student to infancy, and after that to a PLV. Under deep hypnosis the student reported he was Brian O'Malley, a British officer of the Irish Guards who died in a horse accident in 1892. The PLV was very brief and quickly discontinued as the subject was fatigued after the process of hypnosis and regression. A second session was held four days later, and again the volunteer was deeply hypnotized. The investigator was determined to find the contemporary origin of the name. I quote directly from the article:

> Following this the subject was asked: "Where does the name Brian O'Malley come from?" He replied that he did not know but that, "I just know it, it's there." Consequently he was asked if it was part of a story he had read, or whether it was part of some movie he had seen, to both he replied that he didn't know.[5]

Further questioning revealed that he had once heard of a *similar* name, Timothy O'Malley, who had been his grandfather's enemy and was also a soldier. Zolik concludes that story to be the source of the PLV. This may seem logical to him, and certainly to some of his readers who share his assumptions, but certainly his procedures and assumptions are seriously flawed. He spent very little time gathering data from the PLV, and although the words of his entranced volunteer tended to *negate* the assumption of this-life origins of the name, he continued to prod until some similar name was remembered. It should also be noted that there are many who claim that a PLV is merely the result of telepathic suggestion, that the subject comes up with a PLV in order to *please* the hypnotist. Zolik seemed to prove that even in deepest trance, the subject could not "please" the hypnotist and confirm the assumption of current-life origins of the PLV.

More significantly, Zolik discovered something totally unexpected. The PLV, or as he termed it "progignomatic fantasy," related to current emotional problems of the subject and had definite *diagnostic possibilities*. He suggested further research on this last point.[6] No such research ensued. As a matter of fact the academic and professional community assiduously ignored the PLV issue.[7] The mental health establishment in the 1950s was in the grip of behaviorism, that strange theory which stipulates that the internal processes of the mind have no importance because they are beyond scientific examination or consideration. Similarly, not a single Christian theologian was moved to personally investigate the PLV phenomenon. Many religious journals at the time dismissed the Bridey Murphy PLV with a few caustic remarks about the theological unacceptability of reincarnation, and the case was closed for the professional establishments.[8]

This response was a classic case of *data avoidance*. Contrary to popular beliefs about science and scientists, this is *normal*. Data avoidance is not an event restricted to Galileo, when the best-educated minds of the time refused to peer through the newly developed telescopes.[9] It is an ever-present factor in the history of human thought. In the 1960s the liberal bias of the educational and psychological professions ignored, and refused to credit as significant, discoveries by animal behaviorists about aggression and territory.[10] Or again, note how stubborn many medical doctors are in examining the data and research on megavitamin therapy.

The truth is that scientific-professional groups do not like data that is upsetting or radically unusual.[11] Normal scientific progress is based on clarifying, extending, or modifying *already accepted theories*, while working with data of a familiar *kind*. A scientific discipline has what is called a "paradigm," a set of agreed assumptions, bounds of investigation, procedures and instruments that function as a model for further research. Simply put, the data generated by PLV, whether from the Bridey Murphy case or from Zolik, did not fit the paradigms of either the psychological or theological establishments of the 1950s.

As a consequence, further work on PLVs was left in the hands of amateurs or maverick professionals. An amateur is a person who has no professional training, but is usually endowed with curiosity and perseverance. A professional maverick has disciplined training, but operates outside of the professional paradigm, without normal professional supports such as shared journals, seminars, or the criticism of fellow professionals. In effect the professional maverick is an amateur with credentials.

The First Response: Early Manuals by Amateurs

As we indicated earlier, it was only in the 1930s that American spiritualists and metaphysical groups came to adopt reincarnation as a doctrine. But even after that there was little encouragement among spiritualist groups to have their disciples experience PLVs for themselves. Rather the accent was placed on having the local psychic or medium give "life readings" as with Edgar Cayce. This of course reinforced the grip that the spirits had on the disciples, and prevented any experience that might contradict occult doctrine.[12]

There was a gap of a decade and a half from the time of the Bridey Murphy book to the emergence of works specifically concerned with systematic and sustained PLVs. Immediately after the publication of *The Search for Bridey Murphy*, hundreds of curious and adventuresome people went to their libraries and read one or two books on hypnosis and proceded to experiment with PLVs on friends and neighbors. From experience we must assume that the results of these sessions were what they have always been: a mix of a few clear, detailed PLVs with many cases that were muddled, incoherent, or historically impossible. This is discouraging to all but the most determined of investigators. There are hints in the current literature that some of those early dabblers were persons with professional training in mental health fields. Many of the professionals prudently chose not to publicize their experiments and make themselves subject to peer ridicule.[13]

In any case, it was the amateurs, those who had no professional reputations or clients to lose, who published the first manuals for inducing PLVs. Some of these persons were experienced occultists with a good knowledge of the philosophy of reincarnation. Others were weekend investigators, who did some casework in PLVs and read a few books on reincarnation from their neighborhood library. It takes a sophisticated and critical intelligence to be aware that by relying on occult and Eastern descriptions of reincarnation the researcher has both prejudiced and interpretation of the PLVs and limited what he "sees" in the PLVs. Further, by accepting the spiritualist assumptions of occult writings the investigator is susceptible to demonic influence and not infrequently comes into direct contact with spirit guides.

Of the dozens of manuals that came out in the occult explosion of the 1970s we can examine only a few.

The first one I know of was published in 1970 by a small, Miami-based metaphysical group. The author was William Swygard, and he called his procedure for inducing PLVs the "awareness technique."[14] Despite the fact that the author believed that his technique was nontrance, it differs very little from traditional hypnosis. It is based on the old occult technique of inducing out-of-body travel (called astral projection) by hypnotically suggesting deep relaxation, dissociation of body and mind, and finally by guided visualizations.

The Swygard technique was commonly used within a few years by many metaphysical groups. Swygard would have had more influence had he not insisted that the same technique be used to "prove" and experience the existence of twelve concentric worlds that supposedly surround the earth. In other words, Swygard fell into the old Gnostic trap of taking his own visionary experiences at face value. Most of the readers who bothered to read his second volume on the concentric worlds were turned off by his unbridled subjectivity.[15]

The next year saw the publication of two slender volumes on PLVs from an occult publisher. One, *Five Keys to Past Lives* by J. H. Brennan, concentrated specifically on different techniques of inducing PLVs.[16] The first technique suggested by the author is an Ouija board, which is, of course, a spritualistic device used for communication with familiar spirits, but the author believed that valid past-life information can be derived from its use provided it is used with "care." The second technique the author presents is hypnotic regression, which he significantly calls a "popular research tool" and cites the influence of the Bridey Murphy case in this mode of PLV investigation. The instructions he gives for hypnotic regression were actually quite adequate, at least technically, and sufficient to get an enthusiast started on PLV research.[17] A third technique described by Brennan deserves special attention: the trapping of the Akashic Records. In this technique the inquirer is to train himself in visualization exercises to imagine a vast, elaborate library of all of the world's knowledge. Supposedly, this exercise creates a subjective image of an objectively real spiritual phenomenon. Once the student has completed his training he has access to the whole of man's history, including his past life and anyone else's. In reality this is the ultimate form of spiritualist "cheap knowledge."[18] The author did not stop here, however, but suggested several other ways of achieving PLVs: one is long hours of meditation on personal symbols; another is depth meditation, which is the technique used in Eastern religions. Lastly Brennan suggests inducing PLVs through astral travel and describes a technique basically identical with the one elaborated by Swygard. That last technique is again described at length in Colin Bennett's *Practical Time-Travel: How to Reach Back to Past Lives by Occult Means*.[19] Bennett's procedures are similar to Swygard, but less ludicrously subjective, and more in tune with the vocabulary and traditions of Western occultism.

The PLV in the 1970s

Marcia Moore

Marcia Moore is unquestionably the person most responsible in spreading the use of PLVs as a common experience. Her manual, *Hypersentience: Exploring Your Past Lifetime as a Guide to Your Character and Destiny,*[20] first appeared in 1976 and soon came out in paperback. This book contains simple, clear instructions for learning how to induce PLVs in others and how to guide them through the experience. The techniques and procedures are not new, but she was an experienced writer and made the procedure seem simple and safe. Her seminars and *Hypersentience* have been of tremendous importance to all sorts of metaphysical groups and even to professionals in the mental health fields.

A positive contribution that *Hypersentience* makes is the vocabulary established for the PLV procedure. Taken from Carl Rogers, its adaptation for use with PLVs is simple and appropriate. She calls the seer of the vision the "sensor," and the person who induces the PLV and otherwise helps the sensor in the process the "facilitator." I will use Moore's vocabulary in this book with the understanding that these are neutral terms that do not imply any specific theory of the origins of the PLV.

Moore's first book on the theory of reincarnation came out in 1968.[21] The book is little more than a repetition of standard eastern and spiritualistic interpretations of reincarnation. Karma is the supreme law of the universe and God falls into the distant background. She firmly believed that there should be a radical separation between the truth of reincarnation and the doctrines of any "religion."[22]

The procedures described in *Hypersentience* are simple and informal. The clients are carefully briefed on the process, and after their questions are answered the entrancing process is begun with a prayer-invocation. Thereafter several imagination exercises are employed to help to achieve a moderate to deep trance state.

The prayer at the beginning of the relaxation procedures is not a prayer to God. It is an elegant Gnostic hymn to the "self," so that every person becomes aware of his or her own "true identity."[23] Further on in the relaxation technique the sensors are invited to visualize their personal guide (a straightforward invitation to spiritualism) and ask the guide's assistance in the PLV. She personally uses her own guides to direct her in difficult regressions.[24] It is curious that Moore feels so strongly about separating reincarnation from "religion," and then proceeds to accept totally the religion and practice of spiritualism.

Moore has a tendency to turn practically every PLV into a Gnostic-oriented experience. In every case cited in her book there is no sin (nor of course need of repentance), only errors in judgment or ignorance. The authentic nonjudging role of the facilitator is turned into an insinuation that immorality is not serious, and PLVs have the practical effect of becoming rationalizations for present sin. A businessman had a PLV as a bank robber and murderer, but even that was acceptable because now he is a physician and his disregard for the law and the "establishment" in that lifetime has carried over in his ability to be innovative in his current practice.[25] A woman who "by current standards can be called a nymphomanic" had a PLV as a priestess in an ancient fertility religion. This "explains" her attitude towards men. Moore proudly describes the good the PLV did; she is a swinger, but no longer "compulsive."[26]

In essence, Moore has no concept of sin nor any idea of the true depth of evil. The most she acknowledges along these lines is that immorality is "futile," but in no way subject to judgment or the consequences indicated in scripture. In no way does she attempt to lead the sensors to repentance or to God's forgiveness. This of course is the old Gnostic confusion that sin is little more than ignorance.

The spiritualist element is so strong in *Hypersentience* that the author counts it a great success if the sensor does not experience a PLV but goes instead to the spiritual "inner planes" and converses with other spirits and guides. One case Moore is especially proud of is described in detail—of a woman recently divorced, and horrified by the problems of looking after three small children.[27] She came to Mrs. Moore in a state of exhaustion and depression. When she went through the PLV procedures she did not go into a PLV proper, rather she was met by an angel guide who took her to her "spiritual home," that is, her supposed place of rest between lives. There she met her "old and dear" teacher, and after a wonderful conversation was brought to the presence of a "being of cosmic intelligence." She subsequently came away from that experience mouthing a Gnostic hymn of self-exaltation:

> I am an unending force of life and there is nothing to fear by changing forms or places. The essential core of me is immortal and growing toward this knowledge. There is only life, and it is beautiful.[28]

Note also that in her experience she offered no real worship to God, but rather a chain of beings typical of spiritualistic cosmologies. Moore calls this type of vision, of the afterlife between incarnations, "Inner-Dimensionals" and dedicates two chapters to studying these visions.[29]

Among the cases that Moore records for us there is one in which a person's afterlife is spent in a planet called "Melina." In this planet the girl is "educated" by her guides. One of her guides is a spirit called Jesu who incarnated on earth as Jesus. However, as wise and nice as is Jesu there is another guide called Pelu who is even wiser and more loving.[30] In other words, Jesus is really a second-string guide!

Another use, or rather abuse, advocated and practiced by Moore during her PLV sessions is to bring the sensor to an especially deep trance level and contact his or her "higher self." The purpose of this is to allow the higher self to give guidance to the normal conscious self on vocational, and especially spiritual, matters. The problem with this is that it violates the principle of ambiguity, and attempts to gain "cheap wisdom." In practice it invariably becomes a form of fortune-telling where the daily dependence on God is replaced by the advice from some "higher self." It is plain that what results is a *disguised form of mediumship*. In these "higher self" states the voice often changes and the values, knowledge, and language, just as in mediumship, clearly do not originate in the experiences or consciousness of the person.[31]

The Sutphens

While Marcia Moore was putting together her research on PLVs and writing *Hypersentience,* an Arizona man was working with PLVs and developing an eminently marketable technique of mass regressions. Dick Sutphen came from a solidly Presbyterian home, but certainly little of that religious tradition stuck with him into his adult years. As a young man he read casually into the occult and he and his second wife "experimented" with the Ouija board. The biographical details of Dick and his wife, Trenna, are found in Alan Weisman's *We, Immortals.*[32]

Significantly, Sutphen learned his regression technique and hypnotism from a local psychologist, and began to facilitate PLVs. As he developed a seminar and public workshop for PLV he drew many of his aides from observing Pentecostal prayer meetings and revivals.[33] This is another indicator that authentic and counterfeit spitituality are often similar in their externals.

Sutphen's weekend seminars are a potpourri of relaxation and visualization exercises, self-improvement (and self-salvation), pep talks, and metaphysical doctrines. All of these lead to several PLV experiences for every participant. With the Sutphen system one facilitator could theoretically guide thousands of persons through PLVs simultaneously, although Sutphen's seminars rarely exceed one hundred persons.

Sutphen himself went through the PLV experiences and believes that in his last incarnation he was Ed Morrell, a bank robber of the 1890s who had the talent for inducing out-of-body experiences at will.[34] Sutphen is proud of that life and believes that as a result of it he "learned" to be independent-minded, and is now an "outlaw" of the metaphysical movement by his refusal to accept "established" doctrines.

Apparently what that really means is that he studied little, and combined into his metaphysical system any idea that crossed his mind. Sutphen believes that truth is completely subjective and exists only in the mind of the person, with each person's truth being his or her own belief system.[35] Karma is, in reality, "negative programming" and can be erased by wisdom and positive thinking.[36]

In spite of his pretentions to originality, his understanding of reincarnation is little more than a vulgarized version of standard neo-Gnostic and spiritualistic doctrines. Sutphen's view of the cosmos was summarized in his response to a question posed by one of his seminar participants:

> Reality is how you look at it. I, for instance, envision a very simple universe. If there is a God, it's us. We never die, so to speak, but endlessly trade in old bodies for new ones, to learn or maybe just to have a good time. The spark of perfection we think we're trying to attain is already inside us. Once we know our true nature we can stop looking.[37]

Practically every conceivable demonic use of the PLVs is recorded in his two books. He believes in and uses spirit guides to assist in the PLVs; his own is an Indian girl "who acts like a Jewish mother."[38] With this commonly used expression Sutphen unwittingly stumbles on the essence of spiritualism, the erosion of autonomy and decision making. His wife, who has considerable mediumistic powers, often contacts spirits who "assist" her in particularly difficult PLVs. Sutphen routinely takes his sensors through "higher self" sessions in the course of the seminar in addition to the normal PLV experiences. He has been heavily influenced by the Seth books. These books which appeared in the early 1970s were channeled by the medium Jane Roberts. They have been highly influential in metaphysical and occult groups. The demonic entity communicating through Roberts claims that there is an Over-soul which supervises and coordinates the activities of many incarnated personalities. Also, the Over-soul itself can be simultaneously incarnated as several persons (multi-dimensionals). Many of his PLV sessions are based on the "Over-Soul" and "multi-dimensional" personalities and not a few of his "best" cases are transparently mediumistic in nature.[39]

One case, of the many that could be examined, needs special attention. It is the case of a young woman named Eileen who was orphaned at the time of her birth.[40] She knew so little of her origins that she was uncertain of her ethnic origin or even her country of birth. She was a pretty girl, but

suffered from a sense of rootlessness and rejection that she tried to overcome by traveling all over the world to see if she could "feel at home" in
any spot. She had failed thus far and came to a Sutphen seminar in the
hope of learning about her roots.

During a session in which Sutphen led a seminar through "remembering" lives on other planets (yet another demonic distortion and a way to
"cheap knowledge"), Eileen began to cry and sob, "I'm not of this planet."
She was calmed by Sutphen and his wife, but they both decided that she
needed special attention.

Trenna Sutphen decided she would "tune into" the next regression that
Eileen would undergo in order to help uncover the origins of her problem.
Trenna and Eileen went through a "chakra link," which is an occult technique that is supposed to unite people psychically so they experience the
same visions.[41]

Sutphen hypnotized both women and brought Eileen again to the vision
which had provoked the experience of anguish and pain. Trenna could
now describe to the groups what was happening. It seems that Eileen was
indeed not from the earth, and that immediately before her present incarnation she had been judged and banished from her home planet for some
transgression so terrible that she was blocked from remembering. In that
planet the beings were points of light, they had no need for physical manifestation, and that as punishment for her transgression she had to be sent
to a planet like earth to experience physical manifestation. The procedure
involved some sort of silver saucerlike device which was painful, and
as Trenna sympathetically relived this incident she let out a tremendous
scream that panicked the seminar participants.

Trenna quickly went to her "higher self" level and from there was able
to console Eileen and interpret what was happening.

> It is good that Eileen understands this. In so doing she can stop searching
> because she will never find any earthly ties. She is not of this earth, but she
> has much to offer us through her abilities to help people become in tune with
> themselves.[42]

Some further pious pseudoconsolation was added about her forgiving her
judges and helping others on earth. The essential thing, judging from what
we know of the process of demonic obsession, is that Eileen's sense of rejection was confirmed and embedded in the deepest layers of her mind. It
is not a surprise that she was left shaken and dizzy for two days after the
regression, and that is only the physical manifestation of something much
more destructive spiritually: total rejection. Many experienced exorcists

have noted that rejection is a prime opening for demonic possession and destruction of the personality.[43]

The factor that has made the Sutphen books and seminar so successful is not the spectacular or unusual nature of the PLVs, but rather that their work concentrates on the ever popular topics of love and sex. The Sutphens specialize in facilitating conflict resolution between lovers. Dick's view is that incompatibility, fighting, and divorce are only temporary setbacks to the irreversible progression of the soul. They are all the results of incorrectly managed karma or ignorance, and not in any sense the products of sin and selfishness.

The Sutphens attempt to reconcile couples by "understanding" the karmic links or by a "chakra healing" technique. A critical reading of the Sutphen books will show that not surprisingly these procedures do not work.[44]

In all the pages of his two books there is not a single reference to prayer, worship, or repentance as a way to spiritual growth. The center of attention is on *human love* as a sort of cosmic absolute, the only thing that matters or survives time. It goes without saying that the Sutphens are not "confined" to such ideas as that sexual love be bounded by marriage. The Sutphen books accentuate subconscious attraction (desire) as a sign that a long-standing reincarnation or "soul-mate" relationship exists. The demonic potential in all of this is endless.

The Danger of Ego-Inflation

We should not have this section without noting the dangers that PLVs have for the *facilitators*. The problem seems to be a dilemma born of non-discernment. On the one hand the facilitator wishes to validate the PLVs no matter how historically improbable, irrational, or morally repulsive they are, because of the sporadic "good fruit" of healing and self-understanding. There is also an important element of ego involvement: the more a facilitator works with PLVs the more there is a tendency to credit the phenomenon as important. The normal facilitator is not aware of the tradition of Christian discernment that would allow him or her to approach these PLVs with both *detachment* (nonego involvement) and an attitude of selective evaluation. That is, similar visions may have radically different origins, some valid, some not.

Some facilitators maintain a sense of natural discernment, attributing the more improbable PLVs to subconscious imagination (never to demonic sources), but the general tendency is to gradually validate more and more of the visions until practically everything is accepted.

To many facilitators the rejection of any vision is a threat to their ego-energized belief in reincarnation, and they are enticed to accept and integrate every vision into an ever more complex and fantastic system of "multi-dimensionals." The cosmos becomes an unruly collection of dream-like creatures creating their own dream universes. This is the final position of the Seth revelations, and Dick Sutphen adopts his own popularization of this in *Past Lives, Future Loves*.[45] Yet one cannot help but believe that even in the most gullible facilitator there must be a nagging doubt that those visions of Mu, Lemuria, Atlantis, multidimensionals, and so forth, cannot all be real.

It seems as if the hand of Satan is heavy on many of them, eating away at their natural discernment, common sense, and, ultimately, their integrity. I have seen this demonic process in a few PLV facilitators I am personally acquainted with, and the published literature of PLV hints at the same process happening to most. In his book, Weisman shows plainly how Dick Sutphen believed, at *the same time*, in his fantastic theories of multi-dimensionals, yet was aware that many of the vain PLVs experienced by his seminar participants (as high priests in Atlantis, etc.) were false.[46] A facilitator who is not both discerning and absolutely honest with himself will undergo the same type of decline in integrity that is common to mediums.

Secular Evaluation

We end this chapter by noting the perceptions of a few of the secular critics of PLV therapy. What they say is of particular interest, because although they do not use the spiritual vocabulary, one can plainly see that they do in fact point to the lack of spiritual discernment in PLV therapy as currently practiced. Kenneth L. Woodward, a researcher with no particular spiritual or religious commitment, wrote a perceptive article in *McCall's* on contemporary PLV therapy and said:

> . . . past-lives therapy emerges as another in a series of "Me Decade" fads that bolster the sagging ego. It assures the client that he is really more interesting than he feels. And like *est*, it promises the client that he can take responsibility for his life.[47]

The same sentiment is echoed in a short article in a professional parapsychological newsletter by Dr. Arthur Hastings who notes that paradoxically much of the current sloppy research on PLVs by persons untrained in parapsychology is actually *hindering* the work of true professionals such as Dr. Ian Stevenson, whose work we will discuss in Chapter 8. Dr. Hastings observes:

But the trend of current interest [in reincarnation] is more popular than scholarly. One facet of this is curiosity and perhaps ego-gratification. To learn that you were once a princess in Egypt, or a Sufi teacher, may give you a thrill, and add spice to your self-concept or confirm that your life has a particular meaning.[48]

Both authors are groping at the same insight. There is something wrong with visions that on one hand seem "nice" and give a pleasant experience to the sensor, yet produce ego-gratification and self-exaltation.[49]

It is probable that neither of our two secular critics, and certainly not the authors whom we have studied in this section, ever heard of, let alone read, Saint John of the Cross's *Ascent on Mt. Carmel.* Had they done so they might have come to understand that vain and self-exalting visions are not a product of the subconscious mind, but can also originate in a far more sinister realm.

Chapter 8

Induced PLVs: The Professionals

The PLV in England: Kelsey and Grant

For the first report of the systematic use of PLV in therapy by anyone in the professional psychiatric field we must turn to the work of a husband-and-wife team, Dr. Denys Kelsey and Joan Grant in England. It is not surprising that England was the place where this first occurred. English psychologists and psychiatrists were more open to parapsychological phenomena than their American or continental counterparts because of the long-standing interest that the English have had in the paranormal.

Denys Kelsey was trained as a medical doctor and came into psychiatry through a staffing crisis in a hospital where he was serving at the end of World War II. As his practice developed he often used the technique of age regression to help his neurotic patients. Using this technique the patient would be hypnotized and brought back to some previous trauma where the neurosis had started. For example, fear of traveling might have resulted from a loud noise during a car trip in infancy. Kelsey, like many practicing psychiatrists found that reliving the traumatic event, and then bringing it up to normal consciousness would affect a release for the neurosis. As his practice progressed, he found that some fears originated in trauma as early as the fetal stage of development. These he treated with the same type of hypnotherapy. But occasionally Kelsey ran into neuroses which originated from a time before conception. He was puzzled by this, but attributed it to some sort of genetic memory, linked in a way he did not understand to what Jung had identified as the "collective unconscious."[1]

In 1958 he met Joan Grant. She was a well-established writer whose novels were based on her amazing ability to receive detailed PLVs. Her first and most popular book was *Winged Pharaohs* which appeared in 1937.[2] This dealt with her supposed early incarnation as Sekeeta, an

Egyptian princess and co-ruler of the First Dynasty. Kelsey immediately was won over to the idea of reincarnation. Kelsey and Grant married and worked together to form a most peculiar type of psychiatric ministry. Kelsey would treat his patients with his normal procedures, but if there was a particularly stubborn neurosis he would call upon the special talents of his wife. She would go into a lucid trance and "tune into" a PLV dealing with the patient's problem. Kelsey would then hypnotize the patient and take the person to the traumatic event in the PLV where the process of reliving and conscious recollection would normally be sufficient for a total healing. This procedure pioneered and preceded by two decades anything done by other professionals.

One case from the Kelsey-Grant practice was particularly important for our study. It involved an older, professional man, a sincere Anglican, who suffered all his life from loneliness and homosexuality. For thirteen sessions he and Dr. Kelsey searched his present life for the cause of these tendencies, but none was found. At the fourteenth session the gentleman came, feeling near despair. He had recently moved and found that one of his neighbors was a young man to whom he felt deeply attracted. Kelsey proceeded with a hypnotic search of his early life, but this time asked the patient "who" was the cause of his tendency towards homosexuality. Immediately the patient flashed into a PLV sequence. He began to describe a PLV as a woman. She was a wife to a Hittite military commander; she was very beautiful and jealous of others who had influence over him. She insisted on accompanying her husband, in spite of his objections, on a prolonged and hard campaign. There both her health and beauty broke down. He in turn no longer desired her and turned his attentions to a young man. She raved with jealousy. She attempted to place a magic curse on the husband and boy, but it was she who died.

Kelsey knew that the man was totally devout and orthodox in his beliefs and said to him:

> "Imagine that you are a priest. Imagine that a woman has confessed this story to you. She understands the nature and magnitude of her transgressions, and has resolved never to act in this way again. What would you say to this woman?"
> He replied without hesitation, "I would give her Absolution."
> So I asked him to absolve the woman who was part of his total self.
> He knelt in prayer. Of the form of his prayer I know nothing; but even from my chair on the other side of the room I could feel the beneficent energy which was flowing from him. At length he rose to his feet; and I saw that the drawn, anxious expression on his face with which I had become so familiar had changed to a serene contentment. He said, "I know it is finished. I am no longer a homosexual."[3]

The patient never again had problems with homosexuality. The importance of this case should be reemphasized. Here was no mere *phobia*; here was a severe *moral-spiritual problem*. The healing did not come through merely reliving and knowing about the event, rather, through a *Christian prayer for forgiveness*.

The Kelsey-Grant work in PLVs was a pioneer effort in its techniques, and because of their attitude toward PLVs as an essentially spiritual phenomenon which involved special spiritual procedures and laws. This is due principally to Joan Grant's special talents and to her spiritual outlook in general, although she is not in any real sense a Christian.

American Contributions

Across the ocean there was the same eleven-year gap between the Bridey Murphy controversy and the first book by mental-health professionals on the therapeutic applications of PLVs. Dorothy and Robert Bradley, another husband-and-wife team, acting without an awareness of the Kelsey-Grant work, published a brief mention of their use of PLVs.[4] Their work was far inferior to that of their English colleagues, filled mostly with platitudes taken from spiritualist views of karma and reincarnation. This is especially disappointing in view of the fact that Dr. Robert Bradley had years of clinical experience with medical hypnosis, and had even published a book on hypnosis in childbirth.[5]

1978 was the year that saw a real flowering of PLV publications by mental health professionals. Three books came out, of which two were solid contributions to the field. The first was a useful compendium of case studies written by Dr. Edith Fiore, *You Have Been Here Before: A Psychologist Looks at Past Lives*.[6] Fiore based her book on two years of clinical experience of using PLVs as her *principal* therapeutic tool. Like Kelsey and Bradley before her, she had been trained in the use of regressive hypnosis for neurosis elimination. Like other psychologists she had assumed this technique was limited to early childhood or, at most, to fetal memories. On two ocassions, however, she accidentally encountered visions that were clearly not from the present life, but which seemed to have a healing result. At that point she read Dick Sutphen's first book and straightaway attended one of his seminars to learn more about PLV techniques.[7]

You Have Been Here Before has little theory, and what theory it does have is of the usual neo-Gnostic variety. The real value of Fiore's work lies in its case studies. Chapters Two to Eleven deal with individuals who have come to her with specific problems and phobias such as fear of heights, inability to make decisions, major sexual dysfunctions, and so on, which she treats by regressing her patient to a PLV. In some cases the neurotic symptoms are healed by just one PLV session, where the origin of the neurosis is relived and understood (the Kelsey-Grant procedure of decades ago). However, in several of the cases cited there was a pattern of *repetition* of some problem. One man came in burdened by an inability to come to firm decisions. The pattern of PLVs showed that on various occasions in the past wrong decisions had cost him his life. When this was understood his neurotic terror of decision making was lifted.[8]

Our criticism of Fiore's work is that she treats all neuroses as of merely emotional, psychic origins without reference to ultimate spiritual values.

This is clearly shown in the case of a woman called "Becky." She was twenty years old, unmarried, but with a boyfriend with whom she slept. Her "problem" was her total inability to relax during sexual intercourse. It was also discovered that she has been having severe headaches, which started at the age of thirteen. Becky was led through a series of PLVs, the most important of which was as a soldier's prostitute in England where she was ultimately raped and clubbed to death. Reliving this PLV healed her headache problem, but she still had sexual inhibitions. Another PLV revealed a scene where she had been imprisoned and hacked to death by one of her jailers in a grizzly rape death. In her present incarnation that jailer was her father, for whom she had always felt a repressed hatred. Becky's father came with his daughter to the next session, and Fiore and Becky shared with him the PLV from the session before. The PLV seemed to resonate with the father's inner feelings and there was a touching reconciliation between father and daughter. As it turned out, Becky was totally healed of her sexual inhibitions, and for the first time felt trust and warmth towards her father. All well and good, but the "healing" of the sexual problem was at an emotional level only. There was no reference to spiritual values or transcendence. For Fiore the only consideration was to "free" Becky from her neurotic fear of sex without asking the larger questions with regard to moral sexual behavior.

Much better than the Fiore book was one written by a team, Morris Netherton and Nancy Shiffrin, *Past Lives Therapy* (1978).[10] Netherton is a practicing New York psychologist and the book he coauthored is based on *ten years* continuous experience with PLV therapy, and stands as the best single work on PLV therapy to date. It does not deal at all with the theory behind PLVs, but strives to show how PLV therapy can be useful in overcoming certain forms of mental, and even physical, illness.

Past Lives Therapy is genuinely innovative. The authors present a four-step procedure for inducing PLVs with a word association procedure that does not incorporate any form of hypnotic or relaxation techniques whatsoever.[11] The patient comes in and is interviewed at length in reference to his current problems. The therapist listens carefully for any phrases that are repeated and that seem to have an emotional charge. The second step is to select and repeat the phrase that has the most force until a PLV is achieved. This is surprisingly easy once the patient has been briefed as to the purpose of the phrase repetition. After the initial vision, the whole PLV incident, usually a traumatic event, is carefully examined. The third stage is to have the patient repeat the initial triggering phrase while he is having the PLV vision until the emotional charge of the vision runs completely down. The object is to confront the trauma directly and reexperience the emotional agony of the event until the patient reaches a final point of detachment. Needless to say the therapy is not pleasant. But even after this reliving of the PLV trauma there is one final step. The therapist takes the patient through his prenatal and childhood years to see if there were similar trauma that reinforced the PLV, and, using the same technique, the emotional charge from these events is spent.

Of course the PLV induced by this technique is open to the interpretation that it is a mere fantasy, and that the real healing is done in reliving the early present-life traumas. The authors openly admit that PLVs may be no more than a creative dream. They are not interested in making a case for reincarnation; they are interested in healing neurotic patients and wish to share their PLV technique as a therapeutic tool. This is the type of work that should have been done immediately after the Bridey Murphy case and Zolik articles of the 1950s.

An example of Netherton's treatment worth citing is that of a person who was on the verge of developing an ulcer.[12] The person, Carl, headed a small independent engineering firm that was failing. At the initial interview Netherton learned that the patient also suffered from impotency. The phrases that struck Netherton as the key emotion-packed phrases were "losing everything" in relation to his business and in his lower stomach he felt a sensation "like a hot poker being run through me."

Working with these phrases, a series of PLVs were triggered in the patient, all dealing with sexual misconduct and financial ruin. In the first PLV Carl saw himself as an African in a small village. He lost to his rival in the competition for the girl he desired, but after her wedding he found her alone one day and raped her. As the act was consummating her husband appeared on the scene. They fought, and the husband impaled him with a spear through the lower abdomen.

The next PLV showed Carl living the comfortable life of an eighteenth-century businessman. In this vision, too, he was about to commit adultery, but this time, at the moment of consummation, his own body revolted and he experienced a mild heart attack and stomach hemorrhage. The long convalescence led to his business failure. In desperation he turned to a fortune-teller where he lost every last penny and made a complete fool of

himself. This last item is particularly interesting, for a demonically inspired PLV most probably would have encouraged fortune-telling or turned
the story around to show that he missed an opportunity for "higher consciousness" from occult sources.

Carl's last PLV was in nineteenth-century Mexico, where an extramari-
tal affair with a prostitute led to his business ruin and eventual murder by
his wife's family. With that vision the PLV therapy was successfully concluded. Carl came to the conclusion that he did not want the high pressure
of an independent businessman and went to work for a major engineering
firm. His ulcer never developed and he became a more relaxed person, but
we are not informed if his sexual life became normal.

One of the best elements of Shiffrin's and Netherton's work is their
avoidance of metaphysical and occult interpretations of what they do. But
like Fiore, their refusal to deal with ultimate spiritual values sets limits on
their work. In Carl's case, for instance, the obvious need for repentance
and forgiveness for sexual misbehavior was totally ignored. On the other
side of the ledger we note that the book does not slide into the sloppy and
demonic systems of neo-Gnostic spirituality or doctrines. The Netherton-
Shiffrin team worked out a form of "natural discernment" purely from
common sense and experience. They found it destructive for patients to
linger in the afterlife visions, and severely criticize as "spiritual addicts"
those who believe they can learn superior wisdom from that state.[13] In the
last chapter the authors even come to the conclusion that the concept of
karma is inadequate to explain the sequence of past lives of the PLVs are
indeed that.[14]

Like Wilson Van Dusen, who we have discussed in an earlier chapter
(Part I, Chapter 2, p. 19) the Netherton-Shiffrin team worked out their
discernment through attentiveness to clinical experience, and with an em-
pirical sense of what was helpful for the patient and what was not.

However, this "natural discernment" is by no means a substitute for the
authentic spiritual gift. This is shown in a series of PLVs that amazed and
puzzled Netherton. The PLVs in question took place over the course of
several years and came from people who did not know of each other, yet
they all purported to give a new view on the crucifixion of Jesus.[15]

The first PLV took place in a session with a young man, in April of
1970. In the vision the sensor is a disciple of Jesus, walking on the road
to Jerusalem, when another disciple runs to him and exclaims that they are
killing Jesus. Both run to the place of execution, where they find "about
forty" being simultaneously executed. Jesus is screaming in pain, and the
sensor is disturbed that something has gone wrong and that this is "too
soon." As he approaches the crucified Jesus he is dealt a blow on the head
by one of the guards and knocked unconscious. He awakes later, and in

character as in the Christian fundamentalist view. This is along the lines of secular parapsychology's understanding of phenomena such as the poltergeist and house hauntings.

There is nothing unbiblical about this, but it has the danger of tending to ignore the possibility of entities that operate on deeper levels of evil than those experienced in typical "ghost" situations. An example of this confusion is seen in the case of Dolores Jay, the wife of Carroll E. Jay, a United Methodist minister in the Charlotte, North Carolina, area. The case received nationwide publicity through the wire services, and Carroll Jay gave a detailed account of it in his book, *Gretchen, I Am*.[23] Dolores began experiencing PLVs in vivid dreams of a life in nineteenth-century Germany. Jay, who had practiced therapeutic hypnotism for years, hypnotized his wife and induced a PLV as a German girl called "Gretchen." Dolores's trance state was particularly deep, and Gretchen often spoke in German (this is called xenoglossy, a rare event in PLVs). At this point Ian Stevenson was called on for consultation.

The disturbing aspect of this case is that it developed into pure mediumship with clearly diabolical overtones. Soon after the initial PLV sessions, Dolores began "receiving" automatic writings from Gretchen. Soon Gretchen could overcome Dolores's consciousness at will. On one occasion Gretchen materialized and hypnotized the fully conscious Dolores and *caused her to overdose on sleeping pills*![24] Yet the firmest conclusion that Stevenson allowed himself was that the Dolores-Gretchen case was difficult to evaluate and could be either reincarnation or mediumship of a discarnate entity.[25]

Stevenson, however, has been open to the fact that a few hypno-PLVs do seem to produce the type of quality verifiable data that spontaneous PLVs routinely produce. In his opinion, the problem with hypno-PLV research is that most of the sensors do not go into sufficiently deep trance states, and at light trance levels there is either demonic contamination, or total production of PLVs from the subconscious mind of the sensor, or telepathetic "pick up" from the expectancy of the facilitator. My own case experience verifies Stevenson's suspicion of light trance PLVs, and all but the most gullible of authors on PLV induction are aware of the problem. Yet, we should note that a man who has dedicated so many years of work to spontaneous PLVs should naturally have a prejudice about the value of that type of PLV in comparison to hypno-PLVs.

The problem with Ian Stevenson's fine research is that his criteria for validation of PLV, both hypnotically induced and spontaneous, is purely secular. The Christian must have objections to a few of his assumptions. The deep trance levels he values will normally lead to unconscious states of mind which have always been rejected as essentially dangerous and spiritualist. The case of Dolores-Gretchen clearly shows this. In addition, Stevenson makes only incidental references to the emotional-spiritual effects that PLVs have on the lives of the sensors. What he does mention in this area is highly significant. In a landmark and unfortunately little noted, article on the theoretical problems of his research, "Some Questions Related to Cases of the Reincarnation Type," Dr. Stevenson wrote:

> Persons who remember a previous life are by no means always happier for having done so. The majority seem to me less happy than other persons until they forget their memories. As children they are often involved in painful conflicts with their parents when they remember a second set of parents, and perhaps a wife and children as well! And many of the memories recalled by subjects of these cases are of unpleasant events such as domestic quarrels, crimes, and violent deaths. I think it may be better to consider those who remember a previous life as suffering from a defect rather than as having a gift. Memories of a previous life may harmfully intrude into affairs of the present and interfere with adaptation to it. In this connection it is not inaccurate to compare subjects of cases of the reincarnation type with neurotic and schizophrenic persons who think constantly and too much about events of their childhood or early adulthood.[26]

It is interesting to note some of the conclusions that Stevenson has come to regarding the concept of karma. In his worldwide PLV research, he found that reincarnation and karma were associated only in the Hindu-Buddhist traditions and their Western derivatives. The concept of karma does not occur in other cultures and theological systems where there is belief in reincarnation.

In the reincarnation system of the Hellenistic period, defined for us by Plato, the soul is rewarded and punished for its actions in the afterlife, and then reincarnates in a family of its choosing according to its moral needs. In the modern world there are several peoples who currently believe in reincarnation without any attached system of karma. The Eskimos are one group; for them reincarnation has had little development into a theological system. The Druse, on the other hand, an unorthodox sect of Islam based in Lebanon and Syria, have elaborated a systematic theology of reincarnation. In their system the person's multiple lives are added up and evaluated at a future final judgment. Unlike the Hindu-Buddhist system, there is no accent on detachment from the earth nor an attempt to escape the "wheel of rebirth." The earth is a place of opportunities for moral improvement and submission to the will of God. In West Africa, reincarnation is associated with no ultimate judgment but there is a belief that wrongdoers are punished for their crimes by demons in the between-life interval.

More significant than the identification of systems of reincarnation without karma is Stevenson's own conclusion, based on years of work and hundreds of documented cases, that there is no evidence for retributive karma.[27] In his own words, Stevenson states:

> If reincarnation occurs karma may also occur, but it may also not occur, or not occur in the ways that have been popularly taught and widely accepted. I believe that words have a youth, a prime, and sometimes a burdensome senility when thay may delay the development of new ideas. Karma may be such a word that has passed its best period and I find myself feeling freer in thinking about reincarnation when I do not use it.[28]

This viewpoint is both honest and novel. Everywhere else in the literature it is assumed that PLV experiences are blessings and stepping stones to "higher consciousness." We should be on guard, however, not to jump to the opposite conclusion that visionary experiences which produce unhappiness or social maladaptation are necessarily evil. The prophets of Israel were often "unhappy" with their visions, and were often social outcasts because of their unpopular or unwanted messages. Inversely, we have shown that some PLVs which make people happy or make them "feel good about themselves" are likely to be demonically inspired.

I believe that in the not distant future many Christians will recognize the debt we all have to Ian Stevenson, in spite of the fact that he is publicly reticent about expressing any religious beliefs. He used to the utmost the tools of natural discernment: rigorous logic which prevented him from "explaining" more than the data suggests or "proving" things that are unprovable (a fallacy of most metaphysical writers), and the maintenance of scrupulously high standards of research. With these tools he was able to sift among the morass of confusing and even contradictory evidence for PLV and arrive at conclusions that are far above the neo-Gnostic claptrap common in the literature. His findings are important to us theologically, and we will draw on them in our last section. As far as any such judgment can be made, it seems as if the *Logos* used him and his scientific truthfulness to shed light into the darkness and confusion of PLV theories.

Summary

In Part II we have seen the progress of investigation into reincarnation as a doctrine to PLVs as phenomena, from varied sources. Naturally, both the quality of the work and the amount of demonic interference varies from researcher to researcher, but certain patterns do suggest themselves.

There are persons like Marcia Moore who were sucked into the deepest caverns of the spiritualist trap. Others like the Netherton-Shiffrin team and Ian Stevenson managed to proceed with their work relatively free from direct demonic interference. The difference is not in the amount or quality of psychological or psychiatric training (although Ian Stevenson was the best educated among all surveyed), but in their acceptance or rejection of the doctrines of spiritualism and neo-Gnosticism as their guiding theories for PLV research. Nothing in modern psychological or psychiatric training is helpful to a researcher in evaluating the spiritual worth or origins of any PLV. The idea that a secular psychologist is a natural PLV facilitator because he or she has counseling training is a dangerous assumption. Secular counseling techniques alone will give no guidance about the spiritual discernment of PLV, or indeed of any spiritual phenomenon.[29]

What seems to have given both Morris Netherton and Ian Stevenson protection, is not their specific training, but their scientific attitude, and especially their commitment to reason, logic, and the rejection of unproven dogmatisms. In this case the mavericks did somewhat better than the amateurs. The amateurs as a whole have had little appreciation for the logical regularity of the universe (found also in the spirit world), nor did they have much sense of the limitations of speculative thinking. Yet in spite of their many failures one can discern the motion of the Logos among these amateurs. By their sheer popularity they changed the focus of interest in reincarnation from doctrine to personal experience. In so doing they opened the door to the process of reproof and evaluation as never before. Their success in evangelizing the doctrine of higher consciousness through PLVs prodded professionals in the mental health fields to take PLVs seriously. This in turn has led to major advances in discernment and therapeutic usefulness.[30]

PART III

PLVs as Authentic Christian Experiences

We destroy arguments and every proud obstacle
to the knowledge of God, and take every
thought captive to obey Christ.

2 Corinthians 10:5

Chapter 9

Preexistence and the Elijah–John-the-Baptist Relationship

In our discussions thus far we have been able to distinguish truth from shadow truth because we could rely on developed Christian theology and maturity of experience. For instance, we were able to discern authentic Christian healing from its shadow truths in Christian Science and spiritualism. The problem of separating the truth from shadow truth of PLVs is immensely more difficult because we currently have a clear picture only of the shadow truths (occult doctrines of reincarnation and the preexistent state). There is virtually no received tradition or theological thinking to help us discern today what is happening when a person experiences a PLV. There are, however, important biblical texts which point towards an understanding of this phenomenon. It is with these scripture passages that we must begin the process of drawing truth from its shadow truth.

There are two biblical motifs that are important in our search. The first is the motif of the relationship between biblical personalities across time, specifically the theme of the reappearance of the prophets of God. The second motif is that of the existence and "call" of a person at a time before his or her birth.

In reference to the reappearing prophet, the Book of Malachi reads:

> Behold, I will send you Elijah the prophet before the great and terrible day of the Lord comes. And he will turn the hearts of fathers to their children and the hearts of children to their fathers, lest I come and smite the land with a curse (4:5. See also Daniel 12:13).

In New Testament times many Jews had formulated the idea of the "Chasid" of the Lord. This was a person who had special fellowship with God and as a consequence would not be abandoned after death in Sheol

with the rest of mankind. This was a concept of *limited reincarnation*.[1]
The scriptures that support this belief are found throughout the Old Testament, but are especially prevalent in the Psalms. (See Ps. 16:10; 30:2–3; and 49:15; 103:1–5; 116:2–7.)

In the New Testament this motif is fulfilled with the revelation that Elijah did indeed reappear in the person of John the Baptist. The exact nature of this reappearance is both scripturally ambiguous and theologically undefined. Rather than assert with dogmatic assurance what is the nature of this relationship, let us do as we did with PLVs and give the Elijah–John the Baptist relationship a *neutral*, noninterpretive abbreviation: the "EJR."

There are several scriptures that serve as pillars for understanding of the EJR. One is found in the sayings of Jesus which stress the *identity* of Elijah with John the Baptist, especially Matthew 11:13–14: "For all the prophets and the law prophesied until John; and if you are willing to accept it, he is Elijah who is to come." The same identity relationship is repeated in Matthew 17:10–13.

> And the disciples asked him, "Then why do the scribes say that first Elijah must come?" He replied, "Elijah does come, and he is to restore all things, but I tell you that Elijah has already come, and they did not know him, but did to him whatever they pleased. So the Son of man will suffer at their hands." Then the disciples understood that he was speaking to them of John the Baptist.

Mark 9:11–13 has essentially the same dialogue as above. If these were the only scriptures on the issue it would be difficult to interpret the EJR as anything other than reincarnation.

However, the matter is complicated by the other pillar for understanding the EJR that is found in Luke 1:1–17. There the angel of the Lord came to Zechariah as he was worshiping in the temple and promised him a son, who would be called John:

> And he will turn many of the sons of Israel to the Lord their God, and he will go before him in the spirit and power of Elijah, to turn the hearts of the fathers to the children, and the disobedient to the wisdom of the just. . . .

Orthodox theologians have stressed the Lucan scripture as the key to an understanding of the EJR. They have seen the relationship between the Old Testament prophet and John is of a force or energy, without continuity of person. What in fact has happened is that there has been an agreement to disregard a difficult scriptural ambiguity by reducing to secondary importance Jesus' equivalency statements.

There are serious difficulties with this approach. It is not clear why the Lucan "spirit and power" should in any way deny the equivalency statements. The Lucan scripture could mean "besides John the Baptist being Elijah, he has reappeared with his spirit and power." John A. T. Robinson, one of the best of modern biblical scholars, and one of the few to address himself to the EJR has made this point.[2]

On the other hand we cannot be sure that Jesus' understanding of the EJR included personal reincarnation. The German biblical scholar Oscar Cullmann has noted that Jewish thinking in New Testament times was structured differently from the Greek-influenced categories that we moderns assume. Whereas the Jews thought in terms of *function*, that is, what function does a person have in God's plan, the Greeks, and we their followers, attempt to analyze persons by their *nature*. The Greeks had a more clearly defined conception of the person than did the Jews.[3] It is entirely possible that Jesus' equivalency statement meant an equivalency of *function* and not of persons. Which brings us right back to the Lucan modification.

In summary, the scriptures give us an ambiguous revelation of the EJR. It can be understood as a *personal* continuity (reincarnation) or as a functional-force continuity (nonreincarnation). Incidentally, the Eastern traditions on reincarnation have a similar split. The more ancient tradition of Hinduism sees reincarnation in terms of a core person reincarnating, while the Buddhist tradition, especially Southern Buddhism, sees reincarnation in terms of the rebirth of karmic forces, not of persons.[4]

The Function of the EJR

Rather than asking the "Greek" question, "What is the essence or nature of the EJR?" let us now turn to the more biblical question of how the EJR *functions*.[5] We will do this by comparing the life of the prophet Elijah with that of John the Baptist.

It is important to note that while the EJR is a *major* biblical motif, it is an issue largely ignored by theologians. There seems to be a spirit of fear and inhibition over any serious discussion of the EJR. This is because the EJR is immediately associated with reincarnation, which in turn is associated with occult and Eastern assumptions about reincarnation.[6] When I reviewed the scripture passages about Elijah and John the Baptist for the section below, I used the standard biblical tool of conservative Christianity, *Strong's Exhaustive Concordance*. To my surprise, under "Elijah" were all the Old Testament scriptures, but not one from the New

Testament. Under "John the Baptist," the most important equivalency statement of Jesus, Matthew 11:13–14, was omitted. It seems that the editors of *Strong* consciously or subconsciously took the position that even though this relationship is in the Bible, it had best not be examined.

In regard to the biblical data, we know nothing about Elijah's childhood except who his parents were. The narrative description of Elijah in the books of Kings begins with Elijah as a mature prophet and miracle worker, already a man of God. We know nothing of his calling or subsequent development. He lived an ascetic life, with animal skins for clothing, and for a while was fed by the ravens. His service to the Lord Yahweh placed him in a direct collision course with King Ahab of Israel and his foreign wife, Jezebel.

She had brought in her alien gods and their worship had become mandatory in Israel. This Elijah denounced both verbally and in writing (2 Chr. 21:12). Elijah called the king and people of Israel to repentance and to the work of the true God, but when they did not repent he called upon God to bring a severe drought. At the end of three rainless years he received word from God to confront the prophets of Baal.

In the famous incident described in 1 Kings 18, he challenged the prophets of Baal to call down fire on their altar, and when they failed he succeeded in calling down fire on his. After this he moved the Israelites to kill the prophets of Baal. He thus reestablished the worship of Yahweh in Israel, but at the price of angering Jezebel, who threatened to kill him. Elijah, fearing for his life, fled. Later he discipled Elisha, who succeeded him as prophet of Israel. At the end of his life on earth Elijah passed on to Elisha his power (spirit) to work miracles, and was "caught up" into heaven.

The outstanding characteristic of Elijah recounted in the scriptures was his miracle-working powers. His prayers brought both drought and rain, they caused a widow's grain and oil to renew themselves as long as they were needed, summoned lightning to ignite the altar of God, and later even used lightning to slay soldiers that were coming to arrest him. At one point he split the rivers of the Jordan in imitation of what Moses had done long before.

Our sources for John the Baptist are of a different order. In the Gospel of Luke we are given details of the events surrounding his birth. He was in fact commissioned *before* his birth to live the ascetic life and to have an evangelical mission (Lk. 1). He was filled with the Holy Spirit in Elizabeth's womb, and leaped with joy as the pregnant mother of his Messiah approached. Nothing is known of his boyhood from canonical scriptures other than that, like Jesus, he had to grow in wisdom. At some point in his life he went to the desert where, like Elijah, he lived off the land and wore animal skins.

Also like Elijah, his troubles started when he was called to denounce the ruling king. And again the root of the problem was a woman, the unrighteous wife of the king. John the Baptist's mission was evangelistic, and although he had great grace in that field he apparently worked no miracles (Jn. 10:41).

The first thing we should note about the biblical description of the EJR is that it was a spiritual relationship that was anterior to any act or desire of John the Baptist. John had the relationship from before birth; he did not grow into it by his developing spirituality. This points to the fact that John was a "spiritual prodigy." He "grew" into his vocation with a single-mindedness of purpose and talent that must have amazed his contemporaries, but the impetus for his vocation anteceded his birth.

Note that both Elijah and John had ascetic life-styles and lived close to nature. Both denounced kings who had erred because of their wives, and both Elijah and John had a fundamental mission of calling Israel back to true worship of the Lord.

The biblical pattern is of repetition of circumstances and life-styles, but with an increase in responsibilities for furthering the Kingdom of God. At first glance one might assume that since John worked no miracles Elijah had a more important calling. This is not scripturally correct. In 1 Corinthians 12:27, Paul quite clearly shows that the ministry of apostle and prophet is greater than that of miracle-worker. In "worldly" terms, John the Baptist was less *spectacular* than Elijah, but in the terms of the Kingdom of God, John the Baptist had a greater office.

If the repetitive aspect of the EJR is not karmic, what then shall we call it? Let me suggest the biblical word "recapitulation." This is a word that has both theological and scientific connotations. Its theological usage is quite ancient. The Greek word is *anacephalaio* and it means "to sum up." Saint Paul uses the word twice, once in Romans 13:9 to express the meaning that the commandment to love others "recapitulates," or sums up, all the other commandments. The second passage, and theologically the more important one, is found in Ephesians 1:10, the famous passage in which all things are recapitulated in Christ.

Saint Irenaeus, the brilliant anti-Gnostic theologian of the second century, used the concept of recapitulation as the center of his theology. Saint Irenaeus, basing his theology on Saint Paul, believed that the redemption purchased by Christ was essentially an act of recapitulation. That is, Christ was represented with Adam's temptation to disobey the Father, but Christ triumphed over sin and death by his obedience where Adam had disobeyed. In the same way, Christ recapitulated all of our temptations and by his perfect obedience triumphed over our sins as well. Thus recapitulation does not mean being *stuck*, but rather being *represented* with the same situation with the opportunity to triumph over it.

In the late nineteenth century a scientific parallel to recapitulation was discovered in biology and developed into the separate discipline of comparative embryology. Scientists noted that the human embryo went through a rather peculiar development in the womb. In its earliest stages the fetus looks like and has the biological structures of a fish. Later it seems to acquire the characteristics of an amphibian, with tail and all; only in its later stages does it shed these parts and become a recognizably human form. In other words, scientists thought that every human fetus "recapitulates" the history of evolution of the species from fish to man.[7]

We are now prepared to apply the concept of recapitulation to the EJR that carries with it both biblical and biological connotations. John the Baptist recapitulated the life-style and circumstances of Elijah in order to build the necessary spiritual momentum for his mission. If we can use an image: a slinger whirls a stone around his head and after a few turns the stone has built up enough energy so that releasing the sling will cause the stone to travel far in an entirely new and purposeful direction. John the Baptist recapitulated in life-style and circumstances (whirling around) what Elijah had done, to the point where (by releasing the sling) he could fulfill his new, Apostolic mission with great force.[8]

John had neither personal vision nor knowledge of his EJR. This seems strange, but it is verified in scripture in John 1:19–22. There the Pharisees sent a spokesman to ask John his spiritual credentials. They asked him if he was Elijah, or another prophet of old, or the Messiah. He answered no to all of these questions. Yet the fact remains that Jesus said he was. Perhaps this is best understood as meaning that John had no PLV experience of Elijah, and did not have a conscious understanding of his relationship with the ancient prophet. This is very significant. For one thing, it implies that because John followed the will of God he had no need for a PLV. Whatever skills, prayer power, tendencies, and talents this EJR created were channeled to John through his spirit, to his subconscious and conscious mind. John the Baptist was so spiritually attuned to God's will for his life that knowledge of his relationship with Elijah was unnecessary. In fact such knowledge might have been a burden on his humility and ultimately to his ability to accomplish his task.[9]

The Motif of Preexistence

The idea of preexistence should not be confused with that of reincarnation in spite of the fact that both ideas are often held jointly by many persons. The idea of preexistence means only that in some manner a person has existed before his or her incarnation on earth. This concept was hotly debated by Christians of late antiquity, and the faction of the Church which was bitterly opposed to preexistence gained the upper hand. By the sixth century belief in preexistence was declared a heresy. This condemnation held its authority through the Middle Ages, and the concept was not publicly entertained again until the post-Reformation era. In the seventeenth century certain Protestant thinkers, influenced in part by Platonic philosophy, adopted a belief in the preexistence of the human soul. The English poet John Milton was one of these thinkers, but the concept soon faded from the mainstream of Christian orthodoxy.

All of this is quite astonishing in view of the clear and repeated biblical evidence for preexistence. In Jeremiah 1:5 the Lord spoke to that prophet and said:

> *Before I formed you in the womb*
> *I knew you,*
> *and before you were born I*
> *consecrated you;*
> *I appointed you a prophet to the*
> *nations.*

That God's calling to a person is not limited to a few *Chasid* or special prophets is abundantly clear from New Testament scriptures. Both Ephesians 1:4 and 2 Thessalonians 2:13 reveal that *all* Christians have been called to membership in the Body of Christ from before the foundations of the world.[10] Precisely what is the nature of the preexistent state, or how much consciousness or maturity a person has in this state is not revealed from scripture. In Chapter 11 we will examine several important personal revelations and visions about the preexistent state. For now, we should note that though scripture asserts nothing about the preexistent state, neither does it forbid speculation about it.

Our next step is to take a necessary digression to examine the newly developed, and grossly misunderstood, ministry of inner healing. We do this because most of the Christian PLVs we will examine can best be understood within a healing context.

Chapter 10

Inner-Healing

Definition

In 1976 a book was published by the sister of the president of the United States, Ruth Carter Stapleton, which quickly became an international best seller. That book, *The Gift of Inner-Healing,*[1] set off a flurry of interest and excitement over the prayer technique called inner-healing. Not a few persons were drawn to read this book ostensibly from curiosity about the Carter family. But anyone who picks up any of her books on inner-healing will find a deeply Christian message written with great simplicity and heartwarming power. Her books do not discuss the theology of inner-healing; they are basically edited transcripts of her prayer-counseling sessions.

Unfortunately, because so little was known about healing prayer by the general public or by professional counselors and theologians, much confusion and some misinformation has clouded attempts to understand her use of it. For example, some of her critics, including scholars who should have known better, believed that Mrs. Carter Stapleton was the inventor of inner-healing. They found fault with her ministry because she gave no theological explanations to justify her work.[2]

Inner-healing is a relatively new form of prayer that directs the healing love of God into injured areas of a person's memory. The inner-healing prayer uses a combination of old and new prayer techniques. At times inner-healing seems similar to the ancient rite of confession in so far as the person uses his conscious, willing mind to ask forgiveness for some act or attitude. At other times the person is healed by someone else's intercessory prayer and may be totally unaware of what has happened. In its more spectacular and well-publicized forms it most resembles spiritual psychoanalysis and modern imagery conditioning.

Let me describe an example of inner-healing from my own ministerial experience during a church-sponsored conference on healing in Atlanta.

The person assigned to us was a woman in her late twenties whom will call Mary. She told us she had difficulty relating to men and recognized that the root cause of this problem was her lifelong animosity towards her foster father. She had been given up for adoption as an infant.

There was a lifelong pattern of rejection and resentment which came to a head when she was seventeen and became pregnant out of wedlock. The father, a prominent deacon of his church, flew into a rage and accused her of forcing him to resign his position and to stop church attendance altogether. He sent her to a maternity home, and after the child was born the grandparents took custody of the child.

We began by ministering to her most recent traumatic memory, her expulsion from her home. Here the inner-healing was most similar to traditional confession. We asked if she was willing to forgive her foster father for his rejection of her. She agreed and we spoke the words of Jesus' forgiveness to her: "The Lord Jesus forgives you for your sin of resentment towards your foster father." But we went a step further and recaptitulated her memory of her rejection and banishment. She closed her eyes and imagined the scene as it was, then invited Jesus to walk in and forgive and heal them all. As she did this her tears stopped and she gave a glowing smile.

We then prayed for the Holy Spirit to give her another memory that needed healing, and she immediately remembered her sixteenth birthday. Her foster father was supposed to bring the cake and ice cream, but he did not. This embarrassed her and ruined her party. We again moved into the cycle of spoken forgiveness and recapitulating the memory in the presence of Jesus. The next scene was of herself as a five-year-old girl wanting her foster father to play with her, but finding that he never had the time. With this memory we added the prayer that the Lord fill with his love that which was lacking from her all-too-human foster father's love.

All during the inner-healing process I had my hands on her head, and my wife held her hand. We both felt a flow of healing energy go through us into Mary (a common sensation in the healing ministry). But it is important to note that Mary was in no way hypnotized, nor in fact particularly relaxed. The last memory of her inner-healing session was thus particularly significant. In some mysterious manner her mind was able to use the healing energy of the Holy Spirit to flash into a vivid memory-vision of herself as an eighteen-month-old infant. Her foster mother had just picked her up at the foundling home and brought her to the family car. At this point Mary, who had never seen a man, let alone one in a hat and overcoat, started to cry hysterically. The father was unnerved and shouted: "Take her back! Take her back! I don't want *her*!" Mary, who had never before experienced a vision, was utterly astounded at the detail of the visionary experience (she could recollect the dials on the car dashboard, etc.). We proceeded as with the other memories, bringing in the Lord's love, forgiveness, and acceptance where before there had been only hidden memory of fear and rejection. In this particular prayer Mary saw herself being carried by Jesus who reconciled her to her father. Mary left in a euphoric state, feeling reconciled to her father and anxious to go home on her next vacation to confirm in action and words the reconciliation she felt in her heart. It is significant to note the rapidity with which inner-healing prayer went to the root cause of Mary's problem. Secular techniques of psychoanalysis might have cost her thousands of dollars and taken months, even years, of counseling to come to the root vision of herself as infant. The Holy Spirit was able to accomplish her healing in less than two hours.

Historical Development

Because it is often so similar to the rite of confession, one could claim that inner-healing has its origins in biblical times when James exhorted his fellow Jewish-Christians: "Therefore confess your sins to one another, and pray for one another, that you may be healed" (Jas. 5:16). Note that James believed that *healing* would be the result of this combined confessing and praying.

The imaging elements of inner-healing prayer have antecedents within Christian mysticism. To my knowledge, the first systematic use of the imaginative powers of the mind for prayer was described by Saint Bonaventure (1221–74), a disciple and biographer of Saint Francis. In a devotional book he wrote, *Meditations on the Life of Christ*,[3] Saint Bonaventure leads the reader through the life of Christ as depicted in the gospels and suggests that the reader use his own powers of imagination to join in with the action in the gospel story. Let us quote just one example of his approach, this taken from his meditations on the nativity of Jesus.

> You too, who lingered so long, kneel and adore your Lord God, and then His mother, and reverently greet the saintly old Joseph. Kiss the beautiful little feet of the infant Jesus who lies in the manger and beg His mother to offer to let you hold Him awhile. Pick Him up and hold Him in your arms. Gaze on His face with devotion and reverently kiss Him and delight in Him. You may freely do this, because He came to sinners to deliver them, and for their salvation humbly conversed with them and even left Himself as food for them.[4]

Saint Teresa of Avila was a great enthusiast for this type of prayer. She discovered that this prayer was even more effective when done in the darkness of her cell as she lay in her cot before going to sleep. Her favorite image was to be with Jesus during his agony at the Garden of

Gethsemane.[5] Saint Teresa did not use this type of prayer for healing, but rather as a way to come closer to the Lord and to worship him. In modern terms we could say she was saturating her subconscious mind with his grace and presence. As a prayer technique this type of visualization has been passed on within Catholic devotional groups, but it was not developed as a healing prayer for specific emotional wounds.

But inner-healing as a specific form of healing prayer is really a modern American invention, and it would not be far wrong to say that Agnes Sanford (died 1982) invented it. Mrs. Sanford may be considered the grandmother of the modern Christian healing movement. Others before her, like Aimee McPherson, had established great healing ministries before World War II, but it was Agnes Sanford who wrote on the whys and hows of healing. Directly or indirectly, Mrs. Sanford was the major factor in the establishment of healing prayer among mainline denominations and independent prayer groups.[6]

Her healing career began in the 1930s after a severe personal crisis (brought about by the illness of her six-month-old firstborn son). Since there were no orthodox Christians writing about healing at that time, she had to go to unorthodox sources. She read anything and everything about healing she could find including the literature of the Christian Science movement. She was particularly impressed by the works of Emmet Fox, and especially by his *Sermon on the Mount*.[7] She also included in her readings the orthodox C. S. Lewis, the unorthodox Russian metaphysician Ouspensky, and the psychologist C. G. Jung. In her biography Mrs. Sanford points out that in all of these exploratory readings, she kept herself centered in the essential Christian faith by comparing all of her readings to the standard of the four Gospels. That for her was her anchoring principle of discernment. We might say, in the terminology we have developed, that she used the Gospels to sift the truth from the "shadow truth" of unorthodox sources.

At approximately the same time that Agnes Sanford was exploring the potential of her healing prayer ministry, Glenn Clark's ministry of healing and writing was flourishing. Clark came from a devout Christian family, and although he did not choose the formal ministry he was always active in the Church.[8] Throughout his active teaching, writing, and healing career, which extended from the 1920s to the 1950s, he published scores of books on prayer and the spiritual life. In 1930 he had the idea of establishing a Christian summer camp to train Christians to pray more effectively, which he called Camps Farthest Out (CFO). The CFO was successful from the start, and by the 1940s there were CFO camps in every section of the country and several overseas. Unfortunately the CFO never sought or received nationwide publicity. Its influence did not extend to mainline ministers and counselors until well into the 1960s. By then, ironically, much of what was innovative and unusual with the CFO had become part of the charismatic renewal.

In 1940 Clark published *How to Find Health Through Prayer*, a great pioneer work of Christian healing.[9] A large section of this book is dedicated to the relationship between negative emotional states (sin) and illness. That is what we had earlier identified in Proverbs as the act-consequence relationship (ACR) of illness.[10] He recognized that although there is a relationship between disease and negative thoughts, there was considerable ambiguity in the relationship:

> If it is true that bad thoughts and bad emotions are reflected in bad health, and that hate thoughts become boomerangs upon those we love, then we certainly have the Grace of God to thank for tempering justice with mercy. Most of us would have suffered far worse than we have, had the Lord exacted the full measure of justice.[11]

It should also be pointed out that in this early book Clark mentioned as one of the successful techniques of prayer the use of positive visualization, that is, seeing the person prayed for in good health in the mind's eye.

In 1946 Glenn Clark decided to call a special CFO meeting of proven Christian healers. Twenty-two Christian healers made it that year to the shores of Lake Idi Hopi, Minnesota, to exchange notes on healing prayer. Among those who were there were Agnes Sanford, Genevieve Parkhurst, and Roland and Marcia Brown,[12] all of whom were to carry on important prayer and healing ministries in the years to come. After this meeting Agnes Sanford became a major speaker at CFO camps on the topic of healing prayer, and for the next thirty years she spread the gospel of physical and inner-healing to all those who attended CFO camps.

In 1945 Agnes wrote her first book, *The Healing Light*.[13] This slender volume should be considered among the first rank of Christian literature, along with *Pilgrim's Progress* and Saint Teresa's *Life*.

The Healing Light is an easy-to-read book in which the most profound truths of Christian healing are presented in informal and anecdotal ways. Agnes presented a four-step process for self-healing prayer. First, relax; second, recognize God's power to heal; third, invite God's healing power in; and fourth, visualize oneself as perfectly well.

This last item of the healing process (already hinted at by Glenn Clark) was the most radical part of her book. Thirty years later Ruth Carter Stapleton would call this step "faith-imagination" in order to avoid the word "visualization" which by the 1970s had acquired an occult connotation for many Christians. Agnes did not have to contend with that problem in 1945.

Like Glenn Clark, Agnes Sanford urged the reader to use positive healing visualizations, while at the same time praying with words for the same end. This, in effect, was a way of urging the person to pray with the entire mind and has a scriptural basis in Jesus' commandment to love God with all of our mind and soul (Mt. 22:37). In Sanford's view, God's healing love normally flows through us when we pray with words, but it has a double channel when we pray with words and our imagination.

The Healing Light addressed itself to the general topic of healing with only minor specifics on inner-healing, which came only in later works. Even in her first book, however, we have glimpses of techniques that would be developed for use in inner-healing. For example, Sanford suggested an important visualization technique for the forgiveness of our enemies. One pictures the enemy in one's mind with Jesus beside him or her. Then one imagines Jesus blending into this person. One then adds the specific words of forgiveness: "I forgive you in the name of Jesus Christ, and I give thanks to God because you are now forgiven. Amen."

Further on in the book Sanford adds a ten-page chapter on the topic of "The Healing of Emotions." At this point in her life she felt that this could best be accomplished through ritual confession. She strove to learn the best elements of the Catholic tradition of oral confession from a Catholic nun and priest in Philadelphia. But as time went on she came to realize that there were often deep areas of guilt, sin, and emotional hurt that formal confession was unable to relieve.

In fact, her earliest experience in inner-healing had taken place just after the war while working as a volunteer at Tifton Army Hospital. A Jewish soldier had experienced a miraculous healing; due to her prayer he had regrown a piece of his thighbone.[14] In the course of his physical healing he had become a dedicated Christian. In spite of his recovery he found himself faced with repeated bouts of depression and anger of the most irrational nature. She prayed for him and received a revelation that the root cause of the depression was his childhood experiences in Nazi-occupied Czechoslovakia. There he was taunted and abused by Gentile neighbors. Sanford then directed her prayers for the healing of those terrible memories and for the forgiveness of his sins of resentment against his tormentors. The young soldier, without knowing why or how, was immediately released from his emotional pain and never suffered again from depression.

In the years following the publication of *The Healing Light*, Sanford wrote religious novels, several of which contained vivid examples of inner-healing. However, the next work that was of major significance for the inner-healing movement was a volume called *Behold Your God* which appeared in 1958.[15] This book is essentially her theological reflections on physical and inner-healing. It is by no means a work in the tradition of academic theology. It has no footnotes nor bibliography nor does she cite the great works of theology. What she does do is explain why spiritual healing takes place, and does so perhaps better than anyone had ever done. Her section on the theology of inner-healing is particularly important.[16]

Her theology of inner-healing was worked out by prayer, meditation, by her discerning reading of New Thought materials, as well as her own experiences with the healing ministry. The vocabulary was taken from her knowledge of Jungian psychology. Sanford placed emphasis on Jesus' agony in the Garden of Gethsemane as a major element in the total redemptive act. She believed that during his hours of prayer in the garden Jesus entered into the "collective mind" of mankind with all its sins, rejections, and hurts. His travail for all human pain was what made healing and forgiveness possible for us. Jesus suffered intensely in the garden, not because of the fright of death, but because of the horror of experiencing the collective sinfulness and pain of human history. She related Jesus' experience in the garden to the prophecy in Isaiah 53:4:

> *Surely he has borne our griefs*
> *and carried our sorrows;*
> *yet we esteemed him stricken,*
> *smitten by God, and afflicted.*

Agnes Sanford believed that Jesus' intervention into the collective human mind was an eternal event, and that he entered into every sin and hurt of history: past, present, and future. Therefore any sin or hurt, past, present, or future could be forgiven and healed.

In her later years the gospel of inner-healing became the most important element of her ministry. She and her husband founded an organization called the School for Pastoral Care which held seminars in many parts of the United States, teaching the techniques of both physical and inner-healing to mainline ministers. When the charismatic renewal broke out in the 1960s she was able to relate inner-healing to the gifts of the Holy Spirit with little difficulty.[17] She had experienced the baptism of the Holy Spirit years before and was long aware of the special healing and spiritual powers of that experience.

We should note that Sanford always felt that she was not professionally qualified to utilize psychological and counseling techniques to probe into the seeker's past. In her ministry it was always a matter of allowing the Holy Spirit to bring up memories during the prayer process. Those who followed her pioneer efforts in inner-healing were less reluctant to combine secular technique with the power of the Holy Spirit. Indeed many of her disciples possessed the type of professional credentials that she never had.

Sanford specifically discipled a group of healers into the techniques of inner-healing through her continued association with CFO. Among these followers were Ann White, Genevieve Parkhurst, and the Reverend Tommy Tyson, a Methodist evangelist from North Carolina. It was Tyson who prayed over Ruth Carter Stapleton for her inner-healing and sent her on her way to pray for others.[18]

The 1970s saw a second generation of inner-healing ministers publishing their own modifications and developments of the inner-healing ministry. Among Pentecostal Protestants there has developed an inner-healing ministry based on the robust confidence in the reality of healing that is their inherited legacy. It is not uncommon to see a pastor pray for the inner-healing of his whole congregation at one time in a ritual that recalls the Catholic practice of emergency mass confession. The Pentecostal disciples of Agnes Sanford have striven to establish a precise biblical warrant for inner-healing and have stressed the use of scriptural quotation during the inner-healing process as a basic prayer technique.

Among the finest of this Pentecostal wing of healing ministers is Betty Tapscott, who received an M.S. in psychology and wrote a small volume called *Inner-Healing Through the Healing of Memories*.[19] This book is particularly good in its appreciation of the fact that inner-healing is often needed to repair the emotions and spiritual damage suffered by the fetus in fetal trauma or rejection.[20] Tapscott points out that consciousness in the womb is biblically validated: John the Baptist leaped with joy within his mother's womb at the arrival of Mary (Lk. 1:41).

The biblical basis of inner healing is extensively elaborated in Pastor Morris Sheats's *You Can Be Emotionally Healed*[21] For Sheats, inner-healing is a three-step process in which one first finds a Christian to pray with, then one prays "conversationally" to God (where the work of inner-healing is done), and then one fills his or her mind with appropriate scriptures. In fact the main purpose of his book seems to be a ferreting out of scriptures for various inner-healing needs. He points out that Psalm 32 is particularly significant for inner-healing.

The other branch of the Agnes Sanford disciples was led by Roman Catholics. In spite of the traditional theological stand that only priests can administer confession, a great lay ministry of inner-healing has developed among Catholic charismatic prayer groups. 1972 saw the publication of the first specifically Catholic work on inner-healing, Father Michael Scanlan's *The Power in Penance*.[22] This pamphlet was the outgrowth of a series of lectures given to seminary students. Its main focus was the integration of inner-healing techniques within sacramental confession. However, it did look favorably on the lay ministry of inner-healing, and Scanlan takes the bold position for Roman Catholics that forgiveness of sins is not a power restricted to ordained persons.[23]

A real explosion of books on inner-healing occurred after 1974. The most influential of these was *Healing* by Francis MacNutt. In a single chapter of thirteen pages MacNutt summarized the basics of inner-healing, and more importantly made it an acceptable technique for all but the most conservative of Catholics. As with Michael Scanlan, MacNutt openly acknowledged his debt to Agnes Sanford as his mentor in inner-healing.[24] That same year, two Jesuit brothers, Dennis and Matthew Linn, published their first book, *Healing of Memories*.[25] Again inner-healing was related to sacramental confession. They also suggested self-guided inner-healing exercises for weekly and daily use. Here we see the Catholic tradition of "spiritual exercises" and examination of conscience adapted to inner-healing.

Catholic authors have taken over the visualization techniques of inner-healing with great gusto. The best of the inner-healing visualizations to appear thus far are found in Michael Scanlan's second book, *Inner Healing*, which was also published in 1974.[26]

One visualization prayer used by Scanlan is a very powerful form of prayer, and worth citing. I use a modification of it in my own ministry of inner-healing to assure that the counselee is freed of serious demonic activity:

> Frequently, the people are first told to visualize the Lord coming to them, touching them and embracing them. This visualization prayer can be healing, for to so visualize is to accept forgiveness and be open to healing. Then the individuals are told to visualize the person with whom they are having the most difficult relationship. Once again, they visualize the Lord coming toward the person, reaching out, touching and embracing. As they visualize this, they know from within the Lord's forgiveness for the other. They recall the Lord's forgiveness for themselves and they open to forgiving the other and accepting forgiveness from him. Then they picture the Lord with arms around each of them slowly bringing them together . . .
>
> This visualization process may seem to some to be too fictional and emotional. Actually, it is a true representation of the action of the Spirit and grace in our lives.[27]

This brings us back to the well-known ministry of Ruth Carter Stapleton, who in a sense stands midpoint between the Catholic and Pentecostal traditions of inner-healing. She was raised a Southern Baptist but can by no means be described as a fundamentalist. More than all the other writers combined, she has brought the inner-healling ministry to public attention.

Her first book, *The Gift of Inner Healing*, contains an important innovation that had not appeared before in the literature: the use of inner-healing as an *evangelistic* ministry. Mrs. Stapleton does not spell it out as such, but matter-of-factly presents the case of a certain Mrs. Joiner.[28] This woman came to Stapleton at the verge of a total mental breakdown. She had been unhappy all her adult life and had tried to disguise that by a hectic social schedule. She was an agnostic, had no prayer life, and had been offended by the tactless evangelistic advances of fundamentalist associates. Stapleton accepted her where she was and did not take her through any form of prehealing ritual of "confessing the Lord" as is often done in more conservative settings. Rather, she skillfully probed for the sources of Mrs. Joiner's unhappiness.

It appeared the problem stemmed from the death of her mother when Mrs. Joiner was only four years old. At that age she could not understand what had happened and took the death as rejection from her mother. Stapleton then asked Mrs. Joiner to go back in her memory to the day of her mother's death and imagine that she was again four years old; and then suggested:

> "Now, Joyce, see the door open and see Jesus walk into your house."
> The mature Mrs. Joiner who considered herself above "religion" could not have done this. Her "adult" thinking had allowed Jesus to be a significant historic figure, maybe one of the most significant. But he certainly was not a Savior; she wanted nothing to do with such medieval ideas. Mrs. Joiner was accustomed to keeping everything under control through careful intellectualizing. What she was about to do, what she had to do to find healing and wholeness, is just what Jesus said was necessary. She had to let go and become as a little child.
> Unlike Mrs. Joiner, little Joyce held no such opinions: "I see him!" There was excitement in her voice.
> "What is he doing?" I probed.
> "He's walking toward me. He has his arms out . . . ."
> Mrs. Joiner's face was bathed in a warm smile. Beyond any theological or rational argument, she had met her Savior.[29]

Mrs. Joiner accepted Jesus as her Lord through the subconscious mind, not the normal adult mind as is customary. This does not mean that one can be an "unconscious" Christian. Rather, it means that the process of entering the Kingdom and accepting Jesus as Lord, can begin on different levels of the mind than normal consciousness awareness.[30]

In spite of Stapleton's best efforts, her ministry, and inner-healing as a whole, has come under considerable attack from several quarters. This was not helped by the fact that a cover story on her by *Newsweek*, "Sister

Ruth,"[31] misrepresented her Christology as quasi-Gnostic. Her repudiation of that article did not get much coverage.[32] In fact, she has attempted to dialogue with non-Christians all over the world, and this activity could be interpreted incorrectly as compromising the essential Christian assertions.[33]

However, we must take note of one very intelligent critique of Mrs. Carter Stapleton that appeared in the April 1980 issue of *SCP Journal*, which focused on the issue of inner-healing. This journal is published by Spiritual Counterfeits Projects, a California Christian group dedicated to exposing occult groups and cults. None of the *SCP Journal*'s articles claim that inner-healing is a cult, or that Ruth Carter Stapleton is a cult leader, although they do pose a somber question as to her close association with occult and holistic circles. The article, "Inner-Healing,"[34] develops important criteria for establishing inner-healing as a biblical ministry and the points made are well worth quoting as a current example of the process I have described as "testing discernment":

> First: Inner-healing should touch the problem at its source. The individual should be freed from the hold of a particular memory and *the false meaning attributed to it* . . . .
> Second: Inner-healing should break the patterns of habitual responses and behavior that were generated in reaction to an initial trauma . . . .
> Third: Inner-healing should produce personal changes which are true to the scriptural revelation of our new self in Christ . . . . [35]

The whole issue is a document on how the living church, through testing discernment (including very human elements of initial conservatism and dogmatism) has moved to accept the "new thing" of inner-healing.

Chapter 11

Christian PLVs

In my limited search of the writings of the early Church I encountered only one recorded visionary experience that suggests an EJR. It was written down by Gregory of Nyssa, the great theologian of Eastern Orthodoxy, and it pertained to an experience his mother had while giving birth to Gregory's saintly elder sister, Macrina. The mother's vision was hauntingly similar to the past-life revelation of Zacharias in Luke 1:8–17. In the vision she saw an angel holding the yet unborn infant and firmly name it "Thecla." This was the name of a woman who had been a noted witness in the age of official persecutions years before. Christians of Gregory's era had a biblical appreciation of the power and significance of names. Thus, although the family had already decided to call the infant Macrina, they honored the angel's revelation and called the girl Thecla in the intimacy of the family circle.[1]

Still the fact remains, until recently PLVs have been recorded only rarely. There are several important reasons for this. As we saw from our study of the biblical EJR, no such vision or revelation is necessary for a person living in harmony with God's will. This is especially important in understanding why there are no recorded instances of PLVs in the medieval period. Catholic theology had assumed that valid personal revelations come only to those in the religious life who are well along in their spiritual development. This is precisely the class of person for whom the PLV experience would be least helpful.

There were other factors as well. The Church never understood the EJR motif as a significant segment of scripture that might have pastoral implications or visionary manifestations. Visions, as any other spiritual experience, must be understood within some sort of theological framework. Concurrent with this theological failure is the fact that during the Church's early history and through the Middle Ages there were several heretical groups which made the doctrine of reincarnation a central aspect of their Gnostic doctrines.[2]

Thus there would have been a natural tendency for the seer, or his or her spiritual advisor, to interpret a PLV experience in terms of the only available hypothesis, that is, the Gnostic theory of reincarnation. This would have been spiritually harmful. The other alternative would have been for the seer to reject the vision completely as demonic because it conflicted with orthodox theology. In either case nothing positive could be gained. In fact, only confusion could have resulted, and that certainly is contrary to the work of the Logos (1 Cor. 14:33).

We can see why an exception to this was the revelation of Thecla-Macrina cited just above. The household of Gregory of Nyssa belonged to the educated Christian elite of the period, which cherished the writings of the Church Father Origen. His theological system was one of the few in church history to be open to such a strange revelation (see below, p. 204f.).

It was earlier noted, in our study of Ian Stevenson's work, how rare spontaneous PLVs were even in cultural environments that were open to the idea of rebirth in any form. To this must be added that theologians are similar to scientists: for the most part they do not like to investigate anomalies. The object of most theological work, like most scientific work, is to clarify and expand accepted doctrines. In the authoritarian atmosphere of the Church after the sixth century, it is different to imagine theologian or pastor even recording any form of PLV.

Thankfully, since the emergence of the Pentecostal movement at the beginning of this century and of the widespread interdenominational charismatic movement in the late 1960s, there has been a democratization of Spirit-filled visionary experiences, including PLVs.[3] We now have a large number of Christians who are attentive to spiritual experiences and who are not discouraged from describing them.

A Pentecostal or a charismatic Christian is a person who has a special relationship or indwelling of the Holy Spirit. The initial experience of this indwelling is termed the "Baptism of the Holy Spirit" and is described clearly in the Book of Acts. This baptism is manifest in the believer through one or more of the spiritual gifts enumerated in 1 Corinthians 12:8–10. These gifts are the "word of wisdom," "word of knowledge," faith, healing, the power to do miracles, prophecy, discernment of spirits, tongues, and the interpretation of tongues. Another list of gifts of a less spectacular order are listed in Romans 12:7–8. These are service, teaching, exhortation, liberality, and mercy. Tongue-speaking is the gift that has received the greatest attention in recent decades and may simply be defined as praying in an unknown language under the influence of the Holy Spirit. Saint Paul calls this gift "praying in the Spirit."

As in traditional Catholic theology, the Pentecostal-charismatics believe that spiritual experiences such as visions, locutions, and personal revelations are legitimate, even "normal" to the Christian life. In this respect the Pentecostals broke with mainstream Protestantism, which discouraged such spiritual experiences. Unlike Catholic theology, the new Pentecostals and charismatics believe that the Holy Spirit speaks to all Spirit-filled believers, and not just to individuals of "higher" spiritual attainment.

In the years that I have spent in the charismatic movement I have come across several accounts of Spirit-filled believers who have experienced brief PLVs in association with either ministry prayers to others or as a result of the intense spiritual-emotional experience of being baptized in the Holy Spirit. One person described the experience he received as he was being prayed over by a group of fellow believers for the baptism. He felt transported to another time and place where he was in a prayer circle, holding hands and praising the Lord in German with people dressed in nineteenth-century attire. The seer interpreted the vision as a special gift from God signifying the spiritual unity among believers past and present (Heb. 12:1).

Interestingly, it is in relation to exorcism that one often finds references to PLVs and the ACR in the literature of the charismatic movement. R. Kenneth McAll, an English charismatic psychiatrist who is a strong believer in the ability of sin to flow down the blood line of ancestors (the transtemporal ACR), has ministered to many cases where the sins of the past were manifesting in the present. One case was especially dramatic. A young English woman was held in a padded cell of a mental institution, diagnosed as incurable. She had an intense compulsion to gouge the eyes out of her children. McAll, who is also an Anglican priest, inquired about the woman's ancestors and found that they included nobility who in centuries past had tortured their serfs by gouging out their eyes in the family castle. The young woman was totally and instantly healed when McAll held a communion service for the forgiveness of those terrible sins.[5]

An amazing visionary experience is recorded for us in a book on exorcism written by a fundamentalist charismatic, Pat Brooks.[6] Mrs. Brooks spent years in the Sudan as a missionary, but learned about exorcism from Don Basham, whose books and tapes on exorcism have had a preeminent influence among contemporary charismatic exorcists.

The case in question referred to a ten-year-old girl, Cindy, who had had severe emotional disturbances since birth. The exorcism was performed by Pat and her husband, Dick, with assistance from their two sons and in the presence of Cindy's parents. It started out as a conventional exorcism; after the opening prayers two demons manifested through Cindy, one of hate and one of murder, and both were promptly expelled. However, when the challenge was given to any further demon to identify itself a most unusual thing happened:

> . . . a strange faraway look came into Cindy's eyes, and she got up, walking behind her father and staring off . . . a voice began to talk out of the child, a very agitated woman's voice. "December 14, 1934," the voice said. "Where?" several of us asked in unison. "Nova Scotia," came the self-assured reply. "It's too bad. Bill fell overboard, and now nobody will be able to rescue him. He's gone all right. I can't even see him."
> The child's eyes began to lock down at a point about ten feet away, as if over the side of a boat . . .
> "No, no, that's not the truth," the voice continued. "I pushed him. I pushed him overboard, I killed him. I killed him!"

The Brookses believed a demon of "pushing" was being manifested and commanded it to leave. Cindy shook violently and continued the tale; this time the woman's voice described her suicide by drowning. The Brookses commanded the demon "drowning" to leave the little girl, and again the narrative continued. Cindy described the waters that surrounded the drowning woman. Again the command of exorcism, this time against the demon "water." Cindy continued with silent pantomime, of a grisly stabbing murder, after which the same woman's voice went on:

> "That was Mary, the other woman," the cunning female voice explained. "She deserved it; she was the real troublemaker. I'm glad it hurt so much. That fiend had no right to him; he was mine, he had no right to look at other women."

The Brookses cast out the demon of jealousy. But that was not the end of it. Cindy's foot began to curl downward and the child screamed with pain. The parents immediately explained to the Brookses that Cindy had been born with a defect in the very foot she was holding. The child's abnormality had taken three operations to correct. Pat then commanded the demon "foot" to leave Cindy and the curling phenomenon stopped, but Cindy began to say a few words in French, a language she never learned, and began to describe Paris and Canada, neither of which she had visited. Again the parents quickly interjected that Cindy's first words were in French, though no one in the family spoke that language. Significantly, Cindy did have French-Canadian ancestry.

Finally this strange exorcism came to an end; the child, healed but exhausted, went to bed. The Brookses ended their ministry to Cindy's family by warning the parents not to interpret Cindy's vision-pantomine as rein-carnation, but rather as a manifestation of how cleverly the demonic realm could fool others to believe in that dreadful heresy.

Certain things are clear from this exorcism; other things can be inferred; and yet other elements will not be understood until the Christian healing community has gathered more case studies of this nature. It is clear that in spite of the theological assumptions of the exorcism team, the PLV itself was a spiritual good. That is, the PLV story of the jealous wife who com-mitted murder and suicide in 1934 pointed to the source of the demonic entry of Cindy's emotional and physical problems. Though the fundamen-talist hypothesis of demonic counterfeit declares that all PLVs are in them-selves demonic and deceptive, the Brookses were inspired in the heat of their ministry to Cindy to accept the PLV as important and allow the story to flow.

Thus, although the Brookses had no conscious knowledge of the transtemporal ACR, they functioned as if they did. They essentially did what Kenneth McAll had done for the insane woman. McAll had prayed sacramentally for the absolution of the sins of the transtemporal ACR that afflicted the insane woman (the ancestor's sins). The result of that prayer was an exorcism of the demonic forces which held the woman in mental confusion and bondage. The Brookses reversed the procedure: they spoke the words of exorcism that cast out the demons that had attached them-selves to Cindy due to the sins of 1934.

At an inference level, let me suggest that much of the success of the heal-ing and deliverance of Cindy was due to a factor that was only hinted at in the Brookses' transcript: confession. Christians often mistakenly assume that confession is a two-step process. First the confession of sins, and sec-ond the forgiveness of sin through the spoken words of a Christian, saying the words of absolution. The key scripture of confession is James 5:16, which demands only the confession of sins to other Christians. The confes-sion process is in fact the forgiveness process. Of course that does not mean that it is not better to say words of absolution. I am simply pointing out that the biblical minimum for effective confession is the telling of sins to a Christian. Applying this to the Cindy case, we can see that the sins of the jealous wife were fully confessed in the PLV. Whether or not the Brookses understood it, they ministered the rite of confession which, when combined with their commands of exorcism, broke the ACR between the jealous wife and Cindy.

The last item I wish to note is the fact that the exorcism and healing pro-cedures that Cindy went through would not have been possible had the girl not gone into a trance state. The prayers of the exorcism team acted as catalyst on Cindy's soul or spirit to send her into the trance state. This is an example of the valid Christian use of an altered state of consciousness. Again, the Brookses, in spite of their fundamentalist theology, were inspired not to interrupt Cindy's trance, or denounce it as satanic, but simply accepted it.

Cindy's case also brings to mind the whole problem of child possession. The pattern of adult possession as we know it has always included some sort of cooperation and assent to the demonic. Yet infants and very young children have been known to be possessed by demonic forces long before their capacity to distinguish between good and evil. For conventional theology this has been one of the unsolved mysteries of the demonic realm. Long ago, the great third-century theologian Origen had proposed a solution: the preexistent spirit of these children had committed some sin before they were born.[7] With his condemnation in the sixth century, this very logical speculation was discarded and the mystery remained.

At this point it would not be fruitful to speculate; about what is the ultimate explanation or mechanism behind the transtemporal ACR (i.e., blood line connection, reincarnation, preexistence, etc.). We will discuss the viability of several explanations in Part IV. Let me anticipate, however, and say there is no conclusive evidence to affirm any one interpretation. Rather, it seems that the task for Christians in the immediate future is to be more attentive to this type of spiritual phenomenon, to minister effectively when such incidents do occur, and to openly share information about such cases.

Agnes Sanford

For further evidence on the occurrence of PLVs in an authentic spiritual setting we must again turn to the personal experiences of Agnes Sanford. Her first experience with a PLV occurred when she was a child in China, where her parents were missionaries. She had just lost an extremely close friend, who went to a distant city, and as a result Agnes suffered a period of depression and insomnia. After several nights:

> . . . strange thoughts and pictures were apt to float into my mind and start me quaking and perspiring in utter terror. One of these horror pictures was most strange, because it was not based on anything I had seen in real life. It had popped into my mind full-grown, a complete mental picture, when I was studying the history of the ancient Greeks, particularly their method of human sacrifice. It was as if I had slipped back through time and seen this particular episode. And it was more real and more completely devastating than anything I had ever seen . . . [8]

Agnes suppressed and later dismissed that PLV as a mere fantasy brought upon by her studies and depressed state. Years later, as a world-famous healer and writer, she again came to grips with this "fantasy." It happened at a Camps Farthest Our seminar. At the time John L. Sanford (no relation), a young minister who went on to become an important Christian psychologist and writer, felt called to pray for Anges Sanford's inner-healing. They prayed together for any hurt memory that might be affecting Agnes, and immediately the old childhood PLV came bubbling up. Agnes felt it was unimportant, but John felt that one should pray for this type of vision, as it might signify a spiritual ancestor in need of prayer, and proceeded to pray for the "healing" of that vision.

At first nothing happened, but two days later "amazing things happened to me. (This prayer) . . . had apparently opened the door for my spirit to leap back through time . . . somewhere very far away . . ."9 At this "far away" location, possibly another planet, Agnes had an encounter with Jesus. He sent her with an angel to the planet Earth on a sort of reconnaissance mission. It was to the very same vision of the human sacrifice in Sparta she had experienced in childhood.

> Then again the scene changed. I was once more in the far away valley [of the planet] and in deep grief, though it could not express itself in tears, for I was not in body (II Cor. 12:2). Again Jesus came down the valley and spoke to me in thought, after this manner: "Now you have seen the very worst that can happen upon the planet earth. Would you be willing to go down there, when I deem best, and be born and live on that planet for the purpose of relieving suffering? If so, I must tell you that it will be a hard life."
>
> I do not remember the words, if they were words, but the sense of my heart was that I was willing. Thus I was healed in another manner. For I was never again bitter about the hardships of life nor angry with God, as I have confessed to being, remembering that this had happened long before my birth into this world.10

These are rather strange visions—almost without precedent in Christian literature. But they seem to be inspired by the Holy Spirit and deserve our close attention. The visions do not point to reincarnation; rather they indicate something about the preexistent spirit. The spirit of Agnes Sanford was to some degree spiritually mature and submissive to the Lordship of Jesus Christ even before her birth. Where and how she got her maturity or learned to acknowledge Jesus as Lord is not revealed. In refreshing contrast to the prebirth, "in-between-life" visions cited in Book II, there are no neo-Gnostic motifs in her vision. It is Jesus as her *Lord* who asks her to come to earth. It is not a "karmic board" or any sort of spirit guide which would tend to interfere with a direct relationship with Christ as Lord of all *individuals* on earth. For this the beautiful Song of Hannah provides a scriptural reference point: "The Lord kills and brings to life; he brings down to sheol and raises up" (1 Sam. 2:6). Note also the *timing* of the vision; had it occur as a teenager it might have given her a sense of exaltation or vanity. As it was, the vision was given to her in her mature years, after she had achieved her ministry. Instead of an exaltation, the vision gave her a sense of consolation. Somehow, the remembering that her present hardships were the natural consequence of a covenant with the Lord acted as a great emotional healing. Further, the vision did not give her "cheap" knowledge or wisdom. The setting was much too nebulous for her to believe she had definite knowledge of other planets, and her belief in preexistence was formed *before* the vision.[11]

I wrote that this vision was *almost* without precedent in Christian literature. Yet there is recorded a vision which was given to Julian of Norwich, one of the great medieval English saints (died c. 1420). Significantly, the vision was given as a parable, thus not directly challenging Julian's or her contemporary's theology or cosmology. The vision was in reference to what happens to God's elect before and during their life on earth.

In the vision she saw God seated on his throne with a dedicated servant at his side. The servant was very anxious to please the Lord, and with tremendous eagerness he sets out on a mission to a distant land. The mission will give further glory to the Lord. However, the trip is dangerous and exhausting. The servant at one point falls into a mud-filled pit, and in his exhaustion and confusion forgets his mission and even his former position at the side of the throne. The great Lord sees all this and loves his servant continuously, no matter how fallen the servant finds himself.[12]

Other than the cosmological setting, which would have confused the medieval mind, this is very similar to Sanford's vision. They both agree as to the importance of ambiguity and "forgetfulness" of our specific mission on earth. Again, this should be related to the experience of Saint Paul and his understanding that the things of heaven cannot be fully revealed to us on earth.

Experiments: The "Tongues"—PLV Connection

> For one who speaks in a tongue speaks not to men
> but to God; for no one understands him, but he utters
> mysteries in the Spirit.   1 Corinthians 14:2

I would first like to turn to a description of my own experiments in *induced* PLVs of Charismatic Christians. I was interested in seeing if the "flash" PLVs described earlier could be part of a more complete PLV, and if the whole PLV could be retrieved. I was also interested in experimenting to see if one could come to a PLV by speaking in tongues rather than the normal and lengthy relaxation procedures.

My major problem in carrying out such experiments was in finding

Spirit-filled Christians willing to serve as test subjects. Pentecostal-charismatics historically have adopted the more conservative positions of Christian theology. It has been due, at least partly, to a correct discernment that much of contemporary liberal theology is seriously compromised with Gnostic Christology and other forms of truly *destructive* spiritual ideas. Pentecostal-charismatics therefore "play it safe" by adopting conservative stands on most issues. As we have shown in Part II, practically all of the literature on PLVs is written with the assumptions of neo-Gnostic beliefs in reincarnation. It would take a unique moment of discernment to either separate PLVs from reincarnation theory, or separate the neo-Gnosticism from current theories of reincarnation.[13]

It took me more than two years from the time I formulated the questions on the relationship between tongue-speaking and PLVs before I found Spirit-filled Christians willing to experiment. My first experimental break came when I met a Spirit-filled psychologist at a church social. As we talked, I told him of my work in inner-healing, and as we continued our conversation I sensed his interest and so I went on and briefed him on the PLV aspect of my work. I also described my hypothesis on the relation between the PLV phenomenon and the charismatic experience. He in turn related that he was one of those who had experienced a strange PLV at the moment of his baptism in the Spirit. In that vision he saw himself dressed in a plain robe and worshiping in front of some sort of golden wall or sanctuary. He believed it to be a symbolic vision but was open to the possibility of it being a PLV.

He agreed to be my first charismatic subject. We started with a normal set of prayers and relaxation suggestions (fully described in Chapter 13), but Dr. D, the subject, was already familiar with methods of relaxation and, like many in his profession, was subconsciously resistant to deep relaxation. As I regressed him, he could get no memories of further back than the two-or-three-year age level: a sign of poor relaxation. I tried a different tactic, however: I asked him to relive his experience of being baptized in the Spirit, which had occurred just a few years back. I suggested that he begin by recalling the room and persons involved, and to begin fifteen minutes before the event. He did this with great clarity and devotion, and he went on to relive his experiences at the moment of baptism. He reported that he was reexperiencing the vision of prayer before the golden wall. I then said that, "If the Lord wills," he go on to "six months before." He responded by going into a full PLV. What emerged was a life at some sort of pre-Christian monastic community. It was Jewish, yet celibate and monastic. In fact pre-Christian Judaism had several such sects, including the famous Essene community at Qumram. Without direction, Dr. D slipped from that PLV into another, that of a scholar-philosopher in the

Middle Ages. He was a mystic who got into trouble with the orthodox Catholic establishment, and eventually was tried and condemned as a heretic.

The experiment indicated that one can use the PLV vision experienced during an ecstatic experience of the baptism of the Holy Spirit as an entry point to a full PLV. On a personal level, the full PLV helped Dr. D to understand and to deal, in a more loving and forgiving manner, with his continuing problems with spiritual orthodoxy in *this* life. In this sense the PLV served the pastoral function of consolation. Thus, Dr. D's PLVs, even though intended as experimental, bore good spiritual fruit.

Again, I had trouble in finding another subject, and the research remained at that stage for more than a half year until I met Mrs. K at one of Atlanta's charismatic churches. Mrs. K was a lifelong Baptist who had recently experienced the Baptism of the Spirit. After several conversations with her I felt confident enough to tell her about the PLV research I had done. She was fascinated but cautious. After some private prayer and reflection Mrs. K agreed to be my next subject.

She was in good spiritual and emotional health, so I decided to avoid the inner-healing aspect of the regression. However, I felt that experiments of this nature should not be divorced from a spiritual context, so we decided to do a "praise regression." That is, we would ask the Lord to show Mrs. K positive memories so that we could praise and thank the Lord for his blessings as we moved back in time.

There were four people present at the regression. Mrs. K, her daughter, myself, and my longtime prayer partner who had a gift of prophecy. We began the session with prayers for protection from demonic deception and for discernment. I read the 91st Psalm and we all repeated the Lord's Prayer. We then asked Jesus to take Mrs. K on the first step of her journey back. She prayed momentarily in tongues, and the first vision came to her. She was sitting in her college garden, enjoying the sun and silently praying. We stopped and gave praise and thanksgiving for this memory. This procedure of praying in tongues, vision, and prayers of praise and thanksgiving, was continued throughout. We stopped at teen years, childhood, and infancy. At one year of age Mrs. K's vision was of being outside, on a blanket, with a stuffed white fuzzy dog. We praised God and gave thanks for the stuffed dog! The scene after that was four months old, in the crib, with a rubber toy.

At this point we were forced to take a break; Mrs. K had a stiff neck from her rigid sitting position. Had this been a normal relaxation regression, that would have been very disruptive and we would have had to take time to reestablish the relaxation state. No such problem occurred in this tongues regression; Mrs. K merely prayed in tongues for a few moments and we were right back to a vision of four months old. We then proceeded to the birth experience, and there stopped to do an inner-healing prayer. Mrs. K needed no help on this; she spontaneously broke out into a prayer of dedication of her life to the Lord.

I then suggested to Mrs. K that she ask the Lord to show her "something from before her birth," wording it in this way in case there was need for some inner-healing in the fetal memories.

Mrs. K prayed in tongues for a few moments and began describing a scene: "I'm walking on a cobblestone street. . . . I'm dressed in a silly sort of Pilgrim's dress . . . a brown, long dress. . . ." There followed one of the clearest PLVs I had ever facilitated. We continued the prayer-vision-narration technique throughout. If there was any question we wished to ask, or unclarity in the vision, we merely prayed for a few moments in the Spirit for the appropriate clarification.

The PLV was that of a young girl named Anna, in pre-Reformation Holland. She lived in a solid, comfortable home with an aunt and uncle. At nineteen she had a vivid vision of the Blessed Mother while at church. This was the spiritual turning point in her life, as after the vision she decided to become a nun. She did so and spent the rest of her life in a local convent in prayer and spiritual peace. This part of Mrs. K's narration struck us humorously. Here was a charismatic Baptist having a PLV of being a Catholic nun and seeing the Blessed Mother to boot!

Though Anna was obviously very close to the Lord, I did not want to leave the PLV without asking my usual "repentance" question. She flashed back to childhood with her uncle. He was a huge boorish man, in the process of beating and scolding her. We all prayed and blessed the scene with the Light of Jesus, and Mrs. K extended her forgiveness to her uncle and asked the Lord to forgive her of any resentments held against that uncle. The session ended with prayers of thanksgiving and praise and we all felt a spirit of praise and joy in the course of the PLV.[14]

The second opportunity I had to facilitate another tongue PLV was in London. In August of 1978 I went there by invitation to present a paper on my work of combining inner-healing with PLVs to the International Conference of Christian Parapsychology. At that time I believed that reincarnation was the strongest hypothesis by far for PLV, but had already formed a strong anti-Gnostic and antispiritualist attitude. A woman attending the conference liked my paper, and especially my antispiritualist witness. She was intrigued by my mention of the tongue-PLV of Mrs. K. We met, and Mrs. F volunteered to be my second tongue-speaking subject. Present in the regression were two other Christian observers, one of whom was Mark Albrecht, a representative from the Evangelical antioccult organization Spiritual Counterfeits Project.[15]

Again we used the praise-regression technique, going back in time to infancy, and then asking the Lord to show us if there was "anything else." The PLV was that of London in the 1890s. The person was a "gray lady" of that period. This was a form of Anglican nun whose main task was visitation and social welfare. It was a prayerful but eventful life. The most exciting thing that happened to her was her saving a small child from being lost in a mob scene. When we asked the repentance question she came up with the image of being in her room, with someone knocking at her door. She did not answer or open the door from fear of "getting involved" with the other person's problems. We all joined her as she prayed and asked the Lord to forgive her for this sin of omission. When Mrs. F was finished with her PLV experience, she remarked that she was very glad to know one could serve the Lord more than just one lifetime. She was in fact involved in a very active church and service life.

Chapter 12

The PLV and the Ministry
of Inner-Healing

To now we have examined how PLVs can easily be induced among Christians who have experienced the Baptism of the Holy Spirit and who possess the gift of tongues. In this chapter we will examine case studies from our PLV/inner-healing ministry that pertain to persons from a wide spectrum of faiths. Some were agnostic, some nominal believers, and others dedicated born-again Christians. But before examining these cases it is important to deal with the objections and questions many Christians might already be raising with regard to the fundamental validity of inducing PLVs under any circumstances.

Like all therapeutic disciplines, our PLV ministry proceeds under certain assumptions. Because unexamined assumptions are the most dangerous ones, I will take special care to place them, as well as all the risks inherent in this ministry, "on the table," where they can be subject to Christian reproof.

It is clear that induced visions of any kind violate the admonitions of the whole of medieval Christendom's view of discernment. Even Saint Teresa, who thought visionary experiences valuable, would have exhorted strongly against any form of induced spiritual experiences. Considering that the weight of the tradition is very negative in this matter, why do I think it proper to induce a PLV? The truth is simply that we developed a PLV/inner-healing ministry before we were aware of the theoretical problems involved in induced visions, and we had already built up a substantial number of case histories that showed good spiritual fruit. Upon reflection I have also come to understand that in this area of spirituality the medieval Church was itself unbalanced as a result of its overreaction against Montanism and Gnosticism.

The whole question of asking for wisdom and knowledge was further confused in the medieval Church by its quasi-Gnostic attitude towards humility. This virtue was so stressed that the mystics had difficulty in accepting and exercising the spiritual gifts they received. Saint Paul clearly states that extreme self-abasement was a Gnostic, not Christian, characteristic (Col. 2:18). Medieval mysticism would have been sounder had it placed less stress on humility and more on ministering the spiritual gifts to others. This extreme humility prevented the Christian mystic from asking anything from God other than the grace of union with him.

At the other extreme are the spiritualists. For them there are no legitimate bounds on the nature of communication with the spirit world, and they assume that the human race is entitled to know about everything in the cosmos merely by asking the right spirit.

I believe that biblical revelation shows a middle ground between the negative superhumility of medieval theology and the presumption and gullibility of spiritualism. In this biblical space there is a legitimate role for requested personal revelations.

In Paul's first letter to the Corinthians we find some principles to guide us in this matter. We must keep in mind that the recipients of Paul's letters were small congregations where everyone could participate in the service. When Paul discusses prophecy he is not referring to the sensational variety of prediction as in the major prophets of the Old Testament. Rather, he defines prophecy in terms of practical and pastoral functions for the growth of the Church. In 1 Corinthians 14:3 he wrote: "he who prophesies speaks to men for their upbuilding and encouragement and consolation." Prophecy also has the corrective function of bringing conviction to those who need it (v. 24). Significantly, this type of prophecy-as-personal-revelation is treated as a normative, almost common element in the spiritual life of the Corinthian Church.[1]

A request for a pastoral revelation is a request for knowledge and wisdom of those things which are subliminally known and intrinsic (interior) to the person. This is why when pastoral prophecy occurs in a prayer group it so often "hits home." The person to whom it was directed already "knew" the prophecy but needed an exterior source to bring it to conscious awareness.

I believe that the induction of a PLV is similar to requesting a pastoral prophecy. The PLV is something that is intrinsic to the person's spiritual state. When we induce a PLV we are in effect asking the pastoral question: is there a sinful ACR that needs to be broken for this person? The answer to this through the PLV often gives encouragement, or leads to conviction; that is, to pastoral prophecy.

I understand perfectly that while these arguments have strength, they do not by any means establish certainty. I could very well be wrong, and in this the further discernment of the Body of Christ is needed.

General Principles

Because the PLV ministry of inner-healing is like counseling, disciplined training in certain counseling techniques is useful, but like other forms of spiritual direction, it is ultimately dependent on grace, not methodology. I believe that PLVs should be ministered by a team, with at least one member of the team having the gift of discernment. Further, Karl Rahner's insight, that anything that comes from the spiritual world is distorted or interpreted by the mind of the receiver is a particularly important warning in working with PLVs. For one thing, it is normal to expect that even the best PLVs will have some distortion in historical detail or description, dependent on the subject's expectations. However, a distinction must be made between PLVs with these minor distortions and the blatant PLV fantasies that mix one historical era with another.

The evaluation of the PLV must be made by spiritual criteria first, and then secondarily by secular-historical measures. PLVs that are unclear in historical detail but which bear "good fruit" spiritually are preferable to PLVs that are historically precise but cause spiritual damage to the sensor.

Experience has shown that the trance of the PLV rests on a hair-trigger equilibrium of its natural (psychic-soul) state that can be influenced by either the Holy Spirit or demonic forces. This is analogous to a situation that exists in many Pentecostal-charismatic prayer groups. Often, in a group with inexperienced leadership, a member may have an authentic gift of "prophecy" (upbuilding, encouragement, and consolation) but is pushed into false, demonically influenced utterances when a prophet is asked to *foretell* events in the future. The result is "cheap knowledge" of the spiritual order that masquerades as Christian prophecy. In the same sense there is a subtle but profound difference between "travail" (having someone else's emotions and memories) and "mediumship" (allowing another entity to supersede one's will).

The focus of the PLV session should not be either the amassing of historical knowledge (another form of "cheap knowledge," i.e. the knowledge gained by avoiding the discipline of historical scholarship), or an attempt to gain "higher consciousness" (the belief that advanced spirituality can be gained by knowledge and passivity of emotions). Both attempts lead to neo-Gnostic and demonic distortions of the PLVs. Rather, the minister-facilitator's concern with the PLV should be exclusively focused upon identifying the nature of a person's transtemporal ACR, and of breaking, through the prayer of inner-healing, the negative consequences of that ACR. This of course assumes that most persons do have some sort of sin-ACR that is adding to their self-generated sin-burden.

These principles, then, require that certain procedures be avoided in all circumstances in the PLV ministry. It is imperative not to ask the sensor any question or lead him or her into any vision that will elicit either cheap wisdom or knowledge. For instance, attempts to recover the skills of ancient languages lead to mediumship rather than to accelerated learning. Along these lines, PLV which shows the sensor a life of a person much wiser than he is probably demonic, and will have no good result. Any attempt by a "wiser" PLV personality to advise the sensor is mediumship. Similarly, any attempt to take the PLV into the afterlife for the sake of spiritual wisdom or revelations will result in counterfeit knowledge. I use the moment of death as a point in which the sensor looks *back* on the life experienced in the PLV for the sake of repentance, and that technique bears very good fruit. But to use the death moment to look *forward* into the afterlife is courting the demonic.

The PLV facilitator must avoid any temptation to elicit help from spirits lesser than the Holy Spirit. Any calling upon "guides" to assist the PLV is an open invitation for demonic interference with the PLV and will possibly subject the sensor to uncontrolled "voices" later on.

On the positive side, the facilitator must do the following: assume that the trance state of the sensor is *lucid*. That is, that the sensor has full use of his will and values. Deep trance levels, even if they give "good" historical details, are to be rejected in favor of a state in which the sensor is fully lucid. But this does not exclude the possibility of deep lucid states. In fact those seem to be the best states of a useful PLV.

Procedures

After stating these general guidelines, we will now outline our procedures for facilitating PLV/inner-healing sessions. Presently, at least one assistant (often my wife) and I are the facilitators. The sensor is invited to bring in spouse or friend. As in any form of counseling, facilitating a PLV alone to a member of the opposite sex is not prudent. My wife has the spiritual gift of tongues, interpretation of tongues, and "knowledge." That is, she can often experience the same visions that the sensor experiences, and this is a great help in focusing our prayers. Her gifts are a complement to my gifts of healing and discernment.

Almost always the sensor-to-be telephones me for initial information. I give him or her a brief description of the PLV process and express my "minimum demand" on the sensor — that being that the sensor must allow Jesus to be *Lord of the PLV* and say "Jesus is Lord and came in the flesh" several times during the PLV (the tests for discerning evil spirits, 1 Cor. 12:3 and 1 John 4:2). I explain that this is not a demand that the sensor be either a born-again Christian or an orthodox believer, but my best assurance of the sensor's spiritual protection during the PLV.

This demand offends very few, since most Americans are at least nominal Christians. Some persons in occult and metaphysical backgrounds cannot meet this demand. To these persons I explain my experiences with demonically inspired PLVs and courteously refuse to facilitate them. An exception to this role is made when facilitating a PLV for a Jewish person. I believe that their protection comes from the Old Covenant, and all I ask of them is to pray to God for protection with the 91st Psalm, and the permission for me to *silently* pray Christian prayers.

When the sensor arrives for the PLV we give a detailed briefing that takes thirty to forty-five minutes. This is lengthy, but I believe necessary for the sensor to realize both the healing potential and the uncertainties involved in the PLV process. We carefully explain the prayers, relaxation, and visualization exercises. We include an explanation of the various theories for the origins of the PLV phenomenon: reincarnation, demonic, genetic, subconscious, and empathetic identification. Along with this the need for *detachment* from the vision is stressed. The sensor must have the *emotional* freedom either to reject the vision or to use it for his or her spiritual growth (Saint John of the Cross's insight). We also note the biblical and practical reasons for assuring that his trance state is always *lucid*.

Further we give a description of the inner-healing process and a nontrance exercise in visualizing Jesus in an everyday situation. This introduces the sensor to the process of inner-healing prayer. Lastly we explain the need for debriefing and follow-up. Currently we ask the sensor to make a promise to come back for at least two additional PLV-inner-healings if we feel they are necessary. We also testify to the need for *normal* spiritual growth through regular church attendance, prayer, and Christian fellowship. This is actually the weakest element of our program, for as of now we have no church or prayer group to which we can refer persons. Just imagine someone coming to a prayer group and saying, "I've just had a PLV and have repented of sins of the seventeenth century, and I need more help."

If the sensor has an inner-healing need of recent origins, as in the trauma of recent divorce, we go through a normal, nontrance inner-healing prayer for that situation.

After all of that we are ready for the PLV process. We begin with spontaneous prayers of praise and petitions for protection. We always include the Lord's Prayer and a reading of the 91st Psalm (the ancient prayer of protection and exorcism). We are aware that the prayers that begin the session are not in themselves either proof of the authenticity of the PLV nor a *guarantee* that the PLVs will not have any demonic influence.

In our setting, however, prayer has the power to thwart demonic activity in the mind. Long ago, in the desert of Egypt, Evagrius Ponticus wrote: "The singing of Psalms quiets the passions and calms the intemperance of the body. Prayer, on the other hand, prepares the spirit to put its own powers into operation."[2] This is precisely our goal: to allow the "natural" PLV relationship to come into the mind without demonic distortion.

The sensor is then asked to recline in a comfortable position and a cycle of relaxation suggestions is begun, all of which are standard in self-hypnosis manuals. During the suggestions we add a series of statements that had been presented in the briefing. These include the sentence: "You have dominion over your mind at all times, and you may accept or reject any suggestion, direction, or request we present to you." This statement is effective to the point that on several occasions when the sensor was enjoying the PLV it was difficult to get him or her into the serious work of examining the ethical, emotional, and spiritual problems of the PLV. The point of this suggestion is to assure that the trance state achieved is a *lucid* trance.

When the sensor is in a moderately deep trance we guide the seer through a visualization in which he or she invents a private "chapel." There, just as in the inner-healing visualization described in Chapter 11, the sensor worships and embraces Jesus. This establishes a "safe place" for the sensor where he or she can return if the action in the PLV shows signs of becoming spiritually or emotionally traumatic.

The sensor is given further relaxation suggestions and then the regression proper is begun. We ask the sensor to drift back in time with his mind to earlier periods of his or her life. The general interval is perhaps ten years, although if there is a specific inner-healing needed we go to the hurtful incident. We generally spend ten or fifteen minutes in the early childhood and infancy period, longer if there is an inner-healing needed in those years. After the sensor has established good recall at one year old, and, lastly, at four months old, we suggest to the person that he or she "allow the Lord to show us something from before you were born." This normally triggers a PLV. After the PLV is complete, usually about one hour, we slowly bring the person back up to normal consciousness.

After that we take time to evaluate the vision with the sensor present. Again we stress detachment and monitoring the long-range "fruits" of the vision on the spiritual life of the sensor.[3]

Here we must deal with an important question: Is this procedure nothing more than a disguised form of hypnosis? Classical hypnosis has several salient characteristics. Primarily, the will of the sensor is to one degree or another transferred to the hypnotist. This is manifest even well after the hypnotic session in the phenomenon of posthypnotic suggestion, by which the sensor shows a compulsion to accept an idea or perform an action that the hypnotist had suggested during the trance state. Many Christian commentators have discerned that this transfer of the will, even on a temporary basis and under the best controls, is essentially immoral.

Further, a special bonding occurs in the hypnotic state between sensor and hypnotist that affects the human spirit in much the same way that sexual intercourse does: an actual melding of both spirits. This is particularly dangerous between a Christian sensor and a non-Christian hypnotist.[4] Secular investigators have noted that the hypnotic state can indeed produce a strong "transference" between the parties. In any case, regardless of the vocabulary used, the problem is that the hypnotic state often produces an artificially induced affective bond between sensor and hypnotist.

None of this happens in our trance-induction technique. The person is constantly encouraged to maintain a lucid state of mind with full control over his or her will. Further, whatever affective energies are generated in the trance state are deflected away from the facilitator and towards Jesus in the worship or "chapel" exercise.

Case Studies

All of the following cases are taken from the last years of our ministry. By this time we were aware of the dangers of an uncritical approach to the PLV and had developed most of the procedures just described which minimize the possibility of demonic involvement. The names used in these case studies are fictitious.

Peggy and the Barmaid

Peggy came to us mostly out of curiosity. She was a sincere Christian but, as we found out during the course of the initial interview, she had great inner-healing needs. She married early in life, out of a sense of obligation and not love. The marriage was a disaster from the start, and after one child and ten years it ended in a bitter divorce. During the interview period she broke down into tears on several occasions, and my wife and I ministered to her with prayer. The husband was insensitive to her spiritual or sexual needs and often beat her. The marriage experience had been so traumatic that she was now unable to form serious relationships with other men.

An inner-healing for her marriage experiences was the first priority. The hurts were so deep that, to begin, we had to pray that the Lord give her the grace to be willing to forgive her husband. Only after this step was she able to proceed with the normal inner-healing prayer. The task of forgiving and healing the hurt of that marriage took several hours of prayer. In contrast, her teen years and childhood were good years, happy and uneventful.

After a break for coffee and relaxation we went on to the PLV process.

Her relaxation state was not very deep, but she did manage to receive an initial image of a church in Canada. She was suspicious of this as a PLV because she had seen this church one summer vacation as a teenager. But the image did develop into a normal PLV. She was an indentured servant and had to work as a barmaid at a tavern run by her owner. Later she married this person. The tavern was a dirty, brutal place and she was totally unhappy in her situation. Her husband was himself a crude and rough person who often beat her. It was not a happy life. Her spiritual life revolved around the church she first saw in the PLV, but it was a superficial relation with the Lord, filled with fantasies of escape rather than with forgiveness of her husband. During the PLV she identified her husband in the PLV as the same person she married this lifetime. Again we went into an inner-healing procedure, and again she had some difficulties before she could come to a sincere act of forgiveness towards the husband.

The hours of current-life inner-healing and PLV inner-healing were exhausting. Yet she left refreshed and at total peace. None of us were sure that the PLV of the barmaid was of a real, historical person, but we all knew that she had undergone an intense process of forgiveness in those hours that would change her life.

The Playboy

An earlier case was of a businessman in his forties who came to us solely for the "thrill" of a PLV. Bill presented himself as a playboy with no desire for "spiritual development." This case occurred at a time when we were still doing multiple PLVs. That is, we would brief and do an initial relaxation exercise with six to eight people at a time, but do the actual PLV on an individual basis.

During the briefing and interview period Bill claimed that he had no problem or need for inner-healing, and that he wanted to go straight for the PLV. I chose to be his facilitator and prayed silently that somehow the Lord would use the PLV to bring Bill into a relationship with himself. Just before I took Bill into his second relaxation period and into the PLV he confided with me that he had a major problem. He could not climax sexually with women. I assumed that this was a spiritual problem manifesting on the physical level. I quickly found out that Bill was an agnostic but that he had been raised as a Christian. I asked him if he would allow me to suggest to him during the PLV that he invite Jesus into the experience. He said he would as a matter of fact welcome that procedure (here is a critical point: at some level of his mind he willed to allow Jesus to be his Lord). I had one problem—I would only be able to work with Bill for an hour before I had to leave for a prior commitment. That is much less time than I would normally give to a case of this nature.

Bill went into a deep relaxation state, and we went into his childhood and infancy without any difficulty. I directed him to a PLV that would help him understand his present problem with women. Bill found himself as a captain of a small merchant ship in the 1700s. He was Scandinavian and plied a regular route between Norway and Spain. He brought fish and lumber from his home country and exchanged his cargo for grain and other foods. Nothing particularly daring or exciting happened to him in the course of his life. I asked him about his family life. Immediately, tears of joy came to him as he described his beautiful wife and children. We left that scene and went on to his port of call in Spain. There he had an image of the inn where he stayed and of "Conchita," his mistress there. Ah, she was very beautiful too. I prayed silently: "Lord Jesus, show him your way." I took him through the death experience. He had gotten into a brawl in Conchita's tavern and received a knife that was meant for someone else. I let him float out of body for a few moments and into a gray nothingness. I then asked him to review his life and see if any of his actions then were affecting his life now. He answered immediately: "Of course, my adultery!"

I asked if he would like to ask Jesus for forgiveness. He said, "yes." We went back to his last moments of life. He invited Jesus into the scene and confessed his sin. Tears ran down his cheeks. He was in the presence of the Lord.

I had to go, no time to counsel further. I took him back to normal conscious level and said goodbye. When my assistant called me later on in the evening for a debriefing, she reported that he had spent the remaining two hours of the mass session in a state of conviction and repentance (2 Cor. 7:9–10).

The Leather Goods Merchant

A more recent case, one that my wife and I facilitated, also produced a strong sense of conviction on the sensor. In this case Sam, who was in his early thirties, came to us because of his avid interest in reincarnation. But he also wanted to have prayers of inner-healing said for his adolescent years, which were full of torment. At the initial interview we found out that he had been "saved" as a child but had subsequently lost his churchgoing habits in his adult years. Now, however, he was interested in resuming his spiritual life. Although he was well into metaphysical literature, he was still essentially a Christian, and he was very willing to ask Jesus to heal his memories in this life and in any PLV that we facilitated.

The first need was to bring the Lord's healing and peace into the memories of this lifetime. We started at his eighteenth year when he had an argument with his mother and was forced to leave home. That was easily blessed and healed. Next stop was at age eight. His father had been an alcoholic and often beat his mother. He forgave his father and asked forgiveness of the Lord for his own resentment toward his father. Thankfully, the earlier years were more pleasant; his childhood from years five to birth were happy and there was no need for further inner-healing. We took a break before beginning the PLV session. He had responded prayerfully and sincerely to every inner-healing opportunity and we were all anxious to see what would happen in the PLV.

Sam deepened well, and without difficulty we got into a PLV. He was a prosperous leather goods merchant and tanner in West Virginia. The year was about 1890. He was a "pillar of society" in his small town. He was a church member and well respected by both his children and his neighbors. He had a good relationship with his wife and was especially fond of his sons. He most enjoyed teaching his sons about the business. During the PLV he had a tone of self-righteous satisfaction and respectability that was quite distinct from his more humble conscious personality. But let me add hastily that Sam was still conscious of himself, that this was not a matter of a trance personality. We went on in the PLV to old age. His death was quiet. He was an old man. Children and grandchildren surrounded his bedside. Again there was satisfaction in his voice. At this point I asked the "repentance question." Was there anything in this life that would shame him in front of the Lord?

Immediately his composure changed. His breathing became heavy and a pained and embarrassed expression overcame him. He confessed to us. He had regularly cheated his customers. Further, one day while he was alone at the shop he raped a young woman whose family was in debt to him and who was powerless to complain. All of this was shattering for him to admit. We stopped the action, and he invited Jesus into the PLV. He repented and confessed to the Lord. We then brought him up for a while longer. We again explained that the PLV could come from a variety of sources. Yet, whatever it was, it had some spiritual connection with him. I suggested to him that the fundamental problem of that life was of a superficial religious commitment. If he truly wanted to enter the Kingdom of God it would take more than weekly church attendance (or as in this life, one altar call as a boy). He agreed and left with a noticeable spirit of conviction on his mind.

The Scrupulous Prioress

The next case was a woman in her forties with no obvious spiritual, emotional, or behavioral disorders. She was a longtime Christian friend of mine who knew of my work with PLV. She volunteered to do a PLV at the local monastery in full view of some very skeptical monks. The motivation for the PLV was purely experimental. She had never done a PLV nor had any experience with self-hypnosis.

The relaxation exercise did not go well. She was nervous, I was nervous, the monks were condescending. When we got our first image it was very fleeting and inconclusive. But she remembered that the image was identical to that of a scene she had had years earlier in a vivid dream that had impressed her greatly. I then suggested that she relive the dream. She was deep enough to do that. As she did, she came up with a very clear PLV of a young woman in pre-Reformation Scotland. Her dream scene related to a brief love affair with an aristocratic gentleman. He could not marry her, however, and soon left. At this point we asked her to "go five years" beyond the period covered in her dream. She was able to do so with complete clarity. The young woman had fallen into a state of depression, largely because the affair had violated her religious scruples. She joined a convent out of a sense of penance, and, as the story developed, spent the rest of her life in a severe and guilt-ridden spiritual state, never accepting God's forgiveness for her sin. Later she became prioress of the convent and, due to her guilt, developed a harsh, religiously scrupulous regime in the convent that made life quite miserable for the other nuns. To the utter astonishment of the observing monks she gave a detailed and accurate picture of convent life and practices.

The most important part of the PLV, however, was the death experience. There, in the original PLV, she sensed nothing more than a floating sensation and the hubbub of the convent immediately following her death. At this point I suggested that she invite Jesus to relive that death with her. She accepted the suggestion very readily, confessed her love affair to him, and then, for the first time, felt a real loving forgiveness for herself. At this point she asked pardon for her more serious sins, her scrupulosity and coldness of heart, and again she felt great healing in the presence of the Lord.

As soon as she came to normal consciousness she related the PLV to her present spiritual state. She understood herself as excessively scrupulous and judgmental towards others. In the years of friendship with her since that PLV she has shown a greater closeness to the Lord and a much more accepting attitude toward those around her. In this case the spiritual insight of the PLV produced a definite spiritual change for the better.

It should be noted here that this woman is grateful for her PLV experience and what it did for her spiritual life, but she does not believe in reincarnation. She has chosen to believe the PLV to signify some spiritual connection between her and the medieval nun. She feels that her prayers of repentance released her from scrupulosity towards others and the nun from some state of purgatory for her unconfessed sin of scrupulosity towards her charges. This is the "spiritual empathetic" hypothesis we have mentioned. She arrived at this position following her attendance at a series of lectures by Dr. McAll (see p. 141) who is a strong advocate of praying for the sins of the dead. Very recently she shared with me a "parable" interpretation of the PLV. That she had tried to be "mother superior" to others in this life and that the Lord wished to correct that. I will elaborate this interpretation of PLVs in Part IV.

Evaluation

These facilitations of PLVs were carried out in an atmosphere of Christian prayer and attention to the Lordship of Jesus Christ. The principal reasons we can believe that these PLVs were not demonically produced or distorted is from the *internal data* of the PLVs themselves and from the spiritual effects that they had on the sensors. We can see that there was not *a single* neo-Gnostic or spiritualist motif in these sessions. They in no way stimulated the vanity of the sensor, nor suggested self-worship of the "higher self," nor claimed that knowledge equals salvation, nor implied that sexual or moral misconduct had no serious consequences and was merely a "learning experience." In none of these cases was the Bible "corrected" with "added details," nor was Jesus downgraded from his divinity or Lordship. Note that there is not even a motif of karma. Rather there is a pattern of ACR. A classic karmic relationship of Peggy would have shown a PLV with her as a brutal husband. Instead the PLV showed her a vision of a situation which her current life recapitulated. In fact, the theme of recapitulation ran through all of the PLVs we have described. With playboy Bill, a karmic PLV would have had him as a woman who perhaps teased, angered, or tormented men to the point of impotency. That was not the thrust of Bill's vision.

The PLVs did, however, stimulate various authentic Christian spiritual responses in the sensors. In every case there was a free and sincere worship of Jesus and acceptance of him as Judge and Savior. In all of spiritualist literature or neo-Gnostic doctrine one cannot find a single incident in which these professions of faith occur. For surely the demonic kingdom knows that worship of Jesus leads to its destruction. This is the main reason for eliminating the demonic hypothesis from consideration in these cases.

Further, all the sensors in the cases cited showed that they were under the influence of the Holy Spirit. The sensors were put through the biblical test of saying "Jesus is Lord, and He came in the flesh." However, Bill did not do this. At that time I did not use the phrase as standard procedure, but his worship of Jesus in the death scene was a spiritual equivalent to the discernment phrase. In addition, Peggy forgave her present-life husband for the first time in years. The playboy and leather goods merchant both went through deep experiences of *conviction*. That is, they saw their own sins and felt how unworthy that made them in front of the holiness of Jesus, their judge. Both *repented*. All the sensors, regardless of what PLV hypothesis they preferred, left the PLVs with a realization that there were areas in their lives that needed to be corrected and dedicated to the Lord (1 Cor. 14:24–25). All of these spiritual processes are absolutely and completely against the ability of demonic entities to create or to play a part in.

Now, it is entirely possible that one or even all of these cases were nothing more than subconscious inventions. In that case, what happened was nothing more than the "redemption" of a guided fantasy. If that is all they are, then the PLV has been shown to be a powerful tool for the Christian to use for purposes of defining areas of spiritual weakness, repentance, and even, in the case of the playboy, personal evangelization.

PART IV

Toward a Christian Understanding of the PLV Phenomenon

A revelation, in fact, should teach us something which we did not know. It cannot establish a new doctrine but it should supply something new, whether in a domain other than faith or in the sense that it causes to be understood in a vital way some Christian teaching which has been somewhat forgotten or is only vaguely known.

Laurent Volken

Chapter 13

Evaluating the
PLV Hypotheses

Conclusions

PLVs are a mixed phenomenon that originate from a multiplicity of sources. This is a most important step in developing clear ideas about the nature of PLVs. To attribute PLVs to only one source, be it the subconscious mind, demonic influences, or any other single mechanism leads to insurmountable problems in the attempt to account for all the evidence.[1]

By asserting that PLVs are a mixed phenomenon we are saying that several levels of the person participate in the formation of the PLV. At times the PLV is formed by the natural powers of the mind, but at other times PLVs are forged by virtue of the person's spiritual capacities, which include the ability to receive information and energy from external spiritual sources. This in turn means that PLVs are subject to the same rules of discernment that apply to any vision. Each PLV must be examined independently for its content, short- and (if possible) long-range fruit before the origins of a particular PLV can be determined. As in any discernment judgment, only probable conclusions can be drawn, some stronger than others, some as only tentative discernments awaiting further evidence of "fruits."

Other conclusions follow from what we have described as the Logos' use of shadow truth for its revelatory purpose. Specifically, out of all the occult and metaphysical confusion of theories about reincarnation-karma, the "inner-dimensionals," and the spiritualist's theories of the afterlife and preexistence, there can be found several truths that have been ignored or underdeveloped in traditional theology.

The first truth is that the Elijah–John the Baptist relationship, that mysterious bond that ties one individual in the present with another in the past, is not limited to the few great prophets. Whether the EJR is universal is not clear but, from the range of PLV experiences we have examined, it is fair to say that many individuals are influenced by the reality of ties that connect a living person with persons in the past, for both good and ill.

The second truth that has been outlined by the activities of the shadow truth is an enhanced understanding of the act-consequence relationship (ACR). The biblical revelations of both positive and negative "this-worldly" consequences of moral actions and life-styles must be taken with utmost seriousness. Certain fundamentalist sects already have an appreciation of the ACR which they call the "promises" of scripture. This is movement in the right direction but, on the other hand, Christians must avoid the temptation of attempting to view the ACR in overly rigid and fatalistic terms (karma). There is indeed a moral order to the universe, the laws of which are there to guide and protect us. In the past two centuries certain trends in Western theology have so stressed God's love and mercy that God's demand for righteousness has been all but forgotten. The result is that many Christians, both clergy and laity, have forgotten the centrality of the ACR in their individual, corporate, and national lives.

This does not negate God's mercy, but places it in the perspective of the moral order and of our specific need to call upon God's mercy and forgiveness. The consequences of an evil act may be eliminated by God's mercy, but such a suspension of the ACR is not automatic; it depends on either individual repentance or the authority of the Church to minister Christ's atonement.

The rediscovery of the ACR does not sit well with many contemporary philosophical assumptions, for example, the person's right to shape his or her own moral universe. The ACR implies that regardless of what the individual *thinks*, the moral law will operate and its this-worldly consequences will manifest, either within the same generation or across time and space to another generation. This is a corporate idea of responsibility alien to our thinking, but it is in harmony with older beliefs of responsibility rooted in biblical revelation.

There also seems to be an intimate connection between the EJR and the ACR. Actually one may be little more than a manifestation of the other. We have seen in case after case how PLVs reveal that the acts of a person in the past bring down consequences upon a person living in the present. Our most dramatic cases have been of the negative ACR, such as the case of Cindy and the murders of 1934. Yet good, if more subtle, evidence, such as the revelation of Thecla-Macrina, suggests that the ACR has a positive dimension as well. In association with this we can therefore conclude that some PLVs are indeed authentic personal revelations. We cannot presently interpret them with certainty, but attentiveness to PLVs should have a respected place among the various techniques of Christian pastoral care.

The third truth of biblical revelation brought out by the shadow truth of the occult is the concept of a mature prebirth spirit. In this category the biblical evidence is most clear, but again the information we can glean from personal revelations is limited.

It is hoped that further research and "reproof" by discerning Christians will bring greater clarity to all these issues, though I suspect there will always be a degree of ambiguity, ample room for differing, and yet biblically sound explanations for these motifs.

Interpretations

What will follow will be our theology, our way of interpreting the data we have examined in terms of a meaningful interrelationship of ideas. These ideas are offered in the hope that they will be "reproofed" by fellow Christians and, in the process, false ideas winnowed out and better ideas introduced.[2] It seems that the best way to proceed is to review the original hypothesis of PLVs and see which have been verified and which have been weakened or eliminated. The reader may find it strange that we will eliminate only one of the original hypotheses (and actually reintroduce it in a different form) or hope that we will favor one hypothesis over all others. In conscience we cannot do this, for the evidence is still very limited. In fact it is the characteristic of modern science to entertain more than one hypothesis for a given problem. Astronomy, for instance, gives us an example in the multiple hypotheses currently discussed over the origins of cosmic rays.[3]

PLV as Subconscious Invention

The first hypothesis we examined was that PLVs are the product of the internal processes of the mind. In support of this theory we should cite the fact that many PLVs suffer from gross historical anachronisms. Any experienced PLV facilitator will have had many cases which fall into this category. We should also cite that many PLVs are so vague in details that even if they cannot properly be called anachronistic, their vagueness should be considered evidence for subconscious invention.

Within this discussion, the recent work of Ernest R. Hilgard, whom we mentioned in reference to the Bridey Murphy case, must be noted. Through the years Hilgard has continued to labor in the field of clinical hypnosis and has done some additional work on PLVs. He is convinced that *all* PLVs are a form of disassociation that is natural to the mind. Every night, in our dreams, we create characters with values and experiences different from our known selves. This ability of the mind can become exaggerated and become the mental disease called schizophrenia.[4]

Hilgard discovered that there is a correlation between the sensor's intelligence and his or her ability to form any fantasy, including a PLV. The more intelligent sensors, especially those who frequently daydream and fantasize easily generate PLVs. Those with little developed imagination, had great difficulty in generating any sort of vision.

Another aspect of Hilgard's research has significance not only for our study of PLVs but for all Christians. He has called attention to a part of the mind he calls the "hidden observer." This part of the mind is always conscious, no matter how deep the trance, monitors the other areas of the mind and directs them with an overall set of values and judgments. The hidden observer is more mature and moral than the conscious personality. In Hilgard's view it is this hidden observer that plans the *story line* of PLVs, dreams, and other fantasies.[5]

PLV as Parable[6]

We wish to push this line of thought somewhat further. In fact, many of the PLVs that we have examined, such as the one experienced by the Anglican homosexual, or some of the cases from our inner-healing ministry, show characteristics of being *personal parables*.

In order to understand what we mean by this, we need to examine the biblical usage and meaning of parable. A parable is a *contrived story* used for exhortation. The story is related to the present moral-spiritual situation of the listener, and its purpose it to move the listener from where he is to where he or she should be. The truth of the parable lies not in that the facts or persons in the story line actually happened, but in their moral relationship to the listener.

The Old Testament gives several examples of parables and how they are used. Perhaps the most famous is the one found in 2 Samuel 11–12. There David had just committed the sins of lust for another's wife, adultery, and murder. God sends Nathan the prophet to exhort David to repentance. Nathan does so with the parable of the two shepherds, wherein a rich shepherd who has a large flock steals the only sheep of a poor shepherd. David is enraged at the injustice described in the story and condemns the supposed thief to death. Nathan then points to David and says: "You are the man!" David realizes that he has indeed been the moral equivalent of the thief, and this leads to his repentance and reconciliation with the Lord.[7]

This type of parable, as well as Jesus' parable of the Good Samaritan, (Lk. 10:25–37), goes through a definite sequence to achieve its end. A story line is chosen in which the moral situation is similar to the listener's state, but removed in detail, time, and space. This allows the listener to detach himself from his own situation and make an objective moral judgment based on universal principles. At the end of the story the teller of the parable points to the moral identity between the listener and the fictitious character of the parable. The listener is left with the freedom of accepting that judgment on himself (presumably God's) or of rationalizing and rejecting it.

In his use of the parable Jesus often added an element not found in the Old Testament, the dramatic reversal. The parable ends in a way totally unexpected by the listener, and in fact contrary to the prevalent cultural expectation. In the parable of the Good Samaritan, the audience expected the Jews to be benevolent and the Samaritan to be unconcerned. In another sense, the story of Jesus' life, death, and resurrection, as related in the Gospels, could be considered a living parable whose intent is to reveal the nature of God.

We should also note that a parable is the opposite of myth. A parable is an instrument of *change* by which the listener's sinful status quo is judged and made to feel insecure so that something new and life giving can enter in. A myth is an agent of stability. A myth rationalizes the present in terms of the past, by giving the past sacred authority. This distinction gives us an additional tool for the discernment of PLVs (and other visions as well). A PLV that acts as a myth, that is, which explains a given painful situation in terms of karma that has no possibility of redemption is decidedly not from God. An example of this is the case cited in Part II of Eileen, the girl in the Dick Sutphen seminar who had the PLV of exile from another universe. This myth-PLV rationalized and confirmed her sense of rejection. It offered only the shallow comfort of "understanding" without hope of redemption from her circumstance.

Certain PLVs we presented from our ministry of inner-healing had, on the other hand, a parabolic quality. Many of them did show an ACR, but it was not an inescapable "karma." Most importantly the ACR of sin or neurosis was that of a "parable of recapitulation." There was enough similarity for the sensor to identify with the vision, yet enough distance from it to arrive at detached moral judgments. The PLVs functioned as parables in so far as they served to bring the sensor from where they were, to where God's standards of repentance and righteousness wanted them to go. The PLVs were clear enough to indicate the essential identities of the parable, yet indefinite enough to permit the sensor the freedom to disregard the PLV as "mere invention," and thus free to accept or reject the indicated moral judgments upon himself. Note also, as in the biblical parables, the chief criterion for truth was not the story line, but the moral truths as they related to the sensor.[8]

If we accept Hilgard's position that the spirit (hidden observer) is responsible for the formation of the PLV, certain things become clear. The spirit, like the body, has a natural desire for health and capacity for self-healing. The spirit naturally seeks after God, and most probably knows to one degree or another the essential moral and spiritual laws of the universe. This is the reason why Hilgard found the hidden observer wiser and more mature than the conscious self. Thus it is entirely possible for the human spirit to form a PLV in terms that will bring about healing to the (lower) conscious self. We have evidence for this even in the PLVs generated in neo-Gnostic settings. The PLV of the nymphomaniac described in *Hypersentience* is a case in point. Her PLV as a temple prostitute could have been a parable in search of healing. That the healing did not occur was more a comment on the neo-Gnostic setting than a failure of the girl's spirit.

In this view the prayers and inner-healing visualizations of the PLV ministry do two things. First, they allow the spirit to formulate its parable without interference from outside demonic sources. Second, by bringing the image of Jesus into the spirit's parable they empower the healing potential of the parable to the fullest. This view of PLVs implies no external sources for the PLV, no theory of EJR or of a transpersonal ACR, nothing in fact but a belief in the spirit's desire for healing and God's desire to accommodate that wish.

On this basis many Christian counselors could begin using induced PLVs as one of their therapeutic tools regardless of their theology. Here it is appropriate to remind those interested in this type of ministry of the dangers involved. A quick glance at Part II will remind the reader how devastating a mismanaged PLV can be (remember especially the case of Eileen). In spite of this, PLV therapy does deserve careful attention by Christian counselors and mental health professionals.[9]

Because PLVs function as parables does not mean that this excludes other interpretations. As in so many matters of a spiritual nature, it may not be a case of "either-or" but of "this-and." The biblical Elijah–John the Baptist relationship has a parabolic character. Elijah was the great man of God who called down fire from heaven and dispatched two contingents of the king's troops, but John the Baptist was meekly arrested and beheaded by one. In spite of that there is more than merely a parabolic relationship between Elijah and John the Baptist.

As well, we must remind the reader there is much evidence to suggest that *some* PLVs have paranormal origins. We will examine the evidence for the other hypotheses in short order. Now it is important to recall that Ian Stevenson's study found that spontaneous PLVs had paranormal origins. Further, some induced PLVs seem to have information not attributable to any form of subconscious learning. Recently a series of PLVs done for the BBC under controlled circumstances, and followed up by professional historians, found that PLV data did indeed often contain valid, paranormal information.[10] We must also remember Karl Rahner's insight that valid spiritual revelations often come *through* the subconscious, and are therefore colored by it. This could mean that anachronistic PLVs could have an authentic, paranormal base to them.

All of which means that the subconscious-invention hypothesis is a strong one for a certain number of cases, but not for all. For in many cases there are elements that cannot be attributed to the inner mind.

PLV as Genetic Memory

The hypothesis that PLVs are the product of genetic memory can be dismissed as unacceptable, at least in its materialistic form. Not only do all serious researchers in the PLV field reject it, but the theory is simply incompatible with the data. Genetic information is passed on from one generation to another as a consequence of the fertilization of an egg by a sperm immediately after a sexual act. If the material understanding of the genetic memory hypothesis is correct it could be possible to have PLV data up to the point of the last sexual encounter but not beyond that. Yet some PLVs are of young children who died before puberty, other PLVs include data from very old age, including the last moments before death. In both these types of cases it would have been impossible for any genetic information to have been transferred by a fertilized egg. The Cindy vision is a case in point. Her vision included the suicide-death of the wife.

But a modified and spiritualized version of the hypothesis is altogether tenable. It is that the PLVs are a manifestation of a transtemporal ACR that comes through the biblically defined "blood line," but does not depend upon the material presence of the fertilized egg. I have not seen this modification of the genetic hypothesis in print, though it was suggested to me by Brother Anthony, the monk who witnessed the PLV of the "Scrupulous Prioress." McAll, whose ministry we examined in Part III, might agree to this interpretation of at least some PLV phenomena.

For this "blood-line" interpretation, the work of John L. Sanford supplies us with verification and further detail. Sanford has already been mentioned in reference to the preexistent spirit. His insights into the matter of how sin and the transtemporal ACR affect persons living in the present are not yet down in print and must be gleaned from his taped CFO lectures.[11]

Like McAll, John Sanford has learned, in the course of his counseling ministry, to inquire about the patient's family tree. He especially looks for patterns of premature death by accidents, murder, or suicide; or any form of occult involvement on the part of any ancestor. Sanford believes that the word "loins" is often used in the Bible to mean "genetic inheritance." For Sanford it is a mystery why, when a person becomes a born-again Christian, all the sin-ties of his ancestors' past are not cut. From experience he has learned that a sinful transtemporal ACR must be specifically identified before it can be broken by the blood of Jesus.

Sanford also has an appreciation of the positive side of the transtemporal ACR. He cites Hebrews 7:8 and Genesis 35:11 as well-known examples where scripture shows that blessings are inherited through the generations. In fact, he traces his good rapport with blacks to an ancestor of his who was the person who freed the slave Dred Scott of pre–Civil War fame.

It is important to emphasize that neither McAll nor Sanford relates his understanding of the transtemporal ACR to PLVs. Certainly neither would consider *inducing* PLVs to root out any ACR. Nonetheless, their ability to minister to the transtemporal ACR and their insights on spiritual inheritance through the bloodline must be considered as a major interpretive possibility for understanding many of the authentic PLVs we have described. The attractiveness of this theory is that it is biblically sound, and yet does not depend on a rigorous materialist mechanism for the transmission of the data of the PLV. In other words, since both sin and blessings are of a spiritual order of nature, they do not depend upon a fertilized egg for their transmission.

Presently there are serious difficulties in trying to attribute *all* valid PLVs to the "bloodline" hypothesis. Biblically there is no hint that there was a blood tie between Elijah and John the Baptist, or that their positive transtemporal ACR flowed through the bloodline. There was no apparent blood tie between Thecla and Macrina. To assert that there was a blood tie between the Anglican homosexual and the Hittite woman of 3000 years ago (p. 107f.) is to stretch the biblical revelation of three and four generations to an improbable seventy-five generations or more. Thus while the bloodline hypothesis is a good one, it cannot bear the burden of accounting for all valid PLVs.

Demonic Counterfeit Theory

In reference to the demonic counterfeit hypothesis, we can safely say that for many PLVs it is the most solidly verified hypothesis of all. Many of the PLVs induced in metaphysical or spiritualist meetings have all the characteristics of demonic phenomena. The marks of the demonic presence have little to do with the quality of the visions themselves, either in their clarity or historical authenticity. Rather the indicators of demonic origin are the spiritual fruits that they produce: vanity, self-glorification, separation from an authentic worship relation with God, spiritualistic dependence on other entities, and ethical and moral degeneracy. The evil fruits of PLVs do not flow merely from hypno-PLVs but may also be the product of spontaneous PLVs. Also, many PLVs have shown a special interest in discrediting the ministry and the person of Jesus Christ, another sure sign of demonic activity. In this respect we should remind the reader that several trained parapsychologists, including Ian Stevenson, have noted great similarities between certain PLVs and classical mediumship.

There is growing acknowledgment among even the most sophisticated thinkers that the demonic kingdom is real, that it is active, and that it is capable of interfering with what we consider most private, our minds, although this is still resisted by many who adhere to the more liberal forms of contemporary theology. We noted in Part I that the influential secular psychologist Wilson Van Dusen had quite independently arrived at a demonic hypothesis as the causal factor for certain forms of insanity. Several decades ago this would have been laughed at, but today many mental health professionals not only are *not* laughing, but are cooperating with exorcists in the treatment of mental illness.[12]

On the academic scene, in recent decades, reputable theologians and biblical scholars have been investigating the role that demonology should play in Christian theology. James Kallas made a significant contribution in *The Satanward View: A Study in Pauline Theology,*[13] which convincingly showed how a Christian theology, divested of an appreciation of the demonic world, was seriously unbalanced. According to Kallas, the full Gospel of Jesus (and of Paul) was not only of God's love, but of the delegated power of the Church to deal with radical evil by overthrowing demonic strongholds.[14] Less theologically, but with equal sophistication, John Richards has shown the importance of a deliverance and exorcism ministry at the parish level in his *But Deliver Us From Evil: An Introduction to the Demonic Dimension in Pastoral Care.*[15]

The old-line Pentecostal churches have long recognized the reality of the demonic, and during the great healing revivals of the 1940s and 1950s exorcisms were an integral part of their services. Their particular style of exorcism and belief in the pervasiveness of minor demons (as well as major ones) was surprisingly similar to that of Evagrius Ponticus (see pp. 42f.). The Pentecostal view of demons and exorcism was passed on to the charismatic revival by several persons, but especially through a best-seller by Don Basham, *Deliver Us From Evil.*[16]

The general public has been fascinated by the demonic and exorcism ever since *The Exorcist* appeared as a movie in December of 1973. Subsequent movies on the demonic have taken the road of low theology verging on the occult (believing more in the demonic than in God). Frankly I can see considerable shadow truth in such movies as the *Amityville Horror* and

Poltergeist, and I can sympathize with the confusion among the clergy about these matters in view of their inadequate training on the demonic.[17]

All of these factors are now coming into focus. It is hoped that the Church as a whole will discover that the biblical understanding of the Kingdom of Darkness, with its various principalities and powers, is indeed an accurate description of the other half of the spiritual world. Hopefully, there will be a renewed appreciation of the traditional insights into the demonic and exorcism, and a trust that men of God such as Evagrius Ponticus do indeed have much to teach us moderns. For all the faults of the Christian writers in the Middle Ages, and they had many, they did at least have an appreciation for the necessity of "spiritual hygiene" in keeping the demonic at bay from our minds.

Thus far, what we have shown is that three of the hypotheses of the origins of PLVs, those of subconscious invention, bloodline, and demonic counterfeit, do in fact account for many of the PLVs we have discussed. None of this is alien to, or disruptive of, traditional Christian theology, though the demonic hypothesis would be disturbing to many liberal Christians. As we move on to examine the other two hypotheses about PLVs — reincarnation and empathetic identification — we will be moving into unfamiliar territory, with the boundaries of conventional theology left far behind.

Chapter 14

The Afterlife

The Nature of the Afterlife

At this point in an admittedly lengthy book we must beg the reader's indulgence and once again take time for a theological digression. In Part III we expended considerable effort in describing inner-healing because this form of prayer is indispensable in the pastoral *use* of PLVs. Similarly, we will now examine several fundamental theological issues pertaining to the afterlife and the relationships between the dead and the living. These issues are indispensable for a mature evaluation of two important hypotheses for PLVs: The PLV as empathetic identification and the PLV as personal memory, that is, reincarnation, which will be evaluated in the chapters following.

The modern theology of the afterlife has been dominated until very recent times by two distinct traditions: that of the Roman Catholic Church, first codified into a doctrinal system by Saint Augustine of Hippo and modified by Saint Thomas Aquinas, and the conservative Protestant view developed both in reaction to, and out of, that Catholic tradition.

In the official Catholic view, the afterlife is divided into four locales or spiritual states. There is Heaven proper, which is where the saints and angels experience the presence of God. There is Purgatory, where those who are destined for Heaven must be purified for a season in order to become eligible for the Heaven state. There is Hell, where the damned reside in agony, awaiting the final judgment and the confirmation of their status. Between Purgatory and Hell there is Limbo or the *Limbus Infantum*, where the souls of unbaptized infants reside in relative comfort, but without the experienced presence of God. There was formerly another limbo, one in which the souls of Jewish patriarchs and other righteous souls of the Old Testament stayed until they were freed by Jesus' descent into the underworld described in 1 Peter 3 and 4 (on which we will comment later), called the *Limbus Patrum*.

The traditional Protestant view was developed out of Catholic theology, but with careful attention to avoid any element that would make credible the Catholic practices of prayers, indulgences, and masses for the dead. Thus, Heaven and Hell were retained, but the *Limbus Infantum* and Purgatory were eliminated. Interestingly, many of the Reformers continued to accept the Catholic view of *Limbus Patrum*.

Both the Catholic and Protestant theologies of the afterlife share an inadequate and a highly selective biblical base. They concentrate on Luke 16 (the story of the rich man and beggar), Mark 9:43–47, and the scriptures about the Last Judgment in the Book of Revelations. Ignored are the scriptures about the afterlife found in the Old Testament. Also, both traditions tend to confuse man's ultimate destiny as described in Revelations, with the afterdeath state until the Last Judgment, sometimes called the intermediate state.

This dogmatic bottleneck over the afterlife began to break up in the two decades preceding the turn of the century. The new thinking was apparently stimulated by, but not limited to, stirrings by scholars and divines of the Anglican Church. The Anglican Church was undergoing one of its periodic reexaminations, searching to define itself in terms of scripture, early Christianity, and the Patristic writers. It sought to avoid either the dogmatic assertions of the Roman Catholic Church or the anti-Catholic theology of the Reformation. Part of this reexamination was a fresh look at the belief in the afterlife. F. W. Farrar, Canon of Westminster Cathedral and chaplain to Queen Victoria, was one of the first, and perhaps the ablest, of what might be termed the "Victorian Revisionists." For almost a generation, a score of theologians reexamined the doctrines of the afterlife and the ultimate destiny of mankind.[1] They had the advantages of the system of elite Victorian education, as well as the fruits of modern discoveries in biblical scholarship. These included the rediscovery of many intertestamental writings that had been lost for centuries and which helped considerably to explain the changed ideas about the afterlife in the New Testament from the Old.

As in any group of scholars, not everyone came to identical conclusions, but there was uncommon agreement on some basic findings that are especially important for us. It was agreed that the King James translation of the Bible had unnecessarily muddled the theology of the afterlife by using one word, "hell," for *sheol* of the Old Testament and *hades* and *gehenna* of the New Testament. "Hell" is a good translation for gehenna, but it is a decidedly poor translation for sheol or hades which signified the afterlife in the Old Testament, but did not connote a place of punishment.

The Old Testament uses the word sheol often, but we are never given a precise definition of what it is. It is presumed to be under the earth, and most passages describe it as a place that is dark and gloomy, a joyless place, a mere shadow of life on earth. Not even God can be praised there and the person's consciousness is much reduced (Ps. 6:5, Ec. 9:5–10). In Job 3:13–19 it is lamented that all men, good and bad, come to the same fate in sheol, apparently there being no system of rewards or punishment in sheol. These scriptures indicate that sheol has much in common with the Greek conception of the afterlife, hades. In the Septuagint, the Greek translation of the Old Testament that was in common use at the time of Jesus, sheol was translated as hades.

However, a few passages in the Old Testament hint that there is more to hades than just a neutral gray area. In 1 Samuel 28:8–20 it is also reported to be a place of "rest" and the dead judge complains that his peace has been disturbed by the medium's conjuring. On the negative side, there is a strong suggestion that there is a section of sheol more ominous, called the "pit" (Is. 14:15).

The idea that sheol is divided into different sections was greatly elaborated in many of the books of the intertestamental period. Many of these books were influential in both Judaism and early Christianity, though they became canonical in neither. The book of Enoch was especially influential in establishing the afterlife as a place of rewards and punishments according to the righteousness of the person's life. As a matter of fact, the visionary experiences recorded in Enoch are very much like Swedenborg's tours of the afterlife. By the time of Jesus, the rabbinical literature of the Pharisee advocated a belief in an *accountable* and multilayered afterlife. The names gehenna, "Bosom of Abraham," and Paradise, all of which were utilized by Jesus to teach about the afterlife, came from this rabbinical literature.[2]

Just as the Old Testament is tantalizingly ambiguous about the nature of the afterlife, the Victorian scholars came to see that the New Testament was equally ambiguous about man's ultimate destiny. Canon Farrar had perhaps the strongest sense of scriptural ambiguity in this area,[3] and he identified four separate motifs about the afterlife and man's final destiny in the New Testament. One motif was the final reconciliation of all men to God (identified as "universalism" by theologians), and a current that is particularly strong in the later writings of Paul.[4] A second motif is that the wicked have no hope and will be doomed.[5] Yet another group of scriptures indicates that the wicked will not suffer forever, but will be annihilated.[6] Finally there are a few scriptures which indicate that there is a temporary punishment and cleansing fire (elaborated as Purgatory in Roman Catholic doctrine).[7]

Normative (dogmatic) Christianity, both Catholic and Protestant, has of course stressed the second motif—that the wicked are forever doomed—has given less weight to or ignored the other motifs. This came about historically through the influence of Saint Augustine, who stressed that position.

Canon Farrar goes to great lengths to point out that early Christianity, and especially the Fathers, were as a whole more optimistic than moderns and held out the "greater hope." That is, the vast majority of mankind would eventually come to God, and that the punishment of the wicked would be limited in duration. Origen chose to center his theology on the Pauline scriptures of the restitution of all to God. He was roundly condemned as a heretic, while Gregory of Nyssa, who was more circumspect in describing his beliefs but who essentially believed the same thing, is celebrated as one of the Fathers of Orthodoxy. As a group, the Victorian scholars were sympathetic with the "greater hope," though they shied away from believing the Universalist position that *all* would be saved. They also came to see that the Catholic doctrine of purgatory, though exaggerated and corrupt (a product of trying to derive an unambiguous and complete doctrine from ambiguous scriptures) had a biblical base. They all agreed that the afterlife was not as simple as the common doctrine of Heaven and Hell, and that a characteristic of the afterlife was the opportunity it offered for further growth.

Again Canon Farrar was a pioneer in suggesting that a partial solution to the apparently contradictory nature of the afterlife scriptures in the New Testament was to realize that there is a difference between man's intermediate (afterdeath) state and his final destiny which will be determined at the Last Judgment.[8] New Testament writers were so sure that Jesus' second coming was imminent within their lifetime, that they often did not discern the difference between what was revealed as pertaining to the afterlife in the intermediate state, and the afterlife after the Last Judgment.

After more than half a century, the scholarship of the Victorian Revisionists still stands as a major achievement of Christian theology. Since the 1920s liberal Protestantism increased in influence, and interest waned in the purely spiritual (including afterlife) aspects of theology in favor of the more "practical" and social-action problems of religious life. The "demythologizing" movement in Liberal Protestantism reached a point where many of its theologians denied the concept of personal survival after death.[9]

By comparison to much of the new writing on the afterlife, the Victorian Revisionists strike one as especially solid and scriptural. Current literature such as John A. T. Robinson's *In the End God*,[10] and John H. Hick's *Death and Eternal Life*[11] tends to be heavy on philosophy and light on scripture. However the trend towards "process theology" has rediscovered much of what the Victorian scholars said about growth in the discarnate state, and many process theologians are rediscovering the same biblical and Patristic positions asserted by the Victorian scholars.[12]

A modern theology of the afterlife should begin where the Victorian Revisionists left off. It is plain that there is no scriptural evidence for believing that the sheol-hades levels described in the Old Testament were destroyed. 1 Peter 3 and 4 state that Jesus preached in hades after his death, and Ephesians 4:8 suggests that many in sheol-hades responded to his preaching and followed him to heaven. But there is no indication that sheol-hades was itself destroyed. Indeed there is scriptural evidence to the contrary. In Revelations 20:14, we are given an image of the events *after* the Last Judgment, and hades, personified as a person, is cast into the "Lake of Fire," either ending hades by destruction or converting it into the "hell" we are familiar with. There is no hint that when Jesus preached in sheol-hades his audience suffered the torments of the rich man described in Luke 16. It is more logical to assume he preached to those in the gloom and silence that Job foresaw or the restful level hinted at by Samuel. Further hints in the New Testament verify that the multileveled structure of sheol-hades continued after the resurrection and ascension. Paul had a vision of the *third* heaven, implying that there are at least two heavens at a lower level.

To this we must add the *experiential* evidence of ghosts and ghost-hauntings. Outside the Anglican Church no denomination in Western Christendom deals with or understands this perennial phenomenon. This is because ghosts fit more into the categories of Old Testament sheol than in the post-Augustinian theology of heaven-hell. Ghost manifestations are ignored or written off by Christian ministers and theologians as "occult" phenomena, and therefore to be avoided.[13]

The "Cloud of Witnesses"

Another aspect of the afterlife that we must examine is the relationships that exist between those in the Body of Christ who are living and those who are in the afterlife. In the Roman, Anglo-Catholic and Orthodox Churches there is a well-developed theology about these matters.[14] In Protestant Christianity these questions are given little importance, though not totally ignored.[15] The writer of Hebrews mentions that a "cloud of witnesses" watches over actions, but this is not further elaborated (Heb. 12:1).

The beliefs about the interactions among deceased and living members of the Body of Christ were among the items bitterly debated in the Reformation period. Medieval Catholic devotion to the saints (e.g., prayers to the saints for intercessory help) was seen by the Reformers as little short of idolatry. Prayers and masses for the dead were viewed as mere money-making schemes for the clergy. The net effect has been that most Protestant denominations assert that the biblical prohibitions against mediumship are to be understood as absolute prohibitions against *any* form of communication between the living and the dead.

The Catholic, and especially the Orthodox, religious traditions of spirituality stress that dream contact with the dead is acceptable and not to be feared, though certainly *discerned*. This communication is a function of consolation and comforting grace of the Body of Christ. In its authentic manifestations, it comes spontaneously and is initiated by the deceased. It cannot be sought after by the living in any form of mediumship. A classic example of this is seen in the advice Father Zossima gives to the grieving peasant woman in Fyodor Dostoyevsky's *The Brothers Karamazov*.[16] The most detailed recorded example of this type of dream contact is found in another Russian spiritual classic, *The Way of a Pilgrim*, written in the 1860s.[17] In this book the Christian disciple and pilgrim is encouraged and given direction on such practices as Bible reading through dream contact with his spiritual father (starets).

Dream contact with the dead is not purely a Catholic or Orthodox phenomenon. It has also been reported, though with much less frequency, by the most conventional of Protestants as well. It would seem that the relative infrequency of Protestant experiences of this nature is related to the issue we discussed with regard to spontaneous PLVs: The Holy Spirit does not permit visions or spiritual experiences that would confuse or unnecessarily disrupt the seer's theological stand. Corrie ten Boom, the great saint of the Dutch underground who saved the lives of hundreds of Jews in World War II, had a beautiful and vivid dream about her great-grandfather who lived in the times of the Prince of Orange. In her dream she met the old gentleman and he exhorted her to trust the Bible. For, he added, by the time she is born many things from his age will have changed, but the Word of God is changeless and absolutely reliable.[18]

Contact between the living and the dead has been reported not only in saints' lives, but has been studied since the beginnings of parapsychology in the 1880s. Unfortunately, parapsychologists for the most part lump together all claimed contact with the dead, mediumistic, spontaneous, and dream, as one category which "proves" personal survival. Christian researchers need to do work in this area with more discernment. Spontaneous, nonmediumistic contact with the dead may be more widespread than most people imagine. In 1973 Andrew Greeley, a priest-sociologist, added a question of contact with the dead to a sociological survey he was conducting and received a surprising response. One-quarter of Americans had experienced some contact with the dead. The contacts spread across all religious and denominational boundaries. Unfortunately the survey did not distinguish between mediumship and spontaneous contacts, but certainly very few Americans have been to mediums. The vast majority of cases reported must have been of the spontaneous, visionary, or dream order.[19]

There is one suggestive scripture in the New Testament about the possibility of communication with the dead, though it is definitely not conclusive. It is the transfiguration scene when Jesus conversed with Moses and Elijah (Mt. 17:1–8; Mk. 9:2–8; Lk. 9:28–36). Now some will say that Elijah did not, properly speaking, die, but Moses did (Jos. 1:1). The argument that this communication was a special dispensation for the Son of God, but sinful for us, is rather weak. Jesus explicitly desired to "fulfill all righteousness" (Mt. 3:13–15). The humanity of Jesus placed a limit on his actions insofar as he could do no thing that was humanly sinful. Note also the characteristics of the transfiguration; it was brief, and it was *nonmediumistic*. Jesus did not go into a trance and have the spirits of Moses and Elijah speak *through* him.

The Church's Ministry to the Dead: A Biblical Perspective

The trigger that impelled a young Augustinian monk named Martin Luther to challenge the authority of medieval Catholicism was a fundraising drive by a Dominican preacher, Johann Tetzel, in which indulgences (special prayers for the dead) were sold for a price. Tetzel had an advertising jingle for his product which rhymes even in translation from the German:

> *As soon as the coin in the coffer rings,*
> *The soul from purgatory springs.*

It cannot be our place here to settle this most emotional of Reformation debates, but we will suggest that in spite of the depths of demonization to which the indulgence system sank, at the root is an entirely valid biblical principle: ministering to the dead. This is a ministry that is confirmed by early Christian documents and by continuous practice since then. It is certainly not central to the Gospel, however, and like many other biblical doctrines it is veiled in a cloak of scriptural ambiguity.

The Victorian revisionists studied the problem of ministering to the dead and came to the unanimous conclusion that it was a sound doctrine, though they did not endorse specific Catholic practices with regard to indulgences.[20]

They also found that among the many varieties of belief that circulated in Jewish denominations in the century before the Christian era, one that received wide circulation was the belief that the sins of the deceased could be atoned for by the prayers of the living faithful. This is specifically recorded in 2 Maccabees 12:38–45. The Reformers believed that this book did not deserve a place in the biblical canon and assumed that the passage in question was an aberration of Jewish custom. The Victorian scholars had access to the rediscovered intertestamental writings and realized that praying for the dead was indeed an accepted Jewish practice.[21]

With regard to the New Testament, let us direct our attention to the most important scriptural passage addressing this issue, one found in the first letter of Peter. Like Paul, Peter's literary style leaves much to be desired, and the passages in question are sandwiched between moral exhortations. But the central meaning is sufficiently clear:

> For Christ also died for sins once for all, the righteous for the unrighteous, that he might bring us to God, being put to death in the flesh but made alive in the spirit; in which he went and preached to the spirits in prison, who formerly did not obey, when God's patience waited in the days of Noah, during the building of the ark, in which a few, that is eight persons, were saved through water. . . . For this is why the gospel was preached even to the dead, that though judged in the flesh like men, they might live in the spirit like God. (1 Pet. 3:18–21; 4:6)

What Peter describes is Jesus' preaching ministry in hades (called a spiritual prison in this passage) and this is corroborated in Ephesians 4:8–9, as there it is revealed that Jesus succeeded and led "a host of captives" into the heavenly realms.

There was little confusion among the earliest Christian writers about the meaning of these passages. Between his death and resurrection Christ preached to the dead in hades and those who accepted his word ascended with him to heaven.[22] Several traditions in early Christian literature attempted to elaborate this revelation. For example, in the *Shepherd of Hermas,* which was held as canonical scripture by many churches in the second and third centuries, there is the assertion that the Apostles followed Jesus' example, and at death they too preached to the heathen in hades.[23] Clement of Alexandria (d. circa 214) adds the interesting detail that the Apostles *baptized* the dead in hades.[24]

However, quite early in church circles the good news of Christ's Lordship in hades became adulterated. Late in the third century a spurious version of the gospel, named the Gospel of Nicodemus, was written in which appears a vivid description of Jesus' arrival at hades. There Jesus saves Adam and the Old Testament saints from Satan's dominion and leads them to the gates of heaven.[25] This view of what happened in hades influenced medieval theology, and it was commonly believed that the "spirits in prison" who had been released by Jesus were the Patriarchs of the Old

Testament. This is of course totally unscriptural. Peter clearly defines the spirits to whom Jesus preached as the ones "who formerly did not obey." Further, the famous passage in Luke 16 mentions a heavenlike place called the "Bosom of Abraham" where that patriarch resided in comfort with Lazarus the just beggar. This quasi heaven was not likely to be the "prison" of 1 Peter. In spite of the problems involved, Reformation theologians adopted the Gospel of Nicodemus version of Christ's descent into hades.

In their enthusiasm to overthrow Catholic practices they rejected too much. Luther accepted the concept of private prayers for the dead, though masses on their behalf were definitely forbidden. Calvin was adamant against any form of ministry to the dead. Significantly, in his massive *Institutes of the Christian Religion*, he skips commentary on the two critical passages of 1 Peter 3:20 and 4:6 and posits the interpretation from the Gospel of Nicodemus.

The conservative denominations of Protestantism, in following Calvin's exegesis, are forced into a contradiction by asserting that because the dead were not, and cannot be, preached to, the scriptures in 1 Peter 3–4 do not "make sense."[26]

If 1 Peter were the only scripture on this matter there would be a serious problem in extrapolating a continuing ministry to the dead. It could be asserted that what happened in hades after Christ's crucifixion was a unique event. 1 Peter 3–4 could theoretically refer to an afterlife mission of recently dead Christians as suggested in the *Shepherd of Hermas*. In that case the living church would have no role in this type of ministry. Several scriptures indicate that this is not the case, and that the church on earth does indeed have a legitimate hand in this ministry.

The first scripture passage concerning this issue is one of the most widely known and quoted, Matthew 16:18. It is used by Roman Catholics as proof text for the establishment of the primacy of the Papacy. Protestants use it as proof text for the importance of faith in the individual believer. In all the most recent translations its meaning has been seriously distorted by the use of the word hell (place of punishment) instead of hades (afterlife). The most accurate translation in English is found in the Jerusalem Bible: "So I now say to you: you are Peter and on this rock I will build my church. And the gates of the under-world can never hold out against it." (See also the translation of the New American Standard Bible.)

A common mistake in interpreting this scripture, based on less accurate translations, is to assume that this is a defensive commission, that is, if the demonic attack, the church will have power to stand. That is incorrect. It is an offensive commission. In warfare the "gates" of a fortress do not move and attack; they are designed to resist assault. This passage means that the best-fortified points of hades (the afterlife in Satan's dominion) cannot withstand the assaults of the church.

One more confirmation for this last point must be noted. It is among the most controversial (or most disregarded) scriptures in the whole of the New Testament, 1 Corinthians 15:28–29:

> When all things are subjected to him, then the Son himself will also be subjected to him who put all things under him, that God may be everything to every one. Otherwise, what do people mean by being baptized on behalf of the dead? If the dead are not raised at all, why are people baptized on their behalf?

Neither Catholic nor Protestant commentators like this passage. For Protestants it implies a sacramental ministry to the dead; for Catholics it is a ministry for the dead that has no "tradition" behind it. That is, no other documents of the early church take note of any such practice and the peculiar practice of the Corinthian congregation must have been short-lived. In the modern world the Mormons have taken this scripture literally, and have an ongoing ritual for the baptism of their ancestors. A few very independent prayer groups have also taken up the practice in recent decades.

In spite of our reluctance to accept it as meaningful, the passage is there. The living church was ministering to those who had passed away, and, unlike some of the other practices of the Corinthian Church, Paul does not criticize it but rather uses this practice to buttress his own argument. The great biblical scholar Rudolf Bultmann notes that in spite of the strangeness of this passage, it represents the authentic sacramental viewpoint of Saint Paul and of the earliest church.[27]

There is a subtle but definite progression of revelation in the Bible with regard to what happens in the afterlife. In Psalm 6:5 we are told that those in sheol cannot praise God. The famous story in Luke 16 implies that those in the quasiheaven (Bosom of Abraham) are not permitted to assist those in the "pit" areas of hades. Finally, in 1 Corinthians 15 Paul shows us that the living members of the church are the ones who minister to the deceased. This is different from traditional Catholic doctrine on the matter, which insists that the church members in the heaven state can minister to those in purgatory (hades).

With regard to church practice, there are several documents that indicate that ministering to the dead, in the form of prayers, was a customary practice in the early church. Among the earliest is an apologetical work by Arnobius of Sicca, called *The Case Against the*

Pagans, written about 305. In it the author protests the destruction of Christian churches and describes their prayers:

> Why should our meeting places be savagely torn down? In them the Supreme God is prayed to, peace and forgiveness asked for all magistrates, armies, rulers, friends, enemies; for those still living and those freed from the bonds of the body. . . . [28]

A second often-quoted source, and one written about the same time (and possibly edited by Tertullian) was a description of the martyrdom of Saints Perpetua and Felicitas. This account is particularly significant because it describes how Saint Perpetua received a vision about the sufferings of her brother in the afterworld, and after several days of earnest prayer had a dream signifying that he was now healed and happy. This type of travail for others in the afterworld occurs periodically in Christian literature of all ages. It happened to Agnes Sanford as a little girl in China. After she saw the execution of a Chinese criminal, she had a dream in which he was pleading for her prayers. She did so, not knowing that as a Presbyterian she was not supposed to pray for the dead, and the next night she saw in a dream the same criminal happily waving to her with Jesus by his side.[29]

We can now begin to understand the role of spiritualism. It is the shadow truth, the demonic distortion, of two profound truths of the Kingdom of God. Firstly, it is true that the afterlife is multileveled, and that some of these levels are of the sheol type described in the Old Testament and not of the ultimate heaven or hell that will exist after the Last Judgment. In this regard, souls in the sheol state occasionally do manifest in apparitions and hauntings. Secondly, it is true that the Kingdom of God does allow some forms of limited, nonmediumistic communications between the living and the dead. Both these truths have been slighted in modern theologies, Catholic and Protestant, with the result that many spiritual phenomena are either misunderstood, ignored, or dismissed. This creates an *interpretive vacuum* which is often filled by the demonic in the form of neo-Gnostic spirituality.[30]

The research of the Victorian Revisionists bore fruit in the Church of England where there evolved a mature theology of the afterlife. This is reflected in pastoral practice by the fact that the Anglican Church is the only modern Christian Church that has an official rite for dealing with ghosts and haunting apparitions. The rite is called "laying a ghost to rest." The assumption is that a ghost is an earthbound soul, trapped in a sheol state, and it does not need to be cursed as in exorcism, but instead needs prayers to assist it in reaching a better place in the afterlife. To this end prayers are said for the forgiveness of its earth-life sins, and at times a communion service is offered for this purpose right at the place of the hauntings. At times the hauntings are of a seriously diabolical nature and can be ended only by a "place exorcism." The choice of what type of prayer or exorcism is needed is a discernment problem that can only be decided on a case-by-case basis.[31]

The Way of Exchange

On the theological level the Anglican Church has been gifted with some remarkable thinkers and theologians who have developed biblically sound concepts of the afterlife. These contemporary thinkers built on the legacy of the Victorian Revisionists, but also took into account all the different types of spiritual phenomena studied by English psychical researchers. The most popular of these writers was C.S. Lewis, whose novels about outer space and the afterlife brought many new concepts to the public attention in a nonthreatening manner.

Perhaps more profound than Lewis in these matters was his friend Charles Williams (d. 1946).[32] At the center of Williams's theology lies what he calls the "way of exchange." This is the human ability to share joy, pain, burdens, and gifts with others. It is the central spiritual act. Persons who cultivate exchange, by truthful communication and selflessness, can enter into the Kingdom of God, while those who refuse pariticipation in the way of exchange, by hoarding and secretiveness, dig their own pit into hell.

Williams strongly asserted the atoning work of Jesus as sin-bearer before God, but he also believed that it was the necessary work of all Christians to share one another's burdens. As described in his essays and novels, Williams shows that the work of burden-bearing was not limited to time sequence as lived on earth, but that in the Kingdom of God one could reach into the past and help bear the burdens of those who had lived before. In his most famous novel, *Descent into Hell,*[33] the spirit of a dead man (ghost) is freed from its sheol state by the burden-bearing concern of a Christian.

Williams's theology is based on a radical understanding of the mystical Body of Christ which stresses the corporateness of human life in a way that is strange to modern Christians for whom salvation is understood as an individual responsibility.

In fact, the "way of exchange" has solid biblical foundations in both the Old and New Testaments. It is closer to the Semitic concept of corporate responsibility expressed in Jude 3 than to our contemporary views. A distinction must be made, however, we do not "save" each other, Jesus saves us, but we do participate in the corporate activity of the Body of Christ by bearing each other's burdens.

The way of exchange makes understandable that little-understood passage by Paul in Colossians about suffering:

> Now I rejoice in my suffering for your sake, and in my flesh I complete what is lacking in Christ's afflictions for the sake of the body, that is the Church . . . (Col. 1:24)

Chapter 15

The EJR Ambiguity:
Empathetic Identification

The Unresolved Ambiguity

We will first consider the implications of the EJR independent of its specific interpretation. That is, what we will discuss in this chapter will hold true of the EJR if interpreted either as empathetic identification or reincarnation. It has already been noted that there is good, though not yet conclusive, evidence to believe that the EJR is an interconnecting force that operates upon most normal men and women.

In view of this, what can we safely assert about the EJR that would be of help in the Church's pastoral ministry? Naturally, we will first have to sift from consideration all PLVs that show Gnostic, spiritualist, and Eastern motifs. Of the remaining few PLVs that can be judged spiritually authentic, such as the revelations of Thecla-Macrina or Cindy, a few things may be posited. Here again we must lament the dearth of reliable evidence and await further case studies and clarification from Christians.

Yet it is clear that the key word for the EJR as it pertains to normal men and women is the same as that of the specific Elijah and John the Baptist case: recapitulation. We say that in the case of John the Baptist, where the recapitualation process went according to God's plan, no PLV was either necessary or helpful. The same holds true of countless saints of the Lord who have cooperated with God's grace to achieve notable levels of sanctification. For a person who has given his or her life to the Lord, and who is presently experiencing the spiritual joys of the Christian life, no induced PLV experience need be undertaken.

Along these lines, we should take note of the phenomenon of child prodigies who appear in such areas as math, science, art, and music. History is dotted with such prodigies as George Frederic Handel (1685–1759) who, in spite of a family environment that was antipathetic to music, became one of the world's great composers and musicians. Metaphysical writers love to cite these persons as "proof" of reincarnation.[1] This is going beyond the evidence, and certainly a spiritual empathetic or "force" continuity could account for the prodigy factor just as well as the reincarnation hypothesis. From the biographies of such persons it is apparent that, like John the Baptist, prodigies are not aware of their specific EJR. Whatever talents, skills, and inclinations the EJR may feed to the living person is done by way of the spirit in a manner that does not burden the child with the personal history of the earlier person.

A different case holds for Christians who are in emotional-spiritual crisis or who feel that their spiritual life is shallow or stagnating. For these Christians a PLV might identify a "recapitulation bottleneck," in which a past moral-spiritual crisis was not overcome and is influencing the current life. This happened with the woman who had the PLV as the "scrupulous prioress" (See p. 161). She discovered she was recapitulating a sinful pattern of scrupulosity and judgment towards others. That pattern was identified, confessed, and broken with the assistance of the PLV. Whether there was a personal continuity between the prioress and the living woman (reincarnation) or a force continuity of similar faults (empathetic identification) cannot be known at this time. All we can do is identify the similarities as recapitulation.

When we reexamine the literature of PLV therapy by such authors as Edith Fiore and Morris Netherton we see patterns of recapitulation that are aggravated by the attempt to live a life on purely secular levels. Persons who go to secular therapists generally have few prayer resources with which to battle and break out of the recapitulation patterns. For a person in the grip of neurotic distress, recapitulation is not a pattern that breaks loose to a higher level of purposeful activity. Rather it is an endless merry-go-round which manifests in unhappiness and stress. Notice also that the majority of the children that Dr. Stevenson identified as having authenticated PLVs had some sort of "problem" in the PLV or were "unhappy" as a result of the visions. This could indicate that the spirit of the child was desperately calling for a healing in the EJR and a breakout from the recapitulation pattern or sin-burden of its life.

Long ago, Gregory of Nyssa saw the problem of cyclical entrapment as the principal malady of "natural," that is, non-spiritual man. In his view man without God's grace was doomed to continually strive to fulfill his bodily and emotional desires. Because they could never be completely fulfilled, natural man was trapped in a treadmill that leaves him exhausted and unhappy. Only spiritual man, filled with God's grace is capable of escaping this entrapment to be released to progress to higher levels of achievement. Gregory loved to use Saint Paul's phrase "from glory to glory" to describe the freedom that the Christian possesses.[2]

All of this reinforces our suspicion that PLVs should be induced only when there is a *healing need*. In other words, PLV therapy is most effective in those persons where the EJR has "gone wrong," with sin or misalignment with God's will. This does not necessarily mean the living individual is totally responsible for the problem. But the case of Cindy demonstrates that the burden of sin (ACR) from the EJR can on occasions be so strong that there is little the individual can do to help himself or herself. In these cases it is the church acting through its believers that must break the recapitulation cycle of sin and its demonic entanglements.

In an important sense, ministering to a PLV is analogous to ministering a sacrament. It is of little importance what specific sacramental theology the minister holds; it is only important that the minister carry out the action (baptism, etc.) so that God may act in grace and power. It is perfectly acceptable for the different members of an inner-healing team to hold varying opinions as to the ultimate cause of a PLV. In fact I have ministered PLVs under such circumstances. All that is necessary is that the members of the healing team agree to pray for the healing of the PLV through the Lordship of Jesus Christ. In that way God can act in grace, power, and healing.

As Empathetic Identification

We are now in a better position to confront the last two hypotheses for the origins of PLVs, the one of empathetic identification, the other the reincarnation hypothesis. In none of the preceding theories (demonic counterfeit, subconscious invention or bloodline) was it necessary to assert that the transpersonal ACR was operational upon a living person because of the EJR. In the following two chapters we will assume that the ACR does in fact operate in conjunction with the EJR, and that this combined ACR-EJR is the cause of at least some PLVs.

The empathetic identification explanation of PLVs occurs with some frequency among both secular writers and religious ones. Gardner Murphy, one of the outstanding figures of American parapsychology (d. 1980), produced an interesting article with this viewpoint.[3] He suggested that PLVs are nothing more than the products of "psychic energies" that emanate from a person at the time of death. These energies in no way signify the continuity of a core personality, but rather are an impersonal force. This is the secular equivalent of the Old Testament use of "spirit" of a person. Strangely, the psychic Jeane Dixon, who is deeply influenced by neo-Gnostic beliefs and who might be expected to accept the standard reincarnationist line, also accepts Murphy's general line of argument. She feels that all humans incarnate only once, but that their "spirits" influence others.[4]

The spiritual empathetic hypothesis has a special resonance with the theological views of Charles Williams (see pp. 188–89). Williams had a profound sense of the solidarity in the Body of Christ that transcends space and time. As we have seen, most of the PLV case studies we have examined involve a vision of a person from the past in need of a sin-burden to be lifted and forgiven. For reasons about which we can only speculate, the living person or sensor finds that the burden of the deceased person is directly related to a burden that the sensor experiences in the form of neuroses or other forms of emotional and physical illness. Perhaps the living person is involved through his or her own choice in a pattern of sin that closely resembles that of the person deceased. A dead soul is attracted to the sensor for this reason, and a link develops between the two souls in need of repentance. But only the living person is capable of repenting. If the living person does so, his link with the dead person enacts his or her repentance as well; thus both are freed from the sin-burden incurred as the consequences of their freely chosen sinful acts.

On the other hand, the person might be personally innocent of the sin-burden he or she experiences. In this case, the meaning of the link between the dead person and the innocent sensor is illuminated by the Suffering Servant passages found in Isaiah 53 or in Paul's saying that we are to complete Christ's atoning suffering (Col. 1:24). Such persons, who may have considered their suffering absurd, will, through the experience of an induced PLV, come to understand that they are carrying the sin-burden of someone from the past, and that they are capable, through the inner-healing ministry, of repenting for this person who is incapable of doing it in the sheol state.

Regardless of whether the living sensor is personally guilty or innocent, the main thing is that, in this spiritual web of relationships, the living have the capability and the responsibility to do for the dead what they cannot do for themselves. Williams's "way of exchange," combined with the PLV ministry of forgiveness, opens up a very important area relating not only to the solution of problems experienced by the living, but also in the area of the ministry to the dead.

Again, it must be emphasized that we are only in the initial speculative stages in our attempt to understand the nature of PLVs and their tie to the EJR/ACR. Our discussion is meant only to suggest some of the possibilities that may be opening up for Christian ministry. But, as cannot be sufficiently emphasized, these are murky waters, and anyone who enters into them must do so with the utmost caution and with the support of a

Christian community. The sad history of the elaborate and corrupt indulgence system should alert us to the dangers of any form of ministry to
the dead becoming exaggerated and demonized.

One way of testing this hypothesis would be to induce PLVs in a group
of volunteers at five to ten year intervals to see if new PLVs develop that
reflect the inner struggles characteristic of that person's stage of life. For
instance, a teenager with a vocational crisis might develop an empathetic
link with a deceased soul who never resolved his or her vocational con-
flicts. The same person in middle age might attract a completely different
PLV, relating perhaps to a sexual conflict like that of the "playboy" we
described in Part III.

The empathetic identification hypothesis is, in my view, best suited to
explain the PLV of the Anglican homosexual (see p. 107). I should mention here that this hypothesis was also first suggested to me by one of the
monks who witnessed the PLV of the "Scrupulous Prioress" (see p. 161),
long before I was aware of the writings of Charles Williams. In the following pages I would like to relate another case from my inner-healing
ministry that is also very amenable to this interpretation.

The case pertained to a young woman, "Mary," who was close to my
charismatic prayer partner. The woman had come from another city for
psychological therapy. She was at the point of divorce and suffering from
severe depression. As a child she and her family had been brutalized and
impoverished by an alcoholic father. Her teen years were spent in the drug
and antiwar subculture of the Vietnam era.

When she came to us, she was under heavy sedation for her depression.
My prayer partner and I took her to one prayer group after another to
have her "prayed over." After a week of prayer groups, church services,
and laying on of hands she had shown considerable improvement and we
decided to proceed with an inner-healing and deliverance. We suspected
that her involvement with drugs had opened her up to demonic infesta-
tion, so the first thing we did was pray for discernment as to how to proceed. There were three of us present to minister to Mary: myself, her
friend, and another charismatic lady who had much experience in counseling. As we were praying we received a strong "word of wisdom" that the
deliverance should proceed after the inner-healing.

The first session lasted over three hours. We walked back in time with
the Lord through Mary's memories, and she first asked for forgiveness for
her wild teenage years and drug experiences. We then proceeded, in the
Lord's presence, to relive some of the horrible memories of her childhood.
It was clear that her whole childhood was hate-filled, and so we chose only
a few of the more dramatic moments to symbolize the whole tangle of relationships poisoned by her father's alcoholism. One incident in particular

was grim: as a five-year-old child, she watched helplessly as her father almost beat to death a younger brother. We all joined Mary in prayers of forgiveness for the father and healing of her memories. We continued the session by saying the words of deliverance, and at this time several spirits were cast out of Mary, including the spirit of murder-hatred that entered her in her anger and helplessness at her baby brother's beating.

That was the first day. The second day, again, we all assembled to see if a PLV could shed light on Mary's hard life and further her recovery process. The PLV that Mary received was of Lucy, a young woman in seventeenth-century France. In the first vision Lucy was on trial for her life, accused of witchcraft. After getting the general picture of her life situation, we returned to the trial room and I suggested that Lucy invite Jesus to be with her. She could not and would not do this! She hated Jesus. I tried several things. I tried to shift the center of consciousness to Mary, and have Mary pray for Lucy. Lucy still hated Jesus. I was in a quandary. I could not let Mary return to normal consciousness with the memory of such a negative lifetime so I risked going to a more recent life. That was much better: She was a shepherd boy in Scotland with a good prayer life, and so capable of inviting the presence of Jesus.

We then brought Mary back to normal level, but we all had a sense of incompleteness. The woman who was the experienced counselor had an idea. Why not try to go back to Lucy's childhood and introduce her to Jesus before the bitterness set it. We all agreed it was worth a try.

The next day: session three. We quickly took Mary to the PLV as Lucy. This time we began at five years of age. She was the only child. The household was totally godless and permeated with the occult. We suggested that Lucy invite Jesus into the house. Lucy says that Jesus will not come in. It is too negative. I ask Lucy to go where she likes to play. She visualizes a lake and a small rowboat. She wants to go on the lake. I suggest she invite Jesus to come with her. She tentatively accepts Jesus next to her, but when they come to the boat Jesus stays on shore and she goes out alone. I try every method I can think of to suggest to Lucy that Jesus can come to her. I tell her that Jesus can walk on the water but, in her mind, he does not—an impasse. Then the moment of grace, Our Lord's way of letting us know who is *really* in charge of inner-healing. Lucy loses the imagery, but feels a tremendous warmth all through her body. I have seen the warmth of healing before; I tell her to bear up with it. Lucy regains her image. Jesus is in the boat; holding her. She worships him.

In the next scene Lucy meets her mentor in black magic. She is eleven-years-old when the evil person comes to have dinner and conversation with the parents. Lucy cannot bear to have Jesus come into the contaminated house. Lucy runs out to the woods to meet Jesus and say she is sorry and experiences forgiveness and acceptance. Next scene—at the home of the evil person, her first instruction in casting spells, in front of a pot, throwing in pieces of a dress. Again, too horrible, too much shame to have Jesus walk in. Again Lucy runs out to the woods. Again she finds love and forgiveness. Things move rapidly now: Lucy is sixteen-years-old, beautiful, full of lust. Many men in the village desire her, and she has already known several. Lucy is the manipulator, this time reluctant to tell us what she is seeing. We respect her privacy but we see in her face that there is shame. Again Lucy goes into the forest to meet Our Lord. Her face changes to an expression of peace.

Next scene—Lucy now nineteen-years-old at a Black Mass, laughter, and a naked woman on an altar. And again the reconciliation in the woods. Finally, the capture and trial emerge. The first time around it had been with hate for Jesus. This time she flees again to the forest, she repents, she forgives her judges and she accepts Jesus' love. She goes on to the stake, but this time *with* Jesus, not against him. It is over, the healing is complete, it has been recapitulated. My prayer partner receives word of prophecy, "My work will be done throughout eternity." We all felt awed by this experience.

We will never know if indeed we did "release" Lucy from sheol, or if the whole story was a healing parable from deep within Mary's mind. The latter is a distinct possibility and has scriptural warrant in the fact that the Bible equates rebellion with witchcraft (1 Sam. 15:23). Mary's life in the drug counterculture did, in fact, bring her in contact with some distinctly unsavory spiritual forces. The viability of believing that her PLV was a ministry to Lucy depends upon the acceptance of a theological system similar to that of Charles Williams, which will always be both controversial and unprovable.

Chapter 16

The EJR Ambiguity: Reincarnation

As Reincarnation

We are now in a position to confront the most controversial interpretation of the EJR, that of reincarnation. As we have seen in Part II, it is this interpretation that has been most subject to demonization throughout Church history, yet the demonic link between Gnostic doctrines and reincarnation should not automatically bind us to rejecting all forms of belief in reincarnation as anti-Christian and antibiblical. In fact, much of the biblical evidence points in the other direction. Because this interpretation of the PLV phenomenon has received a lion's share of attention in the last few decades (it is the only interpretation of PLVs that has inspired serious debate), we will dedicate most of the remainder of this book to a careful examination of this hypothesis.

Biblical Evidence

Modern scholarship has developed a picture of Palestinian Judaism at the time of Christ with two salient characteristics: it was mixed with many Hellenistic or "Greek" concepts, and it was amazingly pluralistic in practice and beliefs. Biblical scholars in the early decades of this century believed there was a dramatic dichotomy between Palestinian Jews and the Hellenistic Jews of the Diaspora. It was their belief that the Jews outside Palestine had absorbed Greek ideas and philosophy and become somewhat corrupt in their beliefs, while the Palestinian Jews remained true to their Hebraic origins. Recent scholarship, especially the work of W. D. Davies, has shown that this dichotomy is false. The Jews of the Diaspora and the Jews of Palestine were in fact similar in their beliefs.[1] This was because the

Temple served as a focus of pilgrimage for the Jews of the entire world, and Greek ideas were disseminated through all of Palestine via the "tourist industry." Diaspora Jews themselves kept close contact with the rabbinical schools of Palestine (Saul of Tarsus is but one example of a Diaspora Jew who studied orthodox Jewish theology in Jerusalem). Another factor was that even within Palestine there were many Jews who had absorbed Greek ways. As a matter of fact the Jews of Galilee, Jesus' home district, mostly spoke Greek.

Though there was no noticeable division of Jewish beliefs along geographic lines, there was much denominational and sectarian division *within* all of Judaism. The New Testament gives ample evidence of the difference between the Sadducees and Pharisees. Josephus, the Jewish historian, and a general in the Jewish-Roman War, and other sources reveal further divisions with other sects such as the Essenes, as well as substantial differences or "schools" of Pharisaic theology. All of which means there was an amazing pluralism of thought and freedom of specula-tion in New Testament Judaism. In fact, it would be best not to think of Judaism as a unified religious system, but rather as a way of life that centered on Temple worship and reverence for the Torah.

In view of all this, it would be strange if some Jews of New Testament times had not begun to understand the ancient scriptures of reappearing prophets in terms of reincarnation. Personal rebirth was a belief widely known in various Hellenistic religions. The evidence from both the New Testament and Josephus shows that many Jews were indeed speculating about reincarnation. We see an echo of this in John 9:1–4:

> As he passed by, he saw a man blind from his birth. And his disciples asked him, "Rabbi, who sinned, this man or his parents, that he was born blind?" Jesus answered, " It was not that this man sinned, or his parents, but that the works of God might be made manifest in him."

Jesus' very disciples asked him the reincarnation question. Note that the question implies the possibility of personal continuity. Did *his* sins in a state before birth cause his blindness? Jesus' answer is specific only to the one case at hand but the negative evidence is important. Jesus did not rebuke his disciples for entertaining the reincarnation question. Jesus was not one to hold back a rebuke when needed, either to his disciples (Lk. 9:54–55) or to anyone else.

It is best to call it speculation on reincarnation and not just the EJR, because in spite of what Oscar Cullmann has suggested about Jewish func-tional thinking (see Part III), the reincarnation interpretation is more appropriate for the New Testament setting. The Jews were groaning under Roman occupation and longed for the reappearance of Moses or Elijah *in person*.[2]

Also, the theory that the EJR is a force or nonpersonal spirit relationship is historically a sophisticated development that depends on refined concepts of the personality. In primitive cultures where forms of rebirth are adhered to, it is always a belief in *personal* rebirth, not *force* rebirth. This is the pattern in the East where Hinduism believed in personal reincarnation, but Buddhism which is a "reformation" and more sophisticated development of Hinduism, developed a theory of nonpersonal reincarnation.

The echoes of speculation on reincarnation found in the New Testament are amplified in several passages from the writing of Josephus. In his *Wars of the Jews* he gave a description of the Pharisees' belief in the afterlife (II, 8:14):

> They say that all souls are incorruptible; but that the souls of good men are only removed into other bodies, — but that the souls of bad men are subject to eternal punishment.

He elaborates this sentiment further when he records his own speech to a group of defeated soldiers who were contemplating suicide rather than surrender to the Romans (III, 8:5).

> Do you not know that those who depart out of this life, according to the law of nature, and pay the debt which was received from God, when he that lent it us is pleased to require it back, enjoy eternal fame? That their houses and posterity are sure, that their souls are pure and obedient, and obtain a most holy place in heaven, from whence, in the revolution of ages, they are again sent into pure bodies; while the souls of those whose hands have acted madly against themselves are received by the darkest place in Hades. . . . [3]

In effect Josephus is describing an expansion of the old concept of limited reincarnation. It is no longer only a precious few prophets, the "Chasidim," who return to earth. All good men, after a period in heaven, return to earth, while those who are evil are doomed to the pit areas of sheol. Some writers have attempted to discredit these passages as an inaccurate rendition of Pharisaic beliefs. They have accused Josephus of dishonestly accommodating to his Hellenistic audience by twisting Jewish beliefs into Greek ways of thought.[4] In view of recent discoveries of Essene literature and of their belief in reincarnation, the assumption that Josephus distorted his description of the Pharisees is less likely.[5] Here we should also note that Origen cited a now lost rabbinical tradition which claimed that

Elijah was himself a reincarnation of Phinehas (Num. 25:7–13; 31:6, Jos. 22:13, 1 Sam. 4:11). This Old Testament personage lived in the time of Joshua; he was especially zealous for the Lord, and he slew Israelites who had taken heathen women as wives in disobedience to God's commands. Origen was unique among the Church Fathers in that he knew Hebrew and maintained ties with contemporary Jewish scholars. His account of this ancient tradition is undoubtedly correct.[6]

We must now turn to the most significant evidence of all, the sayings of Jesus. The difficulty with considering anything he said is that our response to his sayings is largely conditioned by the theologies of those who trained us in the faith. Most often our first exposure to the words of Jesus comes from Sunday school or from catechism instructions that essentially are simplified theological presentations of what Jesus said. Later, as we probe for deeper understandings, we are guided by elders, commentators, instructors, and so forth, who, are more likely than not, have conventional understanding of scripture themselves.[7]

First, let us reconsider the original scriptural ambiguity that we found to exist between Luke 1:17 (spirit and power) and Matthew 11:13–14 (John is Elijah). The conventional exegesis on these scriptures is that Luke modifies and essentially dilutes Matthew from a continuity of person (reincarnation) to that of a force continuity (nonreincarnation). There are severe difficulties with this interpretation.

The most serious difficulty in "watering down" Jesus' equivalency description of the EJR is that Jesus used equivalency statements *only when he meant them*. Often his equivalency statements cost him dearly, but he did not back down from them. In John 10:30 he taught "I and the Father are one," and was almost stoned by the crowd. In John 6:49–69 he tells his followers that they must drink his blood and eat his flesh. This causes great scandal and many leave him, but he meant his words and did not back down. Later, with the institution of the Eucharist, these words were understood in their proper context. Further there is no reason why the Matthew and Luke scriptures cannot be reconciled instead of one subordinated to another. Their combined meaning would be: John is a reincarnation of Elijah and, in addition, he has the old prophet's power.[8]

In addition, it should be noted that it is unclear in what sense Luke used the word "spirit." In the Old Testament the word clearly meant *force*, with no connotation of personality to it (2 Kg. 2:9 or Num. 11:17–25). But in the New Testament "spirit" has different shades of interpretation. Paul uses it as a key element in his understanding of the person, and spirit for him is the deepest individual and *personal* level of a human being (1 Cor. 5:5). Further, Christianity has come to accept that the New Testament revelation of the Holy Spirit means more than merely the "force" of God, and that the Holy Spirit is also a personality of God. Thus, the attempt to totally *depersonalize* the EJR on the basis of the supremacy of the Lucan scripture is on weak ground.

Other sayings of Jesus that point to reincarnation of some form have been interpreted for more than a thousand years with an eye to the eschatology (theology of the last things) established by Saint Augustine that became normative in the Western Church. Saint Augustine believed that the present age of world history would continue until the moment of Christ's second coming. That event would be instantly followed by the resurrection of the dead, the Last Judgment, and then the eternal heaven or hell for all of mankind.

It is important to understand that this eschatology has influenced the interpretation of the more this-worldly sayings of Jesus towards a spiritual interpretation that often does violence to their intended meaning. For example, the beatitudes. They are the rule of life for the Christian, with attached promises of specific rewards in terms of what Jesus understood as the ultimate ACR. The conventional interpretation sees the rewards in other-worldly terms, as rewards that the Christian will receive after the Last Judgment in the Heaven life. Some beatitudes fit this interpretation quite well, as in Matthew 5:8, "Blessed are the pure in heart, for they shall see God." One beatitude, however, does not fit this interpretive pattern at all: Matthew 5:5, "Blessed are the meek, for they shall inherit the earth." It is the *earth* that the meek inherit, not heaven. Other beatitudes could be interpreted in both this-worldly and spiritual terms, such as Matthew 5:4, 5:6, and 5:7.

This points to one of the most important and, again, least understood motifs of the Bible, the promises of *advancement in rulership* to those loyal to the Kingdom. The scriptures for this are mostly in the New Testament, but it occurs in the book of Wisdom (canonical for Catholics, 3:7–8). In the New Testament these promises appear frequently: in Matthew 19:28, where the twelve Apostles are promised rulership over the twelve tribes of Israel; in the parable of the good and bad stewards, where the good steward is "promoted" to greater responsibilities of material stewardship; and in the parable of the talents, where an identical theme is proclaimed. Paul confirms Jesus' words with an explicit promise to the Corinthian Christians of future rulership:

> When one of you has a grievance against a brother, does he dare go to law before the unrighteous instead of the saints? Do you know that the saints will judge the world? And if the world is to be judged by you, are you incompetent to try trivial cases? (1 Cor. 6:1–2).

Finally, in Revelations 20:4 there is the famous passage in which the beheaded martyrs come to life (and thus reincarnate at least once!) and are rulers of the 1000-year period before the second, general resurrection and Last Judgment.

In the last century and a half many denominations and sects have developed eschatologies that are different from Augustine's in order to do justice to these this-worldly scripture passages. Among the most radical revisions is that of the Jehovah's Witnesses. They believe that at the second coming only a tiny minority of Christians will go to heaven, while the rest (not Jehovah's Witnesses) will reincarnate and live an eternal life on a perfected earth. Other less extreme views stress the millennium as significant in fulfilling the this-worldly scriptures, but do not limit the heaven life so severely. At the beginning of our current century any such millennial views were considered heretical and extremist, yet these have become normative in most contemporary fundamentalist churches.[9]

In any case, all the attempts to integrate the this-worldly and rulership promises as significant passages of scripture share the belief that a first resurrection of the saints will take place in the millennium at the end of the age, but not in *this age*. In this matter there is one critically important scripture passage which indicates that the this-worldly rewards of the Kingdom are given in *this age*. The implication is very strong that reincarnation extends not only in the next age (Rev. 20:4), the one after the second coming, but is a reality in this age as well. It is Mark 10:28–30:

> Peter began to say to him, "Lo, we have left everything and followed you." Jesus said, "Truly, I say to you, there is no one who has left house or lands, for my sake and for the gospel, who will not receive a hundredfold now in this time, houses and brothers and sisters and mothers and children and lands, with persecutions, and in the age to come eternal life.

Again, let me remind the reader of the interpretive (hermeneutical) problem. This saying is so encrusted with apologetic interpretations about the benefits of Christian fellowship that it is difficult to see it in a neutral and fresh way. A quite possible interpretation is that of reincarnation in this age, and "eternal life" in the age to come. Taken together with Jesus' firm teachings on gehenna, this seems to put Jesus in the same theological camp as the Pharisees described by Josephus: reincarnation for the just, gehenna for the truly wicked (Mt. 23:2).[10] It is also important to note that the subsequent lives will have not only their rewards, but also their hardships for the sake of the Kingdom, "with persecutions." This interpretation of Mark 10:28–30 is in harmony with the mixed this-worldly and other-worldly ACR as described in the fullness of biblical revelation.

We should not leave this section without dealing with three scriptural problems that have been traditionally cited as evidence against any biblical affirmation of reincarnation, or at least that the EJR was a reincarnation one. These problem areas are: Hebrews 9:27, the transfiguration of Jesus on the mountain, and the fact that Elijah did not die but was translated into heaven.

Hebrews 9:27 is cited most often as a definitive scripture against reincarnation. It reads: "And just as it is appointed for men to die once, and after that comes the judgment, so Christ having been offered once to bear the sins of many, will appear a second time." When we go to the content of the letter of Hebrews we see that the central theme, stated in Hebrews 6 but repeated with several examples, is the problem of *spiritual death* through apostasy. This is an issue ignored by certain fundamentalist denominations, and the problem that Kenneth Hagin had to face in his experience with the Lord. The antireincarnation meaning of this scripture is dependent on "death" meaning normal bodily death, not spiritual death. This is not at all certain.

Closely allied to the problem posed by the Hebrews scripture is the strange status of Elijah. He was one of the few men in scripture who did not, properly speaking, die, but was translated into heaven (2 Kgs. 2:11). Thus the argument may be made, especially in view of Hebrews, that reincarnation is possible only for those who do not die (Elijah and Enoch). The counter of this argument is a historical one. The Jewish belief in reincarnation, as developed by the scribes and Pharisees, and apparently validated by Jesus (Mt. 23:2), made no distinction in their theory of the reappearing prophet between those who had died and those who had not. It was expected that Daniel and Moses, both of whom died, would reincarnate, as well as Enoch and Elijah, who were translated.

Lastly, there is the problem raised by the transfiguration (Mt. 17:3, Mk. 9:4, Lk. 9:30). In that scene, which took place after the beheading of John the Baptist, it was Elijah who appeared beside Christ, not John the Baptist or a composite of Elijah and John the Baptist. This is a relatively weak antireincarnation argument. From a reincarnation perspective the transfiguration scene merely shows that the spirit has the power to manifest in any of its incarnations, and is not bound to its last manifestation.

Post-Biblical Period: Lack of Continuity of the EJR Motif

To anyone familiar with the sources of early Christianity (the Apostolic and sub-Apostolic periods) it is obvious that there is no continuity of belief in reincarnation. There was instead a strong proclamation about the resurrection and coming judgment. So then the legitimate question must be posed. What happened to all the Jewish speculation on reincarnation and why were the sayings of Jesus not elaborated into a more precise EJR theological system? The answers to these questions must be divided into two parts: first, what happened to the early church that caused it to ignore the EJR motif.

The events of the first century of the Christian era were devastating for Judaism. In A.D. 70 the Temple was destroyed and the Jerusalem population enslaved and scattered. Sixty years later a second Jewish revolt, led by Bar Kochba, came to a further disaster and the expulsion of practically all of the Jewish population from Palestine. In addition, the rise of Christianity as an independent and powerful movement led to bitter disputes within the synagogues. All of this resulted in the pluralism of pre-Temple Judaism being destroyed. The Sadducees, Essenes, and Zealots were massacred out of existence. All that was left was the Pharisaic party. A conservative retrenchment took place as they attempted to pick up the pieces and re-establish Judaism. All the ideas and speculations that the surviving Pharisees believed to have triggered the revolts against Rome were purged from Jewish orthodoxy. Third-century Judaism became agnostic about the afterlife, and speculations about reincarnation, or any form of postdeath survival were minimized in the Rabbinical Judaism that emerged.[11] A few reincarnation beliefs were passed on within esoteric circles and eventually became the Kabbalah. As we mentioned before, Origen managed to salvage one of these traditions, but normative Judaism was no longer interested in such matters.

In regard to the noncontinuity of reincarnation in the early Church, there seem to have been two major factors to account for this. The first Christian writers were so convinced of the imminent second coming of Christ that any speculations on the continued presence of the EJR in any form was irrelevant.[12] The second factor was the avid adoption of reincarnation by Gnostic sects. From our discussion of Jewish-Christ Gnosticism, we saw that reincarnation was *not* an element of its system. Yet after A.D. 200, the period in which Gnostic documents are plentiful, reincarnation became central to most Gnostic sects. The situation must have been similar to what happened to spiritualism during the 1930s. Both the ancient Gnostics and modern spiritualists flip-flopped on the issue of reincarnation within a single generation. In any case, such early Christian writers as Irenaeus saw reincarnation as intimately associated with the deadly Gnosticism that the Church was battling. In view of the Church's problems with persecution and doctrinal stability, there was no incentive to attempt to develop the EJR motif into an independent Christian theology of reincarnation.

There is a single exception to this in the person of Origen (185–225). He is a unique figure in Christian thought, the source and inspiration of most of the great theologians of late antiquity, including such men as Saint Augustine and the Cappadocians (Gregory of Nyssa, Saint Basil the Great, Saint Gregory of Nazianzus) who established the theology of Eastern Orthodoxy. After his condemnation in the sixth century, few would openly recognize the enormous debt that all orthodox theologians have to this "heretic." Only in this century has his rightful place in the history of Christian theology come to be appreciated.[13]

Exactly what Origen believed about reincarnation or many other issues is difficult to establish. The emperor-theologian Justinian of the sixth century had a passionate hatred for Origen's writings and did his best to have them collected and burned. Only about half of his works survived that holocaust. Also, Origen had a good sense for the difference between essential Christian beliefs and areas of doctrine that were open to speculation. In these latter areas, including reincarnation, he felt the freedom to examine, speculate, and change his mind. You must remember that he lived and wrote in the era before the establishment of Christianity as the official religion of the Roman Empire and before the formulation of the creeds. He was not under the burden of subsequent credal theologians of believing that "right theology" was necessarily dogmatic.

This is not to say that he disregarded the dangers of heresy. As a matter of fact, he was known as the great defender of orthodoxy in his day. In a church that had at that time no legal-coersive power, he constantly battled one heresy after another with reason and scripture. He battled against Gnostics (Eusebius, *Ecc. Hist.,* 6:18), and corrected wayward bishops who had strayed away from biblical teachings. In one case he had to persuade a bishop of Arabia that Christ did indeed exist before his incarnation (*Ecc. Hist.,* 6:33), and in another case he had to contend with a sect that had rejected the writings of Paul as inspired (*Ecc. Hist.,* 6:38). We have an example of Origen's persuasive powers in a dialogue that he had with a certain heretical bishop, Heraclidus, who believed that there were two gods (Christ and the Father) instead of one. The dialogue is a case study of applying Logos methodology to a difficult situation. Origen uses reason, logic, scripture, and gentleness (in other words the method advocated in James 3) to win over his opponent.[14]

Now, to the main point. What *did* Origen believe? For one thing he strongly believed in God's perfect justice, so that the unequal spiritual gifts and consciousness of men must have been due to some pre-earth-life situation. He believed that the angels and humans were all created at the same moment in eternity, but that some sinned greatly and became demonic angels, and some sinned less severely and became the human race, and, lastly, others did not sin at all and remained as God's angels. Interestingly enough, he believed that angels have incarnated on earth for special godly tasks (Heb. 13:2) and that John the Baptist was one of these angel-men.[15] Thus, the EJR is not seen in Origen as evidence for reincarnation.

Yet he believed that sinners who rejected God's love would be given new opportunities to accept God in "other worlds," and in other ages (*De Princ.*, 3, 1 23). Whether he ever held to reincarnation in *this* world is uncertain. He most definitely would have accepted Agnes Sanford's commissioning vision and her theories of cosmic transmigration without any trouble. Metaphysical and occult writers claim that Origen believed in reincarnation, but this is really going beyond the evidence and is a simplification to the point of error.

Even in his lifetime Origen's opinions were controversial. Opposition to his writings mounted among conservative churchmen as time went on. Finally Emperor Justinian I of the East Roman Empire, who stands as one of the most pretentious figures in church history, developed a passion against Origen and decided to have him condemned as a heretic. He succeeded in pressuring a local synod to condemn Origen, but had less success when he called a general council.

Exactly what happened at the Second Council of Constantinople is unclear. It met in 553, at the edge of the "Dark Ages," and the documentary evidence is scant. The Pope was not present and did not want the Council, and of all the bishops present only six were from the West. It was thus not truly an ecumenical meeting. What was definitely adopted at the Second Council was something called the "three chapters," which dealt with matters not at all relating to Origen. Origen's theory of preexistence *may* have been also condemned, but that is not clear. The famous condemnation of Origen *may* have been illegally added on to the Council decree by Justinian after the Council dissolved.[16]

In any case the effect of the Council was devastating. Origen's books were declared heretical and burned, and it was soon general belief in Christendom that the Council did in fact condemn preexistence and, by implication, reincarnation. Thus preexistence and reincarnation became by decree part of the "wrong knowledge" that brings about spiritual death. Throughout the Middle Ages this belief was reinforced by several Western councils which explicitly condemned reincarnation. A spirit of fear and guilt settled on any speculation on reincarnation, which even affected the Church's view of the EJR, and this is the reason that motif has been so poorly developed in any branch of Christian theology.

One might logically expect that the reformers should have reexamined the EJR in their break from medieval Catholicism, but this did not happen. Protestantism accepted as one of its assumptions the position of the medieval church on this issue: The EJR was *not* a reincarnation relationship, and it was not significant in terms of general theology. It is only in recent decades, in response to the proddings and stirrings of occult theories of reincarnation, that Protestant theologians have dared to look at reincarnation from a fresh, nondogmatic perspective.[17]

Toward a Christian Theology of Reincarnation

Thus far we have attempted to strip the EJR of all Gnostic, spiritualist, and Eastern motifs. Yet the problem remains: whenever the word reincarnation is used one immediately encounters a series of connotations of the word that owe their origins to Eastern sources. For this reason it is best to probe for a Christian understanding of reincarnation by direct *contrast* with Eastern doctrines of rebirth.

A Christian understanding of reincarnation has an entirely different view of man's destiny than Eastern varieties of the doctrine. In the East the individual is urged to develop his spiritual skills in order to escape the "wheel of rebirth" and enter into the heaven-state of Nirvana. It is all an individual movement and there is no concept of a spiritual entity such as the Church, nor is the earth process believed to terminate at a definite point in anything like a last judgment. A Christian concept of reincarnation must take into account the corporate nature of salvation (the fundamental meaning of the body of Christ) and the clear revelations about the end-time for world history.

From what can be gleaned from scripture, the aim of reincarnation would not be an escape from the earth, but rather the continued service to the body of Christ at a higher level of effectiveness. This is the meaning that can be derived from Agnes Sanford's preexistence vision. Christians have believed that the Malachi prophecy of Elijah means he will reappear a third time at the tribulation times. Again this indicates a corporate aim, not an individual one, for reincarnation. Elijah returned as John the Baptist, not to save himself but to serve our Lord and prepare the foundations of his church. This was well expressed by the English charismatic woman who said after her PLV that it was a pleasure to know one can serve the Lord more than once. Interestingly enough, Saint Teresa of Avila who of course was perfectly orthodox and would not have let the word reincarnation pass her lips, expressed a similar thought when she described her experiences with mystical prayer life. "Such a soul would gladly have a thousand lives so as to use them all for God, and it would like everything on earth to be tongues so that it might praise him."[18]

However, a word of caution is needed here. Eastern doctrines of reincarnation assert that it takes the individual thousands, even hundreds of thousands of lifetimes to reach Nirvana. Everything in Christian scriptures affirms that once a person enters the Kingdom of God (through trust in Jesus Christ) spiritual progress is accelerated enormously. Since there is no karma in the Kingdom of God, one does not have to undo the evil acts of one's godless lives: the blood of Christ washes away *all* sin. The Agnes Sanford vision suggests that rebirth for someone already submissive to the will of Jesus is on a "covenant" basis only.

On another issue intrinsic to Eastern doctrines of reincarnation, the process of self-perfection, we have limited but highly suggestive evidence. John the Baptist went on to a more responsible position of authority than Elijah, yet it is hard to see the biblical account as showing John as more "perfected" than Elijah. Of the two charismatic regressions I have induced, there seems to be no pattern of markedly increased goodness, rather of service in the Body of Christ in different ways. I know of no evidence from the few reliable secular PLVs that show a definite pattern of moral progression. If we take the evidence of a child prodigy into account as reincarnation, we see not necessarily developing moral perfection, but increased skills for service to others.

Possibility of a Mixed System

Eastern religions assert that there is no other way to unloose the burden of sin (karma) than by retributive rebirth that is mediated by various disciplines of "higher consciousness." Thus reincarnation is an indispensable element for the progress of individuals. A Christian understanding of reincarnation would not be shackled by Eastern assumptions. Since the East's rigid understanding of karma is a pseudoproblem, and the biblical revelation of God is of a heavenly father with infinite capacity for forgiveness, then reincarnation could be seen not as a necessity, but as a possibility. The human spirit could very well make progress in the afterlife through either the intercessory prayers of others, or his or her own prayers on behalf on the Body of Christ. In this view, reincarnation is a possibility within God's plan for mankind, not something rigidly mandated by cosmic laws. The afterlife could very well include a mixed system of some souls progressing in the spirit-world, others reincarnation, and some entrapped in sheol and hell states. The determining factor for each individual case would not be either a "karmic board" (spiritualist) or the driving force of karmic energies (as described in the *Tibetan Book of the Dead*), but the Lord himself who would direct each spirit along the path best suited for its development (1 Sam. 2:6).[19]

A legitimate question to ask is from where do the individuals reincarnate? In this regard, the understanding of the multileveled afterlife discussed earlier is significant. The saints of God, persons who have already accepted Jesus as Lord, would reincarnate from a heaven-life with the Lord, and with some sort of "covenant" commission for further service to the Body. We can imagine that persons such as Agnes Sanford briefly recapitulate a sin-life, crisis, and conversion, then go on to spend the rest of their lives moving to higher degrees of service and wisdom. On the other hand, reincarnation for the unsaved would be a process in which they come out of the gray, prisonlike sheol areas of the afterlife. These persons would doubtlessly recapitulate a pattern of spiritual entrapment and emptiness which would place them at a spiritual crisis where they could choose to enter the Kingdom of God.

The concept of recapitulation, however, does not necessarily mean that those who escape the wheel of repetition will go forth in a lineal progression toward goodness and the Kingdom of God. It is entirely possible that the "natural" pattern of earthly entrapment in neurosis and unhappiness can be broken as well by demonic forces. That is, the demonic can "lift" a person out of merely neurotic patterns to a linear progression into intense forms of evil. Such world-demonic figures as Joseph Stalin, Adolph Hitler, and Idi Amin manifest an intensity of evil far beyond human neurosis. In a sense, a neurotic person is one who has an internal struggle of some sort and there is still a possibility for salvation. The type of intense evil of the Hitler-Amin type, or of the mugger who enjoys kicking the teeth out of old women, represents an order of evil far beyond the neurotic entrapment of the "natural" man identified by Gregory of Nyssa.[20]

Another type of evil may be just as serious. That is the evil of those who have known the Kingdom of God and then turned away from Christ. This is the central concern of the letter of Hebrews, and in Chapter 6:1–6 it is plain that for those persons there is no forgiveness. This was the meaning of Kenneth Hagin's vision (see p. 59), to remind Christians that the doctrine of salvation preached in Romans, which gives comfort and assurance to Christians that they need not be anxious about their salvation, is bounded by the warning in Hebrews.

Chapter 17

Testing the Fruit

In the West

There are several ways we believe the "fruit" of EJR-ACR-based theologies can be monitored so that the Body might either "approve what is excellent" (Phil. 1:9–11) or reject these theories as destructive. The first would be on a pastoral level. By this we mean that healing teams, professional and semiprofessional, with experience in inner-healing could begin to use PLVs as part of their Christian service. Indispensable would be the consistent monitoring of the sensors for both short- and long-range effects.

There are several healing experiments that might shed light on the extent of the ACR. One such experiment is suggested in John 9:1–3, the incident of the man born blind. As we noted, Jesus said that there was no ACR in this case, but, significantly, he did not rule out such a possibility for other cases. The Cindy dialogue hinted that at least some cases of birth defects may be related to sin and its transtemporal ACR. It has long been noted by Christian healers that persons with birth defects are particularly difficult to heal. Could this indicate a block to healing prayer caused by an unredeemed ACR? If so, could the blockage be broken by an inner-healing PLV? The possibility is worth testing.

More difficult to test, though still accountable, is the possibility of utilizing an EJR-ACR theology in evangelization. This could be done on an individual basis by inner-healing PLVs, but it also has potential for mass evangelization. Whether preaching with a theology based on the EJR-ACR can be more effective to large numbers than orthodox preaching is something that must be left to testing discernment. Much modern evangelization is based on the method of preaching the sinfulness of man and the consequence of this sin, eternal loss and hellfire. This is a product to a great extent of Augustinian theology, developed among those already exposed to the Gospel. The emphasis is on individual choice and responsibility for accepting the call of the Lord. This is neither wrong nor ineffective. It is especially effective as a revival technique where the public has some prior instruction in the Gospel and where there is already a sense of guilt. Many persons respond dramatically to this sort of evangelization.

Yet it is based on an unbalanced interpretation of scripture. The primary meaning of salvation is not to get to heaven and avoid hell, but "to enter into the Kingdom of God," and escape the Kingdom of Satan. Modern biblical scholars have shown this in important studies. For example, James Kallas in his *The Satanward View: A Study in Pauline Theology*[1] noticed that Saint Paul changed his vocabulary in preaching from the "Kingdom of God" to "salvation" after he was misunderstood as preaching political revolution (Acts 17:1–9). The major meaning of salvation is "earthy." It is salvation from the enslavement of sin, sickness, and demonic control. A further consequence of salvation is eternal life in the next age (heaven). This was the central message of Jesus' teaching. Until the coming of the Pentecostal-charismatic renewal, most Christian churches did no spiritual healing or exorcism, and for practical purposes becoming a Christian, aside from a genuine sense of inner peace, did not mean an escape from illness or demonic oppression.

This unconsciously forced a restricted connotation for "salvation" to mean "other-worldly," eternal life (dispensationalism). As a consequence, a common evangelistic technique has been to teach about hell in order to make the people desire something to be saved from. This is not "Good News."[2]

Yet even in the individualistic West, this form of evangelization is not universally effective. The concept that God would punish limited sin with infinite torture is disturbing to many people. They are not likely, they reason, to punish a child for lying with a term of life imprisonment. Why should God, if he is a loving Father, punish some sinner with eternal torture. Jesus did indeed preach hellfire and damnation, but only to those who were already believing Jews. As believers they needed correction and exhortation (Mk. 9:42–50). In the book of Acts (Ch. 17), and wherever we see Paul preaching to Gentiles, he preached truly good news of release from sin and demonic entanglements. He did *not* preach hellfire to unbelievers. He performed miracles to back up his proclamation that the Good News frees from the Kingdom of Darkness.

Presently in America we have a serious situation with the growth of a vast inner-city "underclass," people of little education who are mostly "unchurched" and ignorant of the most elementary gospel teachings. Many of these persons have smatterings of occult knowledge, especially in its most diabolical forms of magic and Caribbean spiritualism. For this underclass, a Gospel of Jesus Christ based on the theology of the EJR and ACR might have profound resonance due to the shadow truth elements in the underclass cults. It is certainly worth a try.

Implications for Third World Evangelization

The preaching based on the corporate salvation scheme of the EJR has special significance for the evangelization of the non-Western world. In many places in Asia and Africa, many a well-meaning missionary of the past century and a half has attempted to evangelize with a Western version of the "Good News." This was the terribly bad news that their unfortunate ancestors were in the flames of hell, but *if* they accepted Christ they could be saved.

In the century of fervent and systematic evangelization of China by Western preachers (from the 1850s to 1949), less than *one percent* of the Chinese were converted to Christianity. There were many factors to account for this, among them a confusion of Western manners, clothing, and education with the *essential* gospel message. But there may have been another serious theological error in associating the gospel with Augustinian-Calvinistic theology that only a few are saved. To a culture that revered its ancestors and had a finely developed concept of the corporate responsibilities of mankind, this was definitely *not* Good News. The concept that the unsaved ancestors were in hell was a terrifying thought to many a Christian convert in China. The most that the more liberal-minded missionaries of the nineteenth and early twentieth centuries could say is that they *might* not be damned, and that God's mercy was great. Catholic doctrine forbade praying for unbaptized ancestors, and Protestant theology had no concept at all of ministering to the dead.[3]

In spite of thirty years of Communism, most Chinese still greatly revere their immediate ancestors, even if they no longer have a religious cult of the dead. In the coming reevangelization of China it might be helpful to have a theology that takes into account the EJR and the corporate nature of salvation more seriously. For the Chinese, that sort of theological understanding of scripture would definitely be much better "Good News."

The EJR-ACR Theology for India

It is in India, however, where a Gospel that incorporated both the EJR and the ACR might be most helpful in the evangelization of India's Hindu population. The sad fact is that in spite of the presence of the Christian Church in India from early times (legend has it from the ministry of the apostle Saint Thomas) less than 2½ percent of the Indian population is Christian.

Many reasons have been given for this unsatisfactory state of affairs.

Most Christian observers, both indigenous and Western, have noted the overly close association of Indian Christianity with specifically Western patterns of thought, theology, liturgy, and all the things that make up "religious culture." This has had the effect of forcing a convert from Hinduism to forsake almost every element of his culture, his dress, eating habits, philosophical orientation, and so forth, to be accepted into the Christian community. This "cultural imperialism" was especially characteristic of Indian Christianity up to the last decades of the nineteenth century.

Recently, a completely different style and approach to Indian evangelization has developed. The newer approach has two sources, one Western and the other indigenous. In the last four decades a group of prominent Catholic monk-theologians have sought to form a dialogue with Hindu believers. The thrust of this effort, brought forth by such men as Thomas Merton, Dom Aelred Graham, and Bede Griffiths, is that, through dialogue, Hindu and Christian can discover that at the center of all authentic religious quest (especially contemplative-meditative disciplines) is found the same God.

Not all the monk-scholars came to the same conclusions. Bede Griffiths has maintained a good sense of the evangelical imperative that all Christians should have, and used dialogue and cultural accommodation as a way of sharing Christ with the Hindu seeker.[4] This is in the best tradition of Saint Paul's evangelical technique of being a Greek among Greeks and Jew among Jews. At the other extreme lies Dom Aelred Graham. His studies of Hindu mysticism finally led him to the astonishing conclusion that Christianity has little to offer to the Hindu sage, and that Western Christians are boorishly ignorant about the basics of contemplative prayer and therefore cannot really teach anything to the Hindu about God.[5] Dom Graham's position places the experience of contemplative prayer and meditative technique at the heart of the Christian faith instead of the faith-trust relationship with Jesus. It also assumes a "dispensationalist" view of Christianity, that the miracle-working, healing, exorcising, and liberating power of the trust relationship with Jesus is something that belongs to the mythical past. Thus it assumes that the Hindu believer is "above" the base desire to be healed, delivered, and liberated from the powers and influence of the demonic kingdom.

From a completely different direction there has been an attempt by Hindu-Christian thinkers of various denominations to redefine the essential Gospel in Hindu vocabulary and philosophy. These persons are Christian in that they accept the Bible as the definitive word of God and acknowledge the Lordship of Jesus Christ. At the same time they have retained much of their Hindu cultural and philosophical heritage. It is not possible here to examine specific Hindu-Christian writers who have labored mightily and produced great fruit in this area. Much has been and continues to be written about Hindu-Christian theology.[6]

The major thrust of Hindu-Christian theology has been the attempt to adapt the extensive Hindu vocabulary to the use of traditional Christian doctrines. Much attention has been given along these lines in efforts to define the concept of the Trinity in Hindu terminology, and to suggest that Hindu scriptures had a positive shadow-truth revelation about the Trinity centuries before Christian scriptures. Other Hindu-Christian thinkers have attempted to relate the divinity of Jesus in terms of the Hindu Avatar.

Strangely, reincarnation and karma have received little positive attention from Hindu-Christian thinkers. On the one hand this is surprising because belief in reincarnation is a basic assumption of the major non-Muslim sects in India. So much is this the case that one of the earliest indigenous Hindu-Christian denominations in India, the "Chet Ramis" of the 1870s drifted naturally into a modified doctrine of reincarnation. This sect was established in the Punjab by Chet Ram after he experienced a vision of Jesus, who told him to build a church and to place a Bible in it. He acquired a considerable congregation and the church lingered on to the 1920s, but after his death his followers began to venerate Chet Ram as a reincarnation of Jesus. This certainly would not have encouraged more-sophisticated Hindu-Christians to consider the issue of reincarnation.[7]

There are more important reasons why the problem of reincarnation was not addressed. Christian missionaries who imparted the faith to the Hindu brethren were aware that both rebirth and karma were central to Hinduism and heretical in terms of normative Western Christianity. The result was that Christian thinkers in India, indigenous or missionary, have laid great stress on the proclamation of the resurrection of the body as the antithesis to the belief in reincarnation, and that true "rebirth" is rebirth into belief in Jesus Christ.

What we have is one of those gentle ironies that have occurred in the history of Christianity. For over a century Hindu-Christian theologians had striven to recast Christianity that is both authentically Christian and biblical, yet does justice to Hindu thought and culture. Yet they never gave serious thought to reopening the question of reincarnation or karma. It was the academic theologians of the West who did the pioneer world in this area.

In any case, a Christian Gospel incorporating both the EJR (as either "force" or personality-continuity) and the ACR has great evangelical possibilities in the Indian subcontinent. The Hinu-Christian may rightly proclaim to his nonbelieving countrymen that Christ breaks the bonds of karma (ACR), and then back up this amazing proclamation by *demonstrating it* in PLV prayer. For the pious Hindu who struggles constantly to form an attitude of acceptance (or, as it would be called in this country, "higher consciousness") of his caste situation, that could be a wonderfully liberating revelation. This does not mean that a Hindu would be miraculously liberated from his painful economic situation, but rather that the burden of passive acceptance and caste guilt (guilt based on the concept that birth in a low caste is the result of sin in a past life) would be lifted. To a great extent current Hindu-Christian evangelization does the same thing. The advantage of preaching an EJR-ACR Gospel is that it could proclaim Christ's liberation while allowing the Hindu to maintain what is familiar to him, the concept of karma-reincarnation. This would be in harmony with Paul's technique of maximum accommodation with Gentile culture. In regard to the substantial differences between the ACR and classical definitions of karma, Bible study would clarify that situation. In India we have a situation where the word karma serves as a positive shadow-truth and the word itself need not be avoided.

The Final Accountability: Jesus as Lord of All History

For Christians, the most important criterion for any theology must be, does it glorify the Lordship of Jesus of Nazareth? We believe that a theology that integrates a concept of a widespread EJR-ACR does in fact glorify Jesus naturally to a greater extent than the traditional view.

In ways we can only dimly see, the EJR means that the Body of Christ extends not only geographically, but temporarily to such time-places as Egypt in the fifth century B.C. or Gaul at the time of the Punic Wars. This is not so much a new idea as a refurbishing of an old one. The great biblical scholar Oscar Cullmann described in his book *Christ and Time: The Primitive Christian Conception of Time and History*[8] that the apostolic church believed the cross to stand at the midpoint of history and that its salvation and influence extended both *forward* and *backward* in time. Cullmann saw 1 Peter 3–4 as a *central* scripture in the primitive church's trust that Jesus was Lord of all time and could extend his kingdom even to those who lived and died before his sojourn on earth.[9]

Either interpretation of the EJR (empathetic identification or reincarnation) asserts this spiritual truth. If the EJR means reincarnation, it implies that sooner or later *everyone* will have an *opportunity* to accept the Gospel before the Last Judgment. If the EJR is really a spiritual empathetic phenomenon, then the Kingdom of God can be extended to them via the inner-healing of a PLV. Either way, Jesus is glorified as the head of his body, which includes many more members than formerly imagined. A problem in accepting this biblical view is that we have become accustomed to the Augustinian-Calvinistic theologies which proclaim a limited

Kingdom of God, a kingdom limited to the tiny minority of those believing the "right knowledge" of orthodoxy and who were fortunate enough to be born within earshot of Christian preaching.

We must, however, make a distinction between the idea that the Gospel will be preached to all mankind and the concept that all mankind will be saved. The latter concept is called universalism, and, as we pointed out in Chapter 2, it is a motif that has many scripture passages to support it, especially 1 Corinthians 15:27–28. The problem, of course, is that there is an opposing motif in the Bible about the eternal punishment of the wicked. What the ultimate reality and reconciliation of these two motifs may be is perhaps a mystery in the mind of God not intended for us to understand. The EJR implies universal proclamation of the Gospel rather than the necessity of universal salvation. In this manner Jesus, through his body, offers salvation to all men, but does not force it on anyone. This is a much better and glorifying vision than the Augustinian-Calvinistic view that Jesus restricted the opportunities for salvation to a select minority.

An appreciation and elaboration of the EJR-ACR continues this trend by extending the dimension and complexity of the relationships in the Kingdom of God. Jude's "common salvation" and Saint Paul's concern for the organic unity of the "body of Christ" acquire a fuller meaning. Just as the Christian's appreciation of God's awesome power was expanded with the development of astronomy, so our appreciation of the headship of Christ will be increased as we develop a better understanding of the EJR-ACR.

Notes

Introduction

1. Frederick Lenz, Lifetimes: *True Accounts of Reincarnation* (Indianapolis: Bobbs-Merrill, 1979).
2. Ibid., pp. 66–67.
3. Edith Fiore, *You Have Been Here Before: A Psychologist Looks at Past Lives* (New York: Coward, McCann & Geoghegan, 1978), pp. 96–108.
4. New York: American Society for Psychical Research, 1966; see the last chapter, "General Discussion."
5. In any type of unknown phenomenon it is always possible to invent an infinite number of hypotheses, many of which cannot be immediately disproven. The following five have been chosen because, given minor alterations in vocabulary and accent, they represent the great bulk of belief as to the origins of the PLV phenomenon. I am mindful that the open-minded person must always have an additional category to consider, that of "none of the above." The history of science has been filled with examples where the early theories were *all* discredited, as for instance the early theories of electricity.
6. *Journal of the American Institute of Hypnosis* 16:1 (January 1975), pp. 35–48.
7. George Gallup, Jr., and William Proctor, *Adventures in Immortality* (New York: McGraw-Hill, 1982). See Chapter 11, and especially the tables on pp. 192–193.
8. See: Pat Brooks, *Out! In the Name of Jesus* (Carol Stream, IL.: Creation House, 1972), p. 122
9. Mark Albrecht and Brooks Alexander, "Interview With Dave Hunt," *SCP Journal* 4:2 (Winter 1980–1981), p. 8.

The demonic counterfeit hypothesis is not limited to Protestant fundamentalist circles. In 1976 Malachi Martin, an ex-Jesuit, published an important work on the processes of demonic possession called *Hostage to the Devil: The Possession and Exorcism of Five Living Americans* (New York: Reader's Digest Press, 1976). One of the cases described in the book was of the possession of a prominent university parapsychologist who became possessed during a series of experimental PLVs. The fundamental error made by the parapsychologist was to assume that all psychic phenomena are spiritual and that all things spiritual are by nature positive and good. This is a very common position among investigators in the ESP field and the case described by Martin is an indispensable warning to Christians investigating these fields. (The case of the "Rooster and Tortoise" pp. 321–406).

As valuable as is *Hostage to the Devil*, Mr. Martin has made a serious methodological and theological error. He essentially *believes the Devil!* This ludicrous situation is not uncommon among a minority of Catholic exorcists. They believe that once the exorcist has forced the demon to reveal its name (which is normal in the process of exorcism, see Mk. 5:1–20) it is under the power of the exorcist and can be *constrained to tell the truth*. This is simply not true. The Devil is the "Father of Lies," and although it is both biblical and useful to know the demon's name in the process of an exorcism, to ask the demon anything beyond that is to invite serious confusion. The demon will respond to any question with a mix of error and truth that will fit into the current beliefs of those present while leading them to some unsuspecting error. The information "forced" from the demon is of the same order as any form of spiritualist utterance; it is a form of "cheap knowledge" (discussed in Part II) which blends a little truth with a great lie.

In the case of the possessed parapsychologist, the possessing demon "confessed" that it was a demonic entity that gave the parapsychologist his original PLV. Further, all PLVs are produced by demonic forces, and that there is no reincarnation. Now any or all of those statements may or may not be true. They cannot be taken as truth because a demon was "forced" to reveal them under the power of an exorcist. If the demonic hypothesis is true a different order of evidence must be found to collaborate it.

10. "Reincarnation Research: Method and Interpretation," in Martin Ebon, ed., *The Signet Handbook of Parapsychology* (New York: New American Library, Signet, 1978), pp. 313–24.

11. This book is the result of the normal processes of scholarship as indicated in the notes and bibliography, plus my own involvement in PLV casework. Additionally, I have made extensive use of taped lectures and seminars offered by several Christian institutions. Readers who may wish either to confirm or follow up this aspect of my research are advised to write for the catalogues of the national libraries I have used: Springs of Living Water, Richardson Springs, CA 95973; Lord's Own Tape Ministry, 5529 Granada Rd., Fort Myers, FL 33907; The Cutler Memorial CFO Tape Library, 5516 Lyndale Ave. S., Rm. 108, Minneapolis, MN 55419.

Chapter 1 — The Logos and Its Shadow

1. In Part II there are extensive descriptions of both spiritualism and the Metaphysical movement. The "occult" may be briefly defined here as a loosely tied group of beliefs that include magic, self-salvation doctrines, and cosmologies that are alien to traditional Western Christianity. Certain occult groups participate in witchcraft and Satan worship, but this is not by any means universal.

2. As in the famous *Honest to God* by J.A.T. Robinson (Philadelphia: Westminster Press, 1963) and Harvey Cox's *The Secular City* (New York: Macmillan, 1965). Father Andrew M. Greeley has shown convincingly from solid sociological data that the "crisis of faith" of the 1960s was limited to academic circles, and that, in fact, the faith of the laity was healthy. See his: *Unsecular Man:*

The Persistence of Religion (New York: Dell, Delta, 1972). I doubt that a single academic theologian who preached the "death of God" ever attended any of the huge healing-evangelism rallies of the 1950s and 1960s.

3. My principal sources for this section are: Henry Chadwick, *Early Christian Thought and the Classical Tradition: Studies in Justin, Clement and Origen* (New York: Oxford University Press, 1962); Oscar Cullmann, *The Christology of the New Testament*, trans. Shirley C. Guthrie and Charles A.M. Hall (Philadelphia: Westminster Press, 1963); Jean Danielou, *Gospel Message and Hellenistic Culture*, trans. John Austin Baker (Philadelphia: Westminster Press, 1973); and G.L. Prestige, *God in Patristic Thought* (London: SPCK, 1952).

4. The Logos theology of the Church Fathers placed many of them, such as Origen and Gregory of Nyssa, at ease with contemporary knowledge and philosophy. Had Christians maintained an active Logos theology both the Copernican and Darwinian controversies might have been less violent and more enlightening. There is a passage in Gregory of Nyssa (d. 399) which indicates he believed in evolutionary creation. See: Gregory of Nyssa, *On the Soul and Resurrection*, in: *Ascetical Works*, trans. Virginia Woods Callahan (Washington: Catholic University of America Press, 1967), p. 221.

5. 1 *Apology* 5:2–4. Cited in Jean Danielou, *Gospel Message*, pp. 31–32.

6. Danielou, *Gospel Message*, Chapter 18, "Demonology," pp. 427–33.

7. See a recent book by an experienced missionary, Don Richardson, *Eternity in Their Hearts* (Ventura, CA: Regal Books, 1981). The main point of this fine work is that missionaries should be like Paul, and be alert to the shadow truths of host cultures in order to more effectively propagate the Gospel.

8. Dom Odo Casel, *The Mystery of Christian Worship and Other Writings*, ed. Berkhard Neunheuser (Westminster, MD: Newman Press, 1962). See also Joseph Campbell, ed., *Pagan and Christian Mysteries*, trans. Ralph Manheim and R.F.S. Hall (New York: Harper & Row, Torchbooks, 1963).

9. Walter R. Martin, *The Kingdom of the Cults*, rev. ed. (Minneapolis: Bethany Fellowship, 1968), p. 18.

10. Dom David Geraets, "Theological Perspectives," Tape #EX-64 (Richardson Springs, CA: Springs of Living Water, 1977); and his "Questions and Answers," Tape #EX-70 (Richardson Springs: Springs of Living Water, 1977).

Chapter 2—Ambiguity in the Mature Spiritual Life

1. New York: Harper & Row, Perennial Library, 1973.

2. Ibid., p. 150.

3. Ibid., see Chapter 10, "Hallucinations." Interestingly, he noted that the counter for such "voice attack" was prayer, Bible reading, and an ethical life.

4. Ibid., see Chapter 11, "Mystical Experiences: The Flowering of Understanding."

5. The Wisdom books are Job, Proverbs, Ecclesiastes, plus Ben Sirachy and the wisdom of Solomon of the Catholic canon.

6. This has long been appreciated by biblical scholars. See James L. Crenshaw, *Old Testament Wisdom* (Atlanta: John Knox Press, 1981), Chapter 9, especially p. 220.

7. Ardt and Gingrich, *A Greek-English Lexicon of the New Testament* (Chicago: University of Chicago Press, 4th ed., 1957), p. 16.

8. In: W.D. Davies, *Christian Origins and Judaism* (Philadelphia: Westminster Press, 1962).

9. Acts 15, Peter gives the longer speech, but James has the last and authoritative word.

10. For Kierkegaard's paradoxal theology see his *Concluding Unscientific Postscript* and *Training in Christianity*, both of which are in *A Kierkegaard Anthology*, ed. Robert Bretall (New York: Modern Library, 1946). See also William Barrett's *Irrational Man: A Study in Existential Philosophy* (New York: Doubleday and Co., 1958).

11. Reinhold Niebuhr, *The Nature and Destiny of Man*, 2 vols. (New York: Charles Scribner's Sons, 1941, 1943).

12. Three vols. in one (Chicago: University of Chicago Press, 1967), Vol 3, Chapter 1, "Life, Its Ambiguities and the Quest for Unambiguous Life," pp. 11–107.

13. Paul Tillich, *My Search for Absolutes*, drawings by Saul Steinberg (New York: Simon and Schuster, 1967).

14. Ibid., pp. 132–33.

15. *Systematic Theology*, Vol 3. (Chicago: University of Chicago Press, 1967), p. 245.

16. *The Shaking of the Foundations* (New York: Charles Scribner's Sons, 1948), Chapter 11, "The Yolk of Religion."

17. Ibid. p. 125.

18. See Father Dennis Bennett, "Fellowship in the Spirit," tape (Richardson Springs, CA.: Springs of Living Water), no. DB-22, n.d.; Larry Christenson, "Thursday Evening Session," tape (Ann Arbor Conference Cassettes) CA. 1977; Dr. Howard Ervin, "Quench Not the Spirit," tape (Richardson Springs: Springs of Living Water), no. HE-10, n.d., Don Basham, "Life in the Spirit: Man's Part in Miracles" (Richardson Springs: Springs of Living Water), no, DBB-1, n.d.; Kenneth Copeland, "Campmeeting "82," tape (Tulsa: Faith Library), no. 18523, July 31, 1982.

19. Tillich, *Search*, Chapter 3, "The Absolute and Relative Element in Moral Decisions."

20. *The Moral Judgement of the Child* (New York: The Free Press, 1965).

Chapter 3—Discernment: From the Bible to Saint John of the Cross

1. Catholic writers claim that positive discernment can verify the real presence of Jesus in the Eucharist. A noted Protestant scholar and teacher, Dr. Howard Ervin of Oral Roberts University, points out that discernment extends to the realm of purely human spirits, i.e., that within the spirit of a person there abides certain specific qualities, such as the spirit of hospitality, or of compassion. See his tape, "Miracles, Prophecies and Discernment" (Richardson Springs: Springs of Living Water) no. HE-8, n.d.

2. Laurent Volken, *Visions, Revelations and the Church*, trans. Edward Gallagher (New York: P.J. Kenedy and Sons, 1963), p. 99.

3. For a vivid account of the Pentecostal Armenians' escape from Turkish

massacre during World War I, and of the failure of the more traditional Armenian Christians to heed repeated prophetic warnings see: Demos Shakarian, *The Happiest People on Earth*, "as told by" John and Elizabeth Sherrill (Old Tappan, NJ: Chosen Books, 1975), Chapter 1, "The Message From Over the Mountain."

4. See the excellent study by Morton T. Kelsey, "The Dreams of the Hebrews and Other Ancient Peoples," in his *God, Dreams and Revelation* (Minneapolis: Augsburg Press, 1974), pp. 17–48.

5. Jacques Guillet, S.J., "Sacred Scripture," in Jacques Guillet, et al., *Discernment of Spirits*, trans. Sr. Innocentia Richards (Collegeville, MN: Liturgical Press, 1970), p. 30.

6. Again a chapter by Morton Kelsey, "The Dreams and Visions of the New Testament," in his *Dreams* gives a very adequate survey of the topic.

7. That the trance state focuses the mind on one area of attention has been noted by secular writers in reference to the hypnotic state. See Merton M. Gill and Margaret Brenman, *Hypnosis and Related States: Psychoanalytic Studies in Regression* (New York: International Universities Press, 1959), pp. 47–48.

8. The exception to this is found in a major work of the biblical scholar Oscar Cullmann, *Christ and Time: The Primitive Christian Conception of Time and History*, trans. Floyd V. Filson, rev. ed. (Philadelphia: Westminster Press, 1964). In this book the author sees testing as a major element in Paul's Spirit-based morality. He does not directly relate testing to general discernment. See Part IV, Chapter 2, "The Individual Man and the Present Stage of Redemptive History."

9. See R.A. Knox, *Enthusiasm: A Chapter in the History of Religion* (New York: Oxford University Press, 1950), Chapter Three for an excellent critical evaluation of the Montanist movement.

10. See Eusebius, *The Ecclesiastical History*, 5:16 and 17.

11. I am indebted for this fine insight on the discernment of the early Church to an English scholar, Fr. Simon Tugwell, O.P., *Did You Receive the Spirit?* (London: Darton, Longman and Todd, 1972), p. 72.

12. Knox, *Enthusiasm*.

13. Athanasius, *The Life of St. Anthony*.

14. A truly wonderful edition of two of his major works is now available in paperback: Evagrius Ponticus, *The Praktikos: Chapters on Prayer*, trans. and intro. by J.E. Bamberger (Kalamazoo, MI: Cistercian Publications, 1978).

15. *Chapters on Prayer*, #46

16. "On Various Evil Thoughts," #4. Found in *Early Fathers From the Philokalia*, ed. & trans. E. Kadloubovsky and G.E. H. Palmer (London: Faber and Faber, 1954).

17. *Praktikos*, #54

18. There have been many editions of this forteenth-century classic. Several are in paperback.

19. See the classic description of this state as described by St. Teresa in: St. Teresa of Avila, *The Life of St. Teresa*, trans. E. Allison Peers (Garden City: Doubleday and Co., Image Books, 1960), pp. 177–78.

20. Dionysius the Areopagite, *The Divine Names and the Mystical Theology*, trans. and intro. by C.E. Rolt, (London: SPCK, 1940).

21. An elaboration of this point is found in Judith Tydings, *Gathering a People* (Plainfield, MJ: Logos International, 1977).

22. See his: *The Holiness-Pentecostal Movement in the United States* (Grand Rapids: William B. Eerdmans Publishing Co., 1971).

23. Dr. Vinson Synan, "The Role of the Holy Spirit and the Gifts of the Spirit in the Mystical Tradition," *One in Christ*, 10, 2 (1974), pp. 193–202.

24. "Lesson on Prayer," tape, (FGBMFT: Costa Mesa, CA), no. 5 NYC 66, n.d.

25. See her *Interior Castle*, 5, 4. Available in several translations and in paperback. The book is divided into seven major sections or "mansions" and chapters within the mansions. I used the translation by E. Allison Peers (Garden City: Doubleday and Co., Image Books, 1961).

26. Mansion 4, Chapter 3.

27. Ibid.

28. Several editions available; a paperback one is translated by E. Allison Peers (Garden City: Doubleday and Co., Image Books, 1958).

29. See especially Book 2 of *Ascent of Mount Carmel* for his attack on personal revelations.

Chapter 4—Discernment: From the Reformation to the Present

1. For a classic description of the extremes of Catholic mystical spirituality see William James's *Varieties of Religious Experience*, foreword by Jacques Barzun (New York: New American Library, Mentor Books, 1958), lectures 14 and 15.

2. Bengt R. Hoffman, *Luther and the Mystics* (Minneapolis: Augsburg Publishing House, 1976).

3. A. Poulain, S.J., *The Graces of Interior Prayer: A Teatise on Mystical Theology*, trans. from 6th ed. Leonora L. Yorke Smith (St. Louis: B. Herder Book Co., 1950), Chapter 32.

4. For a definition and sketch of the Pentecostals and Charismatics see Part III, Chapter 11.

5. I remember on one occasion being at an Episcopalian charismatic prayer meeting where they had a ritual of "renouncing the occult." The lead priest rattled off a list of "occult" activities that the congregation had to renounce that included "herbology" and "mysticism." I later found out that he had a high opinion of Christian mysticism but apparently did not want to "complicate" the issue for his group. His public attitude is not atypical of many charismatic leaders who feel that the "safe" way to authentic Christian spirituality is total acceptance of the fundamentalist point of view.

6. New York: Oxford University Press, 1961.

7. Francis MacNutt, O.P. "Resting in the Spirit," in his *The Power to Heal* (Notre Dame: Ave Maria Press, 1977) pp. 189–224. Also, Morton Kelsey, "Slaying in the Spirit: The Place of Trance and Ecstasy in Christian Experience," in *Discernment: A Study in Ecstasy and Evil* (New York: Paulist Press, 1978) pp. 10–50.

8. MacNutt, "Resting," p. 193.

9. Kelsey, "Slaying," pp. 20–25.

10. Among the best recent works is Dennis and Rita Bennett's *Trinity of Man* (Plainfield, NJ: Logos International, 1979).

11. One of the many clearly authentic accounts of a saint who had many psychic-spiritual experiences is *Adomnan's Life of Columba*, ed. Alan Orr Anderson (London: Thomas Nelson & Sons, 1961), written about A.D. 690.

12. For a presentation of this traditional Catholic view of the powers of the soul see the controversial book by Malachi Martin, *Hostage to the Devil* (New York: Reader's Digest Press, 1976), especially the case of the "Rooster and the Tortoise." This is a case of severe possession in which a parapsychologist allowed his psychic powers to fall under the dominion (and deception) of demonic powers. His exorcism was performed by a priest, who like many a good Irishman, had psychic powers from birth, but who allowed his gifts to be used and enhanced by the Holy Spirit in the course of his Christian life.

13. See the wonderful biography of Nee by his friend and Christian missionary Angus Kinnear, *Against the Tide* (Wheaton, IL.: Tyndale House, 1978).

14. New York: Christian Fellowship Publishers, 1968.

15. New York: Christian Fellowship Publishers, 1972. This was originally planned as an appendix to *The Spiritual Man*.

16. Ibid. p. 29.

17. Ibid. p. 33.

18. Ibid. pp. 81–86.

19. 2nd ed. (New York: Fleming H. Revell, 1896).

20. Ibid. pp. 84–85.

21. Ventura, CA: Regal Books, 1981.

22. Ibid. p. 57 ff.

23. See a nationally known Methodist evangelist who has taken the "Catholic" viewpoint: Rev. Tommy Tyson, "Lifting the Natural to the Supernatural," tape #665A (Ft. Myers, FL: Lord's Own Tape Ministry, n.d.).

24. See for example, Karl Rahner, S.J., *Visions and Prophecies*, in *Inquiries* (New York: Herder and Herder, 1964), p. 120 note 34.

25. Translated by Leonora L. Yorke Smith (St. Louis: B. Herder Book Co., 1950). This is an expensive hard-cover edition, but well worth it to any one who values the spiritual dimensions of counseling.

26. Ibid., p. 359 ff.

27. Ibid., p. 380 ff.

28. Originally published as a separate volume, but currently available in English only in an anthology of his works called *Inquiries* (New York: Herder and Herder, 1964).

29. Exactly the same point is expressed by Kenneth Hagin in his *The Gift of Prophecy* (Tulsa: Kenneth Hagin Ministries, Faith Library, 1969), pp. 19–20.

30. *Visions*, p. 92.

31. Cf. the vision recorded in Bede, *A History of the English Church and People*, 5, 12; with Kenneth Hagin's *I Believe in Visions* (Old Tappan, NJ: Fleming H. Revell Co., 1972), pp. 9–16.

32. It is interesting to note that a recent attempt from a conservative Protestant viewpoint to discredit the Moody type of pleasant afterlife experiences and prove that there is indeed a hell came up with many different visions of hell. See Maurice Rawlings, M.D., *Beyond Death's Door* (New York: Bantam Books, 1979).

33. See Kenneth E. Hagin, *I Believe in Visions* (Old Tappan, NJ.: Fleming H. Revell Co., 1972), for his autobiography and details of his main visionary experience.

34. Atlanta: Mockingbird Books, 1975.

35. Hagin, *Visions*, Chapter Two, "Come Up Hither."

36. Ibid., p. 33.

37. Ibid., p. 50.

38. Kenneth E. Hagin, *The Origin and Operation of Demons* (Tulsa: Kenneth Hagin Evangelistic Association, n.d.), p. 26. This pamphlet contains a fuller account of the vision.

39. Old Tappan, NJ: Spire Books, 1963.

40. New York: Pyramid Books, 1974.

41. Still available from Springs of Living Water Tape Library, Richardson Springs, CA 95973. Tape no. DW-8, "The Coming Persecution."

42. In a Charismatic church where I frequently worship we have been met by similar false prophecies. The same essential pattern has emerged: separate from the "unclean" world and obey no one but the voice of the Holy Spirit, break all institutional bounds. On one occasion such a prophecy degenerated into a shrill accusation of "witchcraft in this place!" and the pastor had to firmly ask the ushers to escort the woman out of the Church. It seems the demonic kingdom is especially fearful that the Charismatic movement will remain the "leaven" of the whole church.

43. See "Persecution for Charismatic Catholics?" *New Covenant* 3, 6 (Jan. 1974), p. 13.

44. "David Wilkerson's Vision." *New Covenant*, 3, 6 (Jan. 1974), pp. 11–12.

45. See, for example, Herbert Thruston, S.J., *Surprising Mystics* (Chicago: Henry Regnery Co., 1955), Chapter 14, "The False Visionaries of Lourdes," and Rahner, *Visions*, p. 92, note 8; 143, note 61; 168 ff.; 185, note 131; 186–87, notes 133–34.

46. An exception to this is the classic study of the "Great Awakening" of the 1740s by Jonathan Edwards, *Religious Affection*, ed. John E. Smith (New Haven: Yale University Press, 1959). This work deserves more attention than it currently receives.

Chapter 5—The Roads to Spiritual Death

1. See the novel by the great Catholic writer François Mauriac, *A Woman of the Pharisees*, trans. Gerard Hopkins (London: Eyre and Spottiswoode, 1946); and the earlier classic of Spanish literature by Benito Pérez Galdós, *Doña Perfecta*, trans. Mary J. Serrano (New York: Harper & Brothers, 1896).

2. See Stewart Means, *Saint Paul and the Anti-Nicene Church* (London: Adan & Charles Black, 1903).

3. For a review of the relevant literature see Robert Haardt, *Gnosis: Character and Testimony*, trans. J.F. Hendry (Leiden: E.J. Brill, 1971).

4. R.M. Grant, *Gnosticism and Early Christianity* (New York: Columbia University Press, 1957), Chapter 1, "Nature of Gnosticism."

5. Ibid., p. 11.

6. Walter Schmithals, *Gnosticism in Corinth: An Investigation of the Letters to the Corinthians,* trans. John E. Steely (Nashville: Abingdon Press, 1971); *Paul and the Gnostics*, trans. John E. Steely (Nashville: Abingdon Press, 1972).

7. Taken from part 3, "The Heretical Theology in Corinth," in *Gnosticism in Corinth.*

8. It should also be noted that Schmithals considers proxy baptism (1 Cor. 15:29) as a distinctly Gnostic procedure (*Gnosticism in Corinth*, pp. 256–59). I believe this to be incorrect and probably due to his Protestant roots. Schmithals

went to great pains to explain why sacramental prayer is alien to Gnostic thinking. Why the gnostics in Corinth would believe baptism would help the dead if, in their view, it does not help the living, he does not explain. It must also be noted that praying for the dead is a concept described in *Second Maccabees* 38:45, written much before possible Gnostic influence. Further, Bultmann, Schmithal's distinguished teacher, sees this peculiar rite as part of Paul's sacramental understanding (see R. Bultmann, *Theology of the New Testament*, vol. 1, p. 141).

9. The monk-theologian Dom Aelred Graham has said this of the Catholic Church in his *The End of Religion: Autobiographical Explorations* (New York: Harcourt Brace Jovanovich, Harvest, 1971), p. 91. Cf. Fr. Richard Rohr, "The Gospel of John, #2," tape (Richardson Springs: Springs of Living Water), no. FX-20.

10. Cf. Augustine's and St. Thomas's attitude towards heresy with that of the "heretic" Origen in his dialogue with a certain bishop Hereclidus who believed in two Gods; in Anne Fremantle, ed., *A Treasury of Early Christianity* (New York: New American Library, Mentor, 1960), p. 290 ff.

Chapter 6 — Karma, Spiritualism, and the Metaphysical Movement

1. Frank J. MacHovec, "Hypnosis Before Mesmer," *American Journal of Clinical Hypnosis* 17:4 (April 1975): pp. 215–19.

2. For an extended presentation of the concept of karma by those who believe in it, see Virginia Hanson, ed., *Karma: The Universal Law of Harmony* (Wheaton, IL: Theosophical Publishing House, 1975).

3. L.H. Leslie-Smith, "Karma and Reincarnation," in Hanson, *Karma*, pp. 26–34.

4. For an excellent discussion, both philosophical and biblical, of the inadequacies of the traditional view of Hell, see John H. Hick, *Death and Eternal Life* (New York: Harper & Row, 1976).

5. *Concordant Discord: The Interdependence of Faiths* (Oxford: Clarendon Press, 1970), p. 103.

6. See Harold Hill, *How to Live Like a King's Kid* (Plainfield, NJ: Logos International, 1974).

7. Gerhard Von Rad, *Wisdom in Israel* (Nashville: Abingdon, 1972), Chapter 7, Section 2, "Cause and Effect: The Act-Consequence Relationship," pp. 124–37.

8. Ibid., pp. 126–27.

9. The modern classic of healing prayer which traces the this-worldly ACR between illness and sin and negative thinking is Glenn Clark's *How To Find Health through Prayer* (New York: Harper & Brothers, 1940). This work attempts to correlate specific bodily ailments with patterns of sin and negative thinking. See Chapter 4, "Washing Out the Roots."

10. Wheaton, IL: Theosophical Publishing House, 1967, pp. 62–66. See the same distortion of Galatians 6:7 in Noel Street's *Reincarnation: How to Recall Your Past Lives* (Goose Creek, SC: Lotus Ashram, 1974), p. 17.

11. See also Exodus 34:7; Numbers 14:18; Deuteronomy 5:9.

12. See the very popular work by Raphael Gasson, *The Challenging Counterfeit* (Plainfield, NJ: Logos International, 1966), originally published in England much earlier.

13. The novel, and later movie, by William Blatty, *The Exorcist* (New York: Harper & Row, 1971), correctly describes the Roman Catholic position on this matter. You may remember that the demon tried to confuse Fr. Damien by speaking with the voice of his recently deceased mother.

14. See the pioneer work by John L. Nevius, *Demon Possession and Allied Themes* (New York: Fleming H. Revell, 1896), especially the chapter "Spiritualism." This classic work has been newly reprinted: Grand Rapids: Kregel Publications, 1968. The earliest specific identification of mediumship as demonic counterfeit that I have found in Christian writings has been a couple of booklets printed by the Seventh Day Adventists in response to the American spiritualist revival of the 1850s. See John C. Bywater, *The Mystery Solved: or, A Bible expose of the spirit rappings, showing that they are not caused by the spirits of the dead, but by evil demons or devils* (Rochester: Advent Harbinger Office, 1852). Another one, by an anonymous author was entitled *Mesmeric and spirit rapping manifestations, scripturally exposed, as neither from electricity nor spirits of the dead, but rather from internal evil spirits . . .* (New York: R.T. Young, 1852).

15. Vol. 5, *The Collected Works of C.G. Jung* (New York: Bollingen Foundation, 1956).

16. Cf. with the work of Wilson Van Dusen described in Part I, Chapter 2.

17. See "Healing and the Afterlife," Tape #3, Pecos, TX: Dove Cassettes, 1981.

18. Walter R. Martin, a meticulous Christian scholar on the cults calls Spiritualism a "masquerade of demonic forces" in his *The Kingdom of the Cults*, rev. ed. (Minneapolis: Bethany Fellowship, 1968), p. 199.

19. For a sympathetic, non-Christian view of Swedenborg see Wilson Van Dusen, *The Presence of Other Worlds: The Psychological Spiritual Findings of Emanuel Swedenborg* (New York: Harper & Row, 1974). For the seer's single most important book see Emanuel Swedenborg, *Heaven and Its Wonders and Hell*, trans. John C. Ager, (New York: Citadel Press, 1965).

20. See Colin Wilson, *The Occult: A History* (New York: Random House, 1971), the note on p. 278 for a succinct summary of nineteenth-century spiritualism.

21. J. Stillson Judah, *The History and Philosophy of the Metaphysical Movement in America* (Philadelphia: Westminster Press, 1967), p. 53.

22. For an excellent critical study of this fraud see Gertrude Marvin Williams, *Madame Blavatsky, Priestess of the Occult* (New York: Alfred A. Knopf, 1946).

23. Judah, *Metaphysical Movement*, p. 73.

24. When I first became interested in the occult I assumed a total correlation between spiritualism and reincarnation. In the summer of 1976 I attended the South East regional convention of the Spiritual Frontiers Fellowship (SEF) in Charlotte, N.C. and was astonished to hear the world-famous psychic healer and medium Olga Warrall denounce reincarnation and tell us how "her spirits" assured her that it was all foolishness. I and practically everyone else in the audience thought this was strange and even "heretical." It was only later that I learned that her view was the one of classical spiritualism. For a biography of Olga Warrall see Edwina Cerutti, *Olga Warrall: Mystic With the Healing Hands* (New York: Harper & Row, 1975).

25. Wilson, *Occult*, p. 279, cited from Swedenborg's *Earths in the Universe*.

26. For an example of this tragicomical process of false scientific revelations and engineering secrets see the incident taken from the early years of spiritualism that is described in Slater Brown's, *The Heyday of Spiritualism* (New York: Pocket

Books, 1972), Chapter 11, "The New Motive Power." A group of "engineering spirits" led by none other than "Ben Franklin" directed a Unitarian minister-turned-medium to build an "electrolizer" which was to provide mankind with unlimited amounts of energy. He spent a small fortune and exhausted himself assembling a Rube Goldberg-type device that quivered once and did nothing thereafter.

27. In the several years I spent attached to an Atlanta metaphysical and spiritualist group, The Foundation of Truth, I earned a reputation as something of a pest for asking embarrassing questions like: "How do you know that is true?" or "What are your sources for that?" One psychic told me that I was reading too many books and that I should "slow down" and absorb the "teachings" better.

28. Saint Paul is difficult to understand much of the time. Many readers assume that to be the product of cultural differences or translation. That is not true; Saint Paul wrote in *terrible* Greek. The poor quality of his prose was considered by some early Christians as evidence that his letters were *not* inspired by the Holy Spirit.

29. A tragic and unnecessary controversy has continued for a century over the scientific meaning of the creation story in Genesis. It is only the spiritualist writings which are intentionally precise, unambiguous, and "scientific" in their revelations. The irony of the current debate on evolution is that fundamentalist-literalist Christians insist that the Bible be interpreted as if it were a spiritualist document.

30. By far the best history of the metaphysical movement is Judah's *Metaphysical Movement*, but also useful is the work by Nat Freedland, *The Occult Explosion* (New York: Berkley Medallion Books, 1972).

31. Martin, *Cults*, p. 20.

32. Jacob Needleman, ed., *The Sword of Gnosis* (Baltimore: Penguin Books, 1974). See also how the main beliefs of the metaphysical movement as described by Judah, *Metaphysical Movement*, pp. 12–15, are amazingly similar to the theological tenets of Jewish-Christ Gnosticism as described by Schmithals.

33. On New Thought see Abel L. Allen, *The Message of New Thought* (New York: Robert M. McBride, 1924); also Judah, *Metaphysical Movements*, Chapter 5, "New Thought." On Emmet Fox see: Harry Caze, *Emmet Fox: The Man and His Work* (New York: Harper & Brothers, 1952). Fox's most important works are *The Sermon on the Mount* (New York: Harper & Brothers, 1934), *The Ten Commandments* (New York: Harper & Brothers, 1936), *Power Through Constructive Thinking* (New York: Harper & Brothers, 1937).

34. "The Magic of Tithing," in Emmet Fox, *Alter Your Life* (New York: Harper & Brothers, 1950).

35. See especially his *Power Through Constructive Thinking* (New York: Harper & Row, 1940), and *Stake Your Claim* (New York: Harper & Row, 1952).

36. There is a hint in Colossians 2:18 that the Jewish-Christ Gnostics advocated the worship of angels. Was there a mediumistic source for this? Perhaps there were demonic spirits claiming to be angels, thus avoiding the literal biblical prohibition against mediumship. The demonic accommodates any belief system, just as today there are many mediums who claim they channel entities from outer space.

37. Various Christian writers have examined the Cayce systems over the past decades and have conclusively exposed how it is in contradiction with authentic Christianity. See: Paul Siwek, S.J., *The Enigma of the Hereafter* (New York: Philosophical Library, 1952) and Philip J. Swihart, *Reincarnation: Edgar Cayce and the Bible* (Downers Grove, IL: InterVarsity Press, 1978).

Chapter 7—Induced PLVs: The Amateurs

1. The following is based on an excellent review article by C.J. Duncan, professor of Philosophy at Brown University. "Bridey Murphy Revisited," in Martin Ebon, ed., *Reincarnation in the Twentieth Century* (New York: New American Library, Signet, 1970).

2. Morey Bernstein, *The Search for Bridey Murphy* (New York: Lancer Books, 1965); this second edition contains a very effective rebuttal of the original "debunking" articles. Doubleday published the first edition.

3. Milton V. Kline, ed., *A Scientific Report on "The Search for Bridey Murphy"* (New York: Julian Press, 1956).

4. Edwin S. Zolik, "An Experimental Investigation of the Psychodynamic Implications of the Hypnotic "Previous Existence" Fantasy, *Journal of Clinical Psychology* 14 (1958), pp. 179–83.

5. Ibid., p. 181.

6. Ibid., p. 183.

7. Dr. Helen Wambach, a professional psychologist who during the 1970s was to take PLVs seriously, noted that during her graduate studies, when the Bridey Murphy case first came to public attention, her professors treated the whole issue "scornfully" and dismissed it from discussion. See Helen Wambach, *Reliving Past Lives* (New York: Harper & Row, 1978). The exception to this is the work done by Ernest R. Hilgard (see Part IV, pp. 169f.).

8. See, for example, L.G. Miller, "Bridey Murphy and Her Brood," *Ligourian* 44 (June 1956), pp. 348–54; and C. Keenan, "Riddle of Bridey Murphy," *America* (March 31, 1956), p. 716.

9. Giorgio de Santillana, *The Crime of Galileo* (Chicago: University of Chicago Press, 1955), p. 9.

10. I remember during the late 1960s waiting anxiously for *Psychology Today* to do an article on Konrad Lorenz or Niko Tinbergen. It never happened. See the Christian psychologist Paul C. Vitz, *Psychology As Religion: The Cult of Self-Worship* (Grand Rapids: William B. Eerdmans, 1977), p. 39, for the potential of animal behavior studies for formulating a more accurate view of man.

11. My understanding of the entire data-avoidance process was greatly clarified by two works of Thomas S. Kuhn, a scientist and historian of science, *The Structure of Scientific Revolution* (Chicago: University of Chicago Press, 1962), and *The Copernican Revolution* (New York: Random House, Vintage Books, 1959).

12. When I first joined a local Theosophical lodge in 1974, I was surprised to find that the leadership adamantly preached reincarnation as a *doctrine*, but refused to have anything to do with PLVs as an *experience*. When I invited them to witness a PLV, they responded with the same restlessness and avoidance behavior I had observed in priests and ministers in a similar situation. They wanted no data that might disturb their belief system.

13. See the article in *Time*, "Where Were You in 1643?" (October 3, 1977), p. 53, which suggests that many psychiatrists had been discreetly using PLV therapy for the past fifteen years.

14. William Swygard, *Awareness Techniques, Book One* (Wellesley Hills, MA: privately published, 1970).

15. All three books were published in 1970; only Book One deals with PLVs.

16. J.H. Brennan, *Five Keys to Past Lives: Practical Aspects of Reincarnation* (New York: Samuel Weiser, 1971).

17. Ibid., pp. 20–28.

18. Not surprisingly, people who claim they can read the Akashic records are quite ignorant, and most have delusions of being both wise and knowledgeable. I personally know of one deluded person who believes that the angels had taught him to read the Akashic records, which were "really" stored deep in Stone Mountain State Park, near Atlanta. See E.C. (Buddy) Cantrell, *Holy Stone Mountain* (Atlanta: privately printed, 1975).

19. New York: Samuel Weiser, 1971.

20. New York: Crown Publishers, 19—. Autobiographical details are given in "Epilogue" to *Hypersentience*, and a description of her life and philosophy in the early 1960s is found in Jess Stern's best-selling, *Yoga, Youth and Reincarnation* (New York: Bantam Books, 1965).

21. Marcia Moore, and Mark Douglas, *Reincarnation, Key to Immortality* (York Cliffs: Arcane Publications, 1968).

22. Ibid., p. 5.

23. *Hypersentience*, p. 26.

24. Ibid., p. 28.

25. Ibid., p. 18.

26. Ibid., p. 4.

27. Ibid., pp. 6–7.

28. Ibid., p. 7.

29. Remember what we discovered in our study of mystical discernment. Saint Paul had a vision of the heavens and stated that it was unlawful to disclose what he had seen, Saint Teresa likewise declared that she was not permitted to remember what she has seen in that spiritual dimension. We had concluded that this type of shielding had something to do with protecting the essential ambiguity of our human knowledge. Yet experiences apostles dare not reveal and the saints cannot remember is exactly where Mrs. Moore delights in taking her sensors. It would be surprising if any of the visions reported of the inner-dimensional were *not* demonic.

30. *Hypersentience*, p. 132.

31. Marcia Moore paid the ultimate earthly price of her lack of discernment: She was murdered and dismembered by a Satan-worshiping group she was researching. Only a piece of her skull was found. See the account by her brother, the famous novelist Robin Moore: Bob Borino, "Satan cult murdered my sister, says top author," *Globe* [West Palm Beach, FL] (April 28, 1981), p. 15.

32. New York: Pocket Books, 1977. Weisman had considerable experience among metaphysical groups, and the book shows he is not impressed by the fantastic claims and assertions of neo-Gnosticism, and he occasionally rises to heights of true discernment.

33. Ibid., p. 88.

34. Dick Sutphen, *Past Lives, Future Loves* (New York: Pocket Books, 1978), Chapter 17, "My Own Case History: The Ed Morrell Story," pp. 176–89.

35. Weisman, *We,* p. 129.

36. Ibid., p. 100.

37. Ibid., p. 179. This reminds us of what the Psalmist says about the "wicked man": "He thinks in his heart, 'I shall not be moved; throughout all generations I shall not meet adversity.' " (Psalm 10:6)

38. Weisman, *We,* p. 145.

39. Sutphen, *Future Loves*, p. 50.

40. Ibid., "Eileen and Pat and the "Light People,' " pp. 190–203.

41. The idea of a chakra link comes out of the early Theosophical literature; see, C. W. Leadbetter, *The Chakras* (Wheaton, IL: Theosophical Publishing House, 1972, 1st ed., 1927).

42. Sutphen, *Future Loves*, p. 197.

43. See, for example, Frank Hammond and Ida Mae Hammond, *Pigs in the Parlor: A Practical Guide to Deliverance* (Kirkwood, MO: Inpact Books, 1973),. p. 117, and Chapter 21, "Schizophrenia." The opposite of this spiritual truth is that *acceptance* is an essential foundation for authentic and healthy spirituality. See Paul Tillich, *The Shaking of the Foundations* (New York: Charles Scribner's Sons, 1948), pp. 160–62.

44. See the case of Carl and Bettye, Chapter 14 in *Future Loves*, especially pp. 160–61.

45. Chapter 19, "Frequency Switch—Another Concept Beyond Reincarnation," pp. 204–12.

46. *We*, p. 119.

47. Kenneth L. Woodward, "Do We Live More Than Once?" *McCall's* 106:9 (June 1979), p. 28. Mr. Woodward regularly reports on religious affairs for *Newsweek*.

48. Arthur Hastings, "Current Interest in Past Lives," *ASPR Newsletter* 5:2 (April 1979), p. 9.

49. Al Weisman noted the same problem in *We, Immortals*, p. 64.

Chapter 8—Induced PLVs: The Professionals

1. Denys Kelsey, and Joan Grant, *Many Lifetimes* (New York: Pocket Books, 1968, 1st ed., 1967). See Chapter Two, "Recognition of a Reality." for an account of Dr. Kelsey's entrance into PLV therapy.

2. Currently in print—New York: Berkley Publishing Corp., 1969.

3. Kelsey and Grant, *Many Lifetimes*, p. 45 ff.

4. Dorothy Bradley M.D., and Robert A. Bradley M.D., *Psychic Phenomena: Revelations and Experiences* (New York: Parker Publishing, 1967).

5. *Husband-Coached Childbirth* (New York: Harper & Row, 1965).

6. New York: Coward, McCann & Geoghegan, 1978.

7. See Weisman, *We*, pp. 293–97.

8. Fiore, *Here Before*, Chapter 10, "It Cost Me My Life," pp. 203–27.

9. Ibid., Chapter 2, "Someone's Got a Club."

10. New York: Ace Books, 1979, 1st ed. William Morrow, 1978.

11. Ibid., Chapter 2, "The Method," pp. 22–42.

12. Ibid., Chapter 4, "Ulcers," pp. 57–67.

13. Ibid., p. 181.

14. Ibid., pp. 218–19.

15. Netherton, *Therapy*, pp. 189–95.

16. Ibid., p. 194.

17. Ibid., p. 195. See the account of yet another demonic "eye-witness" of the crucifixion in Edgar J. Goodspeed's *Strange New Gospels* (Chicago: University of Chicago Press, 1931), "The Crucifixion of Jesus by an Eye-witness."

18. Ian Stevenson, *Twenty Cases Suggestive of Reincarnation* (New York:

American Society for Psychical Research, 1966).

19. Ibid., see chapter entitled "General Discussion." Also see his more recent article, "The Explanatory Value of the Idea of Reincarnation," *Journal of Nervous and Mental Disease* 164:5, pp. 305–26.

20. *Twenty Cases*, p. 304.

21. Ian Stevenson, "Some Questions Related to Cases of the Reincarnation Type," *The Journal of the American Society for Psychical Research*, 68 (October, 1974), pp. 395–416.

22. Ian Stevenson, "A Preliminary Report of a New Case of Responsive Xenoglossy: The Case of Gretchen," *The Journal of the American Society for Psychical Research* 70 (January 1976), p. 67.

23. Carroll E. Jay, *Gretchen, I Am,* intro. Ian Stevenson (New York: Avon Books, 1979).

24. Ibid., pp. 67–68.

25. Ibid., p. xiii. William James had a similar problem in coming to grips with entities that were dedicated to destruction and evil. See his *Varieties of Religious Experience*, section 14.

26. "Some Questions," p. 408. The most detailed description thus far reported of a PLV that was purely spontaneous has been the case of Edward Ryall, an English businessman: Edward Ryall, *Born Twice: Total Recall of a Seventeenth Century Life*, introduction and appendix by Ian Stevenson (New York: Harper & Row, 1974). As a child Edward had vivid impressions of being a certain John Fletcher who died in 1685 in the battle of Sedgmour. The impressions of John Fletcher's life started to bubble up as a small child when he mentioned to his father that he had seen Halley's comet before (in 1682). The boy received a severe scolding for this "lie" and subsequently kept his unusual visions to himself until the later years of his married life.

27. "Some Questions," p. 402. See also the discussion of this point in his more recent "Explanatory Value," p. 323.

28. "Some Questions," p. 405.

29. Karl Stern made this point back in 1954 in his *The Third Revolution: A Study of Psychiatry and Religion* (New York: Harcourt Brace & Co., 1954).

30. The interaction of amateurs and professionals often occurs when new sciences or technologies are first developed. One of the major sparks of the massive industrial and scientific changes we call the Industrial Revolution was set by a group of doctors, ministers, craftsmen, and dilettantes who met for dinner and discussion outside of Birmingham, England. Out of the group came James Watt, Joseph Priestly, and others. The chief characteristic of this group was the atmosphere of free-flowing hypothesis generation and reproof that did not involve ego, class, or professional entanglements. See Lord Ritchie-Calder, "The Lunar Society of Birmingham," *Scientific American*, vol. 246, #6 (June 1982), pp. 136–45.

Chapter 9 — Preexistence and the Elijah–John-the-Baptist Relationship

1. Ryder C. Smith, *The Bible Doctrine of the Hereafter* (London: Epworth Press, 1958), Chapter 5, "The Chasid and Sheol."

2. John A.T. Robinson, "Elijah, John and Jesus," in *Twelve New Testament*

Studies (Naperville, IL: Alec R. Allenson, 1962). Of the Lucan description of John the Baptist, Robinson says that one "cannot in view of the functions predicated of him be interpreted as a denial that John *is* Elijah." See also Sang-Ho Lee, "John the Baptist and Elijah in Lucan Theology," PhD dissertation (Botson University School of Theology, 1972), p. 166, for the same evaluation.

3. See an excellent discussion of this in reference to later Christological arguments in Cullmann's *The Christology of the New Testament* (Philadelphia: Westminster Press, 1963), pp. 1–10.

4. See John Hick, *Death and Eternal Life* (New York: Harper & Row, 1976), Chapters 16–19, for an excellent presentation of differences in this regard in Eastern religions.

5. Karl R. Popper has shown that the question of "essence" is antiscientific and produces pseudoknowledge and scholasticism. He terms the essence orientation "methodological essentialism." The natural sciences, which in the past few centuries have made steady progress in the validated expansion of knowledge, long discarded this way of addressing questions by proceeding along the lines of what Popper calls "methodological nominalism." This latter way of thinking concentrates on how a thing functions, and when and where it occurs. See Karl R. Popper, *The Open Society and Its Enemies*, vol. 1 (New York: Harper & Row, Torchbooks, 1963), p. 31 ff.

6. The few scholars who have studied the issue resist using the word reincarnation and instead use the French equivalent *redivivus*. See Robinson, "Elijah," p. 30; Louis J. Martyn, "We Have Found Elijah," in *Jews, Greeks and Christians* (Leiden: E.J. Brill, 1976), p. 182; Erick R. Egerton, "John the Baptist in Lucan Theology," PhD dissertation (Graduate Theological Union and The Pacific Lutheran Theological Seminary, 1968), pp. 88–96.

7. Contemporary biologists do not believe that the development of the fetus does in fact give us much evolutionary information as was believed in the nineteenth century. Yet there is something to embryological recapitulation, especially in regard to "linkage" of similar species. See Garland E. Allen, *Life Science in the Twentieth Century* (Cambridge: Cambridge University Press, 1978), Chapters 2 and 5.

8. My use of the term recapitulation to describe the continuity between persons is not totally original. I found the word used by a PLV practitioner who used it in the medical sense. See James Bryce, *Reincarnation Now!* (Vancouver: F. Forbez, 1978), Chapter 9, "Richard Willard," p. 121.

9. Note that along this line of thought Agnes Sanford entitles her autobiography *Sealed Orders* (Plainfield, NJ: Logos International, 1972). She had no "need to know" of her healing-teaching commission until she suffered from depression in her mature years. See a discussion of this on pp. 000–00.

10. See the plain description of preexistence in the Wisdom of Solomon 8:19–20, which is held as canonical among Catholics.

Chapter 10 — Inner-Healing

1. Waco, TX: Word Books, 1976.
2. See the article by Jim M. Malony and H. Newton, "A Critique of Ruth

Carter Stapleton's Ministry of Inner Healing," *Journal of Psychology and Theology* 8:3 (Fall 1980), pp. 173–84.

3. Translated by Isa Ragusa and Rosalie B. Green (Princeton University Press, 1961).

4. Ibid., p. 38.

5. St. Teresa of Jesus, *The Life of the Holy Mother Teresa of Jesus*, trans. E. Allison Peers (New York: Sheed and Ward, 1946), p. 54.

6. For details of her life see her fascinating autobiography, Agnes Sanford, *Sealed Orders* (Plainfield, NJ: Logos International, 1972). She died in March of 1982.

7. After forty-five years it is still in print. Emmet Fox, *The Sermon on the Mount* (New York: Harper & Brothers, 1934).

8. The biographical information for this section is taken from his autobiography, Glenn Clark, *A Man's Reach* (St. Paul: Macalester Park Publishing Co., 1977); and his son's biography, Miles Clark, *Glenn Clark: His Life and Writings* (Nashville: Abingdon, 1975).

9. New York: Harper & Brothers, 1940.

10. Ibid., Chapter 4, "Washing the Roots."

11. Ibid., p. 32.

12. Genevieve Parkhurst, "What Is CFO," tape # PAg-11 (St. Paul: Cutler Memorial Library, 1968).

13. St. Paul: Macalester Park, 1947; it took two years to find a publisher.

14. The details of this pioneer case of inner-healing are recorded in a talk which Agnes Sanford gave at a CFO camp. See Agnes Sanford, "Healing of Memories," tape #FX-5 (Richardson Springs: Springs of Living Water, n.d.)

15. Agnes Sanford, *Behold Your God* (St. Paul: Macalester Park, 1958). Note that Macalester Park is not listed among the publishers in *Books in Print*, but it may be ordered from Macalester Park Bookstore, 1571 Grand Ave, St. Paul, MN 55105.

16. Ibid., Chapter 8, "The Current of God's Love on Calvary."

17. Agnes Sanford, *The Healing Gifts of the Spirit* (Philadelphia: J.B. Lippincott, 1966).

18. Ruth Carter Stapleton, "Her First CFO Experience," tape #STr-5 (St. Paul: Cutler Memorial Library, 1974).

19. Betty Tapscott, *Inner Healing Through the Healing of Memories* (Houston: privately printed, 1975).

20. Ibid. pp. 22–24.

21. Fort Worth: Harvest Press, 1976.

22. Notre Dame, IN: Ave Maria Press, 1972. Fr. Scanlan has been one of the most important leaders in the Catholic charismatic renewal.

23. Ibid., p. 21.

24. Francis MacNutt, *Healing* (Notre Dame, IN: Ave Maria Press, 1974), pp. 13, 181. See also Scanlan, *Power*, p. 10. It would not be an exaggeration to say that *Healing* has become the single most important source and guide for healing prayer in the Catholic Church.

25. Dennis Linn and Matthew Linn, *Healing of Memories* (New York: Paulist Press, 1974).

26. Michael Scanlan, *Inner Healing* (New York: Paulist Press, 1974).

27. Ibid., p. 69.

28. Stapleton, *Gift*, Chapter Four, "No Place to Hide."

29. Ibid., pp. 57–58.

30. William James knew this was not uncommon in the process of conversion. See his *Varieties of Religious Experience* (New York: New American Library, Mentor, 1958), lectures 10 and 20. The same point is extensively documented in Ernest White's *Christian Life and the Unconscious* (New York: Harper & Brothers, 1955).

31. Kenneth L. Woodward, "Sister Ruth," *Newsweek* (July 17, 1978), pp. 65–66.

32. Brooks Alexander, "Ruth . . . ," *SCP Journal* 4:1 (April 1980), p. 3.

33. Her most recent book, *In His Footsteps* (San Francisco: Harper & Row, 1979), bends over backwards to accent her orthodoxy.

34. Steve Scott and Brooks Alexander, pp. 12–16.

35. Ibid., p. 15.

Chapter 11 — Christian PLVs

1. Gregory of Nyssa, *The Life of St. Macrina*, in *Ascetical Works*, ed. and trans. Virginia Woods Callahan (Washington: Catholic University of America Press, 1967), pp. 164–65.

2. See especially Dmitri Oblensky, *The Bogomils* (Twickenham, Eng.: Anthony C. Hall, 1972) and Joseph R. Strayer, *The Albigensian Crusades* (New York: Dial Press, 1971).

3. See an excellent history of the origins of Pentecostalism in the work already cited in Part I: Vinson Synan, *The Holiness-Pentecostal Movement in the United States* (Grand Rapids: William B. Eerdman's, 1971). For a view of the social and theological distinctions between the Pentecostals and the newer charismatics, see: Kilian McDonnell, *Charismatic Renewal and the Churches* (New York: Seabury Press, 1976), Chapters 4 to 6.

4. For excellent insights into the little-understood "word of wisdom" and "word of knowledge," see Howard Ervin, "Wisdom, Knowledge, Faith and Healing," tape #HE-7 (Richardson Springs: Springs of Living Water, n.d.).

5. R. Kenneth McAll, "Taste and See," in *Demon Possession*, ed. John W. Montgomery (Minneapolis: Bethany Fellowhip, 1976), p. 276, for a brief account of this case. For more details see his recorded lecture: "Releasing Family Ties to God," tape (Atlanta: Cathedral of St. Philip, Sept. 18, 1978). A fascinating and complete overview of his peculiar ministry is found in his newly released book, *Healing the Family Tree* (London: Sheldon Press, 1982).

6. Pat Brooks, *Out! In the Name of Jesus* (Carol Stream, IL: Creation House, 1972). The vision and resulting exorcism-healing is recorded in Chapter 12, "Deliverance of a Child Demoniac," pp. 113–24.

7. Origen, *On the First Principles*, trans. and intro. G.W. Butterworth (Gloucestor, MA: Peter Smith, 1973), III, 3, 5 (pp. 227–28).

8. Agnes Sanford, *Sealed Orders* (Plainfield, NJ: Logos International, 1972), pp. 17–18.

9. Ibid., p. 283.

10. Ibid., Agnes's vision of choosing to come to the earth has some striking parallels with the testimonies recorded in Dr. Raymond Moody's *Life After Life*,

the difference being that Agnes's choice was of being born, rather than of dying. But both Agnes and the persons in Moody's study had a moral option of accepting a difficult task on earth. See *Life After Life*, the section "The Being of Light," pp. 45–49.

11. Agnes Sanford, *Behold Your God* (Saint Paul: Macalester Park, 1958), p. 72. In a talk taped in 1966 Agnes again asserted her belief in cosmic transmigration, but rejected earthly reincarnation because of its association with karma. See "The Redemption of Our Bodies," tape #787-A (Fort Myers: Lord's Own Tape Ministry, 1966).

12. Julian of Norwich, *The Revelations of Divine Love of Julian of Norwich*, trans. James Walsh (St. Meinrad, IN: Abby Press, 1975), p. 131 ff., Chapters 50–51.

13. Recently I have come across another apparently spontaneous PLV of an important charismatic figure. Abbot David Geraets, director of the world-renowned Pecos Benedictine Monastery and experimental charismatic community in Pecos, New Mexico, had a PLV experience years ago which caused him to "half-believe" in reincarnation for a while. He now feels the vision was a dreamlike spiritual message and, in a brief note to me, he was especially anxious that his vision *not* be taken as evidence for any form of reincarnation. See Abbot David Geraets, "Conclusion—Depth Psychology," tape #6 (Pecos: Dove Cassettes, 1980).

14. This PLV raises a double discernment question. Was the PLV of the Lord, and what is the role of Marian devotion in authentic Christianity? We noted in Part I that the Catholic Church, in it discernment obligation, had failed to stop the more extreme forms of Marian practices. Yet throughout the history of the Church there seems to have been a place for this type of visionary experience that is proper to authentic Christianity. It is important to note that Anna's vision was *instrumental* for a life dedicated to the Lord, not an end in itself.

William James recorded for us a similar Marian vision that brought manifest good fruit. It took place in France in 1840. The seer was a young Jewish man, a free thinker and social dilettante, who had a specific antipathy for Christianity. Out of curiosity he visited a small village church where he had a momentary vision of the Blessed Mother. The vision gave him a tremendous sense of the love of God, and, at the same time, of his own sinfulness. The fruit of that brief vision was his conversion to Christianity (at considerable social and family cost) and his eventual service in the Kingdom as a Catholic priest. See William James, *The Varieties of Religious Experience* (New York: New American Library, Mentor, 1958), lecture X, pp. 181–83.

15. Mark Albrecht has subsequently published a very fine book entitled *Reincarnation: A Christian Appraisal* (Downers Grove, IL: Inter-Varsity Press, 1982). In tone and interpretation this book is more conservative than my work, yet we are in basic agreement on many issues, especially the demonic origins of Gnostic theories of reincarnation.

Chapter 12 — The PLV and the Ministry of Inner-Healing

1. The vocabulary of this distinction is mine, though it has been long recognized by those charismatic leaders experienced with the ups and downs of prophetic cycles. Among the books that I am most indebted to on this issue are John and

Paula Sanford's, *The Elijah Task* (Plainfield, NJ: Logos International, 1977), and Bruce Yocum's *Prophecy* (Ann Arbor: Words of Life, 1976).

2. Evagrius Ponticus, *The Praktikos; Chapters on Prayer,* trans. John Eudes Bambeger (Kalamazoo, MI: Cistercian Publications, 1978), *Chapters on Prayer* #83.

3. Our procedures are technically and superficially similar to those described in Marcia Moore's *Hypersentience* (see Chapter 7), but we trust that they are spiritually different and operating in the Kingdom of God.

4. Most fundamentalist ministers will denounce hypnotism as an occult, and thus sinful, practice. One of the few who has attempted to explain why this is so is, again, John L. Sanford. See his tape "Sanctification," tape #3806 (Ft. Myers: Lord's Own Tape Ministry, n.d.).

Chapter 13—Evaluating the PLV Hypotheses

1. For similar, though more conservative, conclusions on the multiple origins of PLVs see Mark Albrecht, *Reincarnation: A Christian Appraisal* (Downers Grove, IL: Inter-Varsity Press, 1982), Chapter 6, "Sorting It Out: Possible Explanations of Past-Life Recall."

2. I also reserve the right to ignore hysterical, doctrinaire reproof which does not subject itself to reason and cannot therefore be part of the wisdom that comes from heaven (James 3).

3. For this point see Karl R. Popper, *Objective Knowledge: An Evolutionary Approach*, rev. ed. (Oxford: Clarendon Press, 1979), especially the essay "Evolution and the Tree of Knowledge."

4. Ernest R. Hilgard, *Divided Consciousness: Multiple Controls in Human Thought and Action* (New York: John Wiley & Sons, 1977).

5. Ibid., Chapters 9. I would suggest that although Dr. Hilgard's research must be discerned, reproofed, and verified by Christian investigators to filter our spiritualistic influences, he may, in fact, have learned to isolate the human spirit in its natural state. This has, of course, important theological and pastoral implications.

6. This approach was first suggested to me by the lovely lady who was the sensor of the "Scrupulous Prioress." I did not consider this possibility seriously until I read the superb little book by John Dominic Crossan, *The Dark Interval: Towards a Theology of Story* (Allen, TX: Argus Communications, 1975), and Michael Shiryon's "Biblical Roots of Literatherapy," *Journal of Psychology and Judaism*, 21 #1 (Fall 1977), pp. 3–11. The definition of parable and its comparison to myth is largely taken from Crossan's analysis. I have subsequently discovered that in this area, too, Glenn Clark was decades ahead of the academic scholarship in the field. In his first books on prayer he clearly understood the use of parables in the spiritual life, and suggested even praying in parables. See his *The Soul's Sincere Desire* (Boston: Little, Brown & Co., 1953). First published in 1924.

7. For further Old Testament examples of the parable see 2 Samuel 14; Judges 9:7–22 and Isaiah. 5.

8. Cf. with the practice of guided imagery described by the Christian psychologist Vance L. Shepperson, "Paradox, Parables and Change: One Approach

to Christian Hypnotherapy," *Journal of Psychology and Theology*, 9, #1 (Spring 1981), pp. 3–11.

9. The problem is that this is a pioneer field and there is no established course work or certification for it. As for specific preparation for the PLV ministry, I can only share what I sense is proper. Training and experience in traditional counseling is helpful, but it must be married to the gift of spiritual discernment. The most important training, however, would be in the practice of "normal" inner-healing.

10. Jeffrey Iverson, *More Lives Than One? The Evidence of the Remarkable Bloxham Tapes* (New York: Warner Books, 1976).

11. See specifically two tapes: John Sanford and Paula Sanford, "Sanctification," tape #3806 (Ft. Myers: Lord's Own Tape Ministry, n.d.); and John Sanford and Paula Sanford, "Captivity and Release," tape #3665 (Ft. Myers: Lord's Own Tape Ministry, June 1978). Both were taped at CFO camps.

12. See, for example, the variety of secular psychologists who contributed to a fine anthology of possession: John Warwick Montgomery, ed., *Demon Possession* (Minneapolis: Bethany Fellowship, 1976), especially Part Six, "Demonology Viewed Psychiatrically."

13. Philadelphia: Westminster Press, 1966.

14. The opposite view, that the demonic descriptions in the gospel are an accommodation to the psychology of the times, but not "real," is taken by Henry Ansgar Kelly in *The Devil, Demonology and Witchcraft: The Development of Christian Belief in Evil Spirits*, rev ed. (Garden City, NY: Doubleday & Co., 1974).

15. New York: Seabury Press, 1974.

16. Washington Depot, CN: Chosen Books, 1973. The best book by far on deliverance in the charismatic tradition is *Pigs in the Parlor: A Practical Guide to Deliverance* by Frank and Ida Mae Hammond (Kirkwood, MO: Impact Books, 1973). This book contains an excellent example of a validated personal revelation that has borne good fruit in the process of healing and delivering persons with hopeless schizophrenia.

17. As in so many matters in the past decades, the laity leads the clergy. See Clyde Nunn, "The Rising Credibility of the Devil in America," *Listening*, vol. 9, #3 (Autumn 1940), 84–100.

Chapter 14—The Afterlife

1. F.W. Farrar, *Mercy and Judgement* (New York: E.P. Dutton, 1881); E.H. Plumptre, *The Spirits in Prison* (London: Wm. Isbister, 1885); Arthur Chambers, *Our Life After Death* (Philadelphia: George W. Jacobs, 1902); Lars Nielsen Dahle, *Life After Death and the Future of the Kingdom of God*, trans. John Beveridge, (Edinburgh: T. & T. Clark, 1896); Lewis Muirhead, *The Terms Life and Death in the Old and New Testaments, and Other Papers* (London: Andrew Melrose, 1908); and J.H. Leckie, *The World to Come and Final Destiny* (Edinburgh: T. & T. Clark, 1918).

2. See, for example, J.H. Leckie, *The World to Come and Final Destiny* (Edinburgh: T. & T. Clark, 1918), pp. 68–102.

3. What we have called ambiguity he calls "antinomies"; see *Mercy and Judgement*, p. 12.

4. Canon Farrar cites as scriptures for this motif: Luke 9:59; John 1:29; 3:17; 12:32; Acts 3:21; Romans 4:13; 5:15, 18, 19; 11:26, 32; 1 Corinthians 15:22–28, 55; 2 Corinthians 5:19; Ephesians 1:10; Philippians 2:9, 10; Colossians 1:20; 1 Timothy 2:4; 4:10; Titus 2:11; Hebrews 2:14; 1 John 2:2; 3:8, Micah 8:9; Isaiah 12:1.

5. The scriptures cited for this motif are: Matthew 13:49, 50; 16:27; 25:46; Mark 3:29; 9:44–50; Revelations 14:10.

6. Matthew 3:12; 5:30; 10:28; Luke 13:1–5; 20:18, 35; Acts 3:23; Romans 6:23; 8:13; Hebrews 10:26–31, Revelations 20:14; 21 ff.

7. Matthew 5–26; Luke 12:5–9; 1 Corinthians 3:13, 15.

8. Farrar, *Justice and Mercy*, p. 13.

9. See Russell Alwinckle, *Death in the Secular City: Life After Death in Contemporary Theology and Philosophy* (Grand Rapids: William B. Eerdmans, 1974), especially Chapter 3, "Theology Without Hope."

10. New York: Harper & Row, 1968.

11. New York: Harper & Row, 1976.

12. See Norman Pittenger, *The Last Things in Process Perspective* (London: Epworth Press, 1970).

13. New Testament writers were not bound by modern categories of "occult" or "nonoccult" and could speak freely about spiritual phenomena. In Acts 12:15, the account of Peter's return from prison shows that the disciples knew of a ghostlike phenomenon which they termed "angel." In Luke 24:39 we see that the disciples know enough about ghosts to discern that Jesus was *not* one (he was material).

14. Catholic theology uses the phrase "Communion of Saints" for its theology of the Body of Christ, a phrase that appeared in the creeds in the fourth century, but it does have a biblical base as Saint Paul uses the phrase interchangeably with the Body of Christ (1 Cor. 1:9).

15. See, for example, Charles H. Dodd, *The Communion of Saints* (Cambridge: Harvard University Press, 1936). Also, Dietrich Bonhoeffer, *The Communion of Saints* (New York: Harper & Row, 1963).

16. Part One, Book Two, "Peasant Women Who Have Faith."

17. Author unknown, trans. R.M. French (New York: Seabury Press, 1965).

18. Corrie ten Boom, *Father ten Boom: God's Man* (Boston: G.K. Hall, 1979), pp. 152–54. See also Joyce Lansdorf, *Irregular People* (Waco: Word Books, 1982), pp. 79–84.

19. Andrew Greeley, *Death and Beyond* (Chicago: Thomas More Press, 1976), Chapter Four, "Sociology Has Its Say."

20. F. W. Farrar, *Mercy and Judgement*; Chambers, *Our Life After Death*; Dahle, *Life After Death*.

21. J.H. Leckie, *The World to Come and Final Destiny* (Edinburgh: T. & T. Clark, 1919), p. 73.

22. Farrar takes special pains to document this: *Mercy and Judgement*, p. 76 ff. Also Plumptre, *Spirits in Prison*, 78 ff.

23. *Shepherd of Hermas*, S. 9:16.

24. *Strom. II*, 9:44. Cited in Danielou, *Gospel Message*.

25. *Gospel of Nicodemus*, Chapters 16–19, in *Lost Books of the Bible* (New York: New American Library, Meridian, 1974).

26. Joseph Agar Beet, *The Last Things* (London: Hodder and Stoughton, 1898), p. 180; and Nelson B. Baker, *What Is the World Coming To?* (Phila-

delphia: Westminster Press, 1965), p. 91. Dr. Baker is professor at Eastern Baptist Theological Seminary.

27. *Theology of the New Testament*, vol. I, p. 136.

28. Translated and annotated by George E. McCracken (Westminster: Newman Press, 1949).

29. *The Second Mrs. Wu* (Philadelphia: J.B. Lippincott, 1965).

30. Among contemporary Christian writers in America I knew of only one, Dr. Morton Kelsey, who believes in the present "sheol" state of the dead and integrates that belief into his understanding of the afterlife. Dr. Kelsey calls the sheol state the "gray area" of the afterlife, neither heaven nor hell. See his *Afterlife: The Other Side of Dying* (New York: Paulist Press, 1979), and especially his tape series "Healing and the Afterlife" (Pecos: Dove Cassettes, 1981). An earlier study, done in the 1940s by Fr. Herbert Thruston concluded only that some ghost and haunting phenomena were *not* demonic; see his *Ghosts and Poltergeists* (Chicago: Henry Regnery Co., 1954).

31. For the Church of England's ministry to ghosts see Fr. Christopher Neil-Smith, *The Exorcist and the Possessed* (St. Ives, Engl.: James Pike, 1974), p. 82.; and especially two works by Dom Robert Petitpierre, *Exorcism: The Report of the Commission Convened by the Bishop of Exeter* (London: SPCK, 1972), and *Exorcising Devils* (London: Robert Hale, 1976).

32. The novels of Charles Williams make for difficult and demanding reading. It is perhaps best to approach his theology by first reading Mary McDermott Shideler's *The Theology of Romantic Love: A Study in the Writings of Charles Williams* (Grand Rapids: William B. Eerdman's, 1962) and then an anthology of his essays: Charles Williams, *The Image of the City and Other Essays*, ed. Anne Ridler (London: Oxford University Press, 1958).

33. Charles Williams, *Descent into Hell* (New York: Pellegrini and Cudahy, 1949).

Chapter 15 — The EJR Ambiguity: Empathetic Identification

1. Geoffrey Hodson, *Reincarnation, Fact or Fallacy?* (Wheaton, IL: Theosophical Publishing House, 1967), Chapter 7, "Child Genius."

2. For a succinct presentation of this aspect of Gregory of Nyssa's theology see his *The Lord's Prayer, The Beatitudes*, trans. Hilda Graef (Westminster: Newman Press, 1954), pp. 126–7; and Jean Danielou and Herbert Musurillo, ed., *From Glory to Glory: Texts From Gregory of Nyssa's Mystical Writings* (New York: Charles Scribner's Sons, 1961), especially the introduction.

3. Gardner Murphy, "A Carington Approach to Ian Stevenson's *Twenty Cases Suggestive of Reincarnation*," *The Journal of the American Society for Psychical Research* 67:2 (April 1973), pp. 117–29.

4. Jeane Dixon, *The Call to Glory* (New York: William Morrow, 1972), Chapter 4, "Elijah Is Come Already."

Chapter 16 — The EJR Ambiguity: Reincarnation

1. See W.D. Davies, *Paul and Rabbinic Judaism: Some Rabbinic Elements in Pauline Theology*, rev. ed. (New York: Harper & Row, Torchbook, 1965).

2. J. Louis Martyn, "We Have Found Elijah," in Robert Hamerton-Kelly and Robin Scroggs, eds., *Jews, Greeks and Christians: Religious Cultures in Late Antiquity* (Leiden: E.J. Brill, 1976), p. 182.

3. Both quotations are taken from the classic William Whiston translation which is available in paperback: Josephus, *Complete Works*, trans. William Whiston (Grand Rapids: Kregel Publications, 1960).

4. See, for example, C.T. Wood, *Death and Beyond: A Study of Hebrew and Christian Conceptions of the Life to Come* (London: Longmans, Green & Co., 1920), p. 17.

5. Jean Danielou, *Gospel Message and Hellenistic Culture,* trans. and ed. John Austin Baker (Philadelphia: Westminster Press, 1973), p. 494.

6. See the Spanish Jesuit A. Orbe, "Textos y pasajes de la Escritura interesados en la teoria de la reincorpación," *Estudios Eclesiásticos* 33 (1959), p. 81.

7. In theological and philosophical circles this problem, of the difficulty of "seeing" past traditional understandings, is given the technical term the "hermeneutical problem." See Hans-Georg Gadamer, *Philosophical Hermeneutics*, trans. David E. Linge (Berkeley: University of California Press, 1976); and Paul Ricoeur, *The Symbolism of Evil*, trans. Emerson Buchnan (Boston: Beacon Press, 1969), especially his chapter "Conclusion: The Symbol Gives Rise to Thought," pp. 347–57.

8. This is what the biblical scholar John A.T. Robinson argues for in his *Twelve New Testament Studies* (Naperville, IL: Alec R. Allenson, 1962), "Elijah, John and Jesus," p. 46.

9. I have found Millard J. Erickson's *Contemporary Options in a Study of the Millennium* (Grand Rapids: Baker Book House, 1977) particularly useful for its sketch of millenniumism and its discussion of current theories of the rapture that are so prominent in fundamentalist circles.

10. Some readers may wish to see a distinction between the phrase "this time" (*tokairo touto*) and "age" (*aioni*). In this passage the first phrase is a synonym for age. The Greek language like other Indo-European languages has an aversion to repeating the same word when another is available. See the discussion on this specific scripture in James Barr, *Biblical Words for Time*, 2nd rev. ed. (Naperville: Alec R. Allenson, 1969), p. 41.

11. See Jacob Neusner, *First Century Judaism in Crisis* (Nashville: Abingdon Press, 1975).

12. The expectation that Jesus will come again very soon has always been a sign of healthy Christianity, and is again a factor in today's revivalist spirit. I vividly remember a conversation with one such expectant Christian not long ago. I explained my work with PLV and gave him my views on the possibility of reincarnation. He listened with more than usual patience and courteous interest. At the end of our conversation he said, "That's interesting. I don't know if there is reincarnation or not, but I do know that within a few years Jesus will return. This is the last generation, now." To him discussion of reincarnation was irrelevant because time had run out. His opinion was identical with that of most New Testament writers; they considered themselves the last generation on earth, and reincarnation a theory that had no *future*.

13. Origen has periodically come into fashion among Christian thinkers. The neo-Classical English poet Milton adopted many elements of Origen's theology, including his belief in individual preexistence. Canon Farrar was one of many who opened the way for the Church of England's renewed appreciation of him, and the

French Jesuit Fr. Jean Danielou, in his book *Origen* (New York: Sheed & Ward, 1955), began the process of his rehabilitation among Roman Catholic scholars.

14. The dialogue was unearthed in Egypt in 1941. See "On the Soul," in Anne Fremantle, ed., *A Treasury of Early Christianity* (New York: New American Library, Mentor, 1960), pp. 290–99.

15. Danielou, *Origen*, pp. 248–49.

16. See Asterios N. Gerostergios, "The Religious Policy of Justinian I and His Religious Beliefs," PhD dissertation (Boston University School of Theology, 1974); F.W. Farrar, *Mercy and Judgement*, Chapter 12, "The Fifth Oecumenical Council," pp. 344–60; and Joseph Head and S.L. Cranston, *Reincarnation: The Phoenix Fire Mystery*, pp. 156–60.

17. See Quincy Howe, *Reincarnation for the Christian* (Philadelphia: Westminster, 1974); John Hick, *Death and Eternal Life* (New York: Harper & Row, 1976) and Geddes MacGregor, *Reincarnation in Christianity* (Wheaton: Theosophical Publishing House, 1978). While all three works have some virtues, it is perhaps the MacGregor book that is most worthwhile. All authors have wisely stayed away from the spiritualist literature on reincarnation and have sought to define the issue of rebirth principally from philosophical and Eastern sources. They are weakened, however, by their failure to examine the scriptural base of the issue, and in this respect their scholarship is not up to the Christian standards set by the Victorian revisionists. Hick has destroyed his credibility among all but the most extreme liberal Christians because of his contribution to the book *The Myth of God Incarnate* (Philadelphia: Westminster, 1977), and MacGregor has made a major discernment error in believing that Gnosticism is an authentic form of Christianity (*Gnosis: A Renaissance in Christian Thought* [Wheaton: Theosophical Publishing House, 1979]). None of these authors relate PLVs to the discernment tradition of the Church.

18. Saint Teresa of Avila, *Interior Castle*, trans. and ed. E. Allison Peers (Garden City, NY: Doubleday, Image, 1973), Mansion 6, Chapter 4.

19. The possibility of a "mixed system" afterlife such as I have just described has assuredly occurred to many people. I have found it recently in a lecture by Morton T. Kelsey that describes a conversation he had with Dom David Geraets. Both Christian scholars agreed that such a system is a "definite possibility." See Morton T. Kelsey, "Healing and the After-Life: Initial Reflections and Some Stories," tape #1 (Pecos: Dove Cassettes, 1981).

20. Essentially the same distinction I am making between a person who is in a neurotic entrapment and a satisfied villain is found in Malachi Martin's book, *Hostage to the Devil*, mentioned in Book One. In Martin's view a person who shows the paranormal symptoms of possession is an indication that the spirit is struggling and crying out for assistance, just as Cindy's paranormal symptoms signified a cry for help. However, persons who are "perfectly possessed" show no symptoms whatsoever, and are, in Martin's view, beyond the help of the exorcist. Thankfully, this one of Martin's theories is *not* based on demonic revelations.

Chapter 17—Testing the Fruit

1. Philadelphia: Westminster Press, 1966.

2. I remember having a conversation with a graduating theology student at the steps of Emory University, and explaining to him the biblical basis for the

possibility of ministering to the dead. He was persuaded of the biblical validity of my arguments, but added, "That's fine in theory. But you can't preach that; the people will lose the fear of the Lord and postpone their salvation." He had a point. To a certain extent this has been confirmed by several people I have met in the metaphysical movement who have relatively happy and prosperous lives and have expressed a belief that they would rather just reincarnate a few more times and enjoy living rather than go into the sacrificial life of a Christian.

3. See the very touching incident between a recent convert and the wife of one of the most famous missionaries of the nineteenth century, John Nevius, in Helen S. Coan, *The Life of John Livingston Nevius* (New York: Fleming H. Revell, 1895), p. 191. The only consolation Mrs. Nevius could offer was that perhaps there is *some* hope for the convert's ancestors.

4. Bede Griffiths, *Christian Ashram: Essays Towards a Hindu-Christian Dialogue* (London: Darton, Longman & Todd, 1966).

5. Dom Aelred Graham, "Can We Learn from Eastern Religions?" *The Ampleforth Journal* 83:2 (1978).

6. See R.H.S. Boyd, *India and the Latin Captivity of the Church* (London: Cambridge University Press, 1974) for an excellent short survey of the principal Hindu-Christian writers to date.

7. See Kaj Baago, *The Movement Around Subba Rao: A Study of the Hindu-Christian Movement Around K. Subba Rao in Andhra Pradesh* (Madras: The Christian Literature Society, 1968).

8. Translated by Floyd V. Filson (Philadelphia: Westminster Press, 1964).

9. See especially Part I, Chapter 4, "God's Lordship Over Time."